THE OLD BRAIN IN A NEW WORLD

Moving from Shame to Self-Care and Understanding

By

Paul D. Pinette MSW-LCSW

XAVIER PUBLISHING
EST. 1994

Between stimulus and response, there is a space.
In that space is our power to choose our response.
In our response lies our growth and our freedom.

— Viktor E. Frankl

CONTENTS

Part I

Understanding the Old Brain. Foundations of the Mind - Biology, Survival and the Roots of Shame

Part II: Domains of Desire, Impulse, and Shame

Chapter 5-The Architecture of Safety: Faith, Fear, Flag and the Old Brain's Search for Certainty..111

Part III-Taking Action

DEDICATION

To the thousands of clients who have shared their stories with me—your courage, resilience, and willingness to face life's challenges illuminate every page of this book.

To my five children: to my four daughters, whose wisdom, compassion, curiosity, and sense of humor have taught me to see the world more clearly, to laugh more freely, and to live more fully; and to my son, whose energy, bravery, and fearless spirit inspire me to reach beyond what I once thought possible, reminding me of the strength and courage inherent in being human.

And above all, to my wife, Mary. As Jack Nicholson said, *"You make me want to be a better man."* Your love, patience, unwavering support—and your remarkable tolerance of my many little annoyances—have shaped the person I am today. Thank you for accepting me with all my faults; without you, this book would not exist.

PREFACE

To those who may be wondering why I would write this book, the truth is simple: my wife told me to.

No, really. She's been saying it for years—"there's a book in you." And she was right, though for the longest time I wasn't sure what that book would be about. But over time, as I listened to my clients, reflected on my own life, and looked out at the world we live in today, the theme became obvious: the intersection of our primitive biology with the modern world. That tension is where so many of our struggles—and our opportunities for growth—live.

Now, I realize this might sound strange. Why write a book about primitive biology in an age of artificial intelligence, digital connection, breathtaking scientific advances, and an ever-accelerating pace of life? Haven't we moved past all that?

I don't think we have. In fact, I think our old biology matters now more than ever. Because while technology races ahead, our brains are still wired for survival in a very different world—a world of scarcity, danger, and tribal competition. This mismatch between old instincts and new environments is at the root of so much of what we struggle with today: sexual shame, overeating, compulsive scrolling, search for safety, competition that turns to conflict, and misunderstanding that breeds prejudice.

That's why this book isn't just about biology. It's about peace. Not the abstract kind that politicians talk about, but the everyday peace that comes from understanding ourselves, our impulses, and each other. If we can see that our drives are not moral failings but part of what it means to be human, we can begin to treat ourselves—and one another—with more kindness and less judgment.

That, ultimately, is what this book is about: trying, in whatever small way I can, to put the "kind" back in humankind.

ACKNOWLEDGEMENTS

My hope is to acknowledge the many people who helped *The Old Brain in a New World* come to fruition—and I offer my sincere apology to anyone I may have unintentionally missed along the way.

First, it goes without saying how deeply grateful I am to the researchers and practitioners whose science, tireless efforts, and guiding principles this book stands upon. These include Stephen Porges, Bessel van der Kolk, Peter Levine, Pat Ogden, Gabor Maté, and many, many others who continue to move the field—and our understanding of humanity—forward.

I would also like to acknowledge those who supported me early in my clinical career. I am especially grateful to Kelli Fox, PhD, LCSW my first clinical supervisor and mentor, whose words of wisdom—*"say what's in your gut"*—along with her steady guidance and support, were instrumental in helping me find my footing and begin my journey into private practice. I would also like to thank Harold Stewart, LCSW, who offered guidance and perspective during those formative years and helped shape my professional path.

Foremost, I want to especially thank my dear friend and colleague of more than twenty years, Adam Dubay, LCPC—my first beta reader—who became the first true ambassador of the Four Pillars. In addition, I would like to thank my many other beta readers. In particular, Danny Pelletier, whose thoughtful, deep discussions with me about Chapter 5 and religion were invaluable, and Linda Berg, LCPC, whose enthusiasm and encouragement fueled my momentum when I needed it most. Gratitude as well to Cheryl Demers, LCSW, for her timely feedback, offered at exactly the moment it was most needed.

A sincere thank you also to Steve Gross, MSW, for taking the time to read Chapter 6. Your wisdom, deep commitment to children and play, and the thoughtful conversations we shared around this work helped shape my thinking in lasting ways. Your feedback and encouragement were instrumental in guiding the book to where it ultimately landed.

I'm also grateful to Chantal Paradis of Paradis Photography for taking the time to capture my photographs in the midst of a very full life with three children—your generosity did not go unnoticed.

And to my five children: thank you for patiently waiting for the final version of this book. Your encouragement, curiosity, and excitement were exactly what was needed to keep going.

A deep and heartfelt thank you to my editor, Deb Landry of Bryson Taylor Inc., for her patience and steady guidance through the technical—and often daunting—process of editing and publishing. I was fortunate to have previously worked alongside Deb in her bullying prevention efforts throughout Maine and across the country—work she continues to this day as both a speaker and writer. Her support helped make the complexities of publishing feel manageable after the long journey of writing.

Although it goes without saying, I want to acknowledge my parents for their gratitude, understand, support, love and long conversations of our complex family history.

I'd also like to thank the many clients I have served over the years. You have taught me more than you will ever know, and this book carries your wisdom.

Finally, without a doubt, this book would not have been possible without the encouragement, patience, and unwavering support of my wife, Mary—ever my *Mary Sunshine*. Thank you for enduring the hours of rambling, the frustrations, the excitement over each chapter, and the constant need to "talk about the book." Your steadiness and love made all this possible.

INTRODUCTION

Humans Between Two Worlds

If you've ever wondered, *"Why did I just do that?"* — welcome to **Club Human**. Membership is automatic, lifelong, and comes with a complicated mix of benefits and challenges. The fine print? You're carrying an ancient brain built for survival in a world very different from the one we live in today.

I've spent most of my life trying to figure out how this all works — the mind, the world, the rules no one explains. (Spoiler: life never came with an instruction manual, so like most of us, I've been improvising.) Every day, we make choices that seem to go against our better judgment. We eat the extra slice of cake, snap at someone we love, ignore biological cues like thirst, scroll long past bedtime, or feel a pull of desire we didn't ask for. And afterward, many of us are joined by a familiar companion: shame.
It lingers like a shadow, whispering, *"Seriously? Again?"*

Here's the truth: those impulses are neutral. They don't care about morality. They don't consult society's rules — or your Instagram or TikTok feed. They're simply doing their job: keeping you alive, alert, engaged, and motivated. Your old brain is doing exactly what it evolved to do.

The challenge, and the opportunity, lies with the newer parts of our brain. This is where we can pause, notice an impulse, and choose how to respond. Notice, **not judge**. That simple act of observation without judgment becomes a central theme throughout this book.

And here's the good news: you're not alone. After more than two decades of sitting across from clients, I can promise you that everyone — and I mean everyone — wrestles with the same impulses. They just show up differently depending on the person, the situation, and the world they live in.

It's not that we're weak or broken. It's that our old brain, designed to keep us alive in caves and small tribes, now has to navigate smartphones, careers, relationships, and a nonstop flood of information. No wonder we feel conflicted, exhausted, and sometimes downright irrational. Even sleep — something we treat as optional or indulgent — is a biological necessity. When the old brain doesn't get it, it gets grouchy.

Before we go further, it's important to be clear about one thing: this book does not claim to have all the answers. It may even fuel more questions. In fact, walking off the stage at graduation with my MSW, I was struck — and honestly a bit frightened — by how little I knew. There is simply too much to know. What's offered here is not a set of absolutes. There will always be exceptions, outliers, and edges of the continuum. What I describe is the broad range of *normal* I've seen and heard in my clinical work over the years. It's offered with humility and curiosity— the same posture that keeps us human.

I've heard countless stories from clients wrestling with impulses: hiding food or sneaking snacks, spending money they didn't have, scrolling long past midnight, saying yes when they meant no, chasing affection that vanishes by morning, or chasing status that never quite quiets the ache for belonging. Some described the shame they felt for resting or playing — how doing "nothing" triggered guilt stronger than hunger. Others searched for certainty, sorting life into right and wrong, good and bad, as if certainty itself might finally bring peace. They sat across from me in tears — embarrassed, aware of how empty the pursuit felt, yet compelled to keep going.

Beneath it all was the same ancient conflict: deep biological imperatives pulling one way, and the rules society teaches us about what is "acceptable" pulling the other.

These same patterns often appear in clients who've experienced sexual trauma as well. Promiscuity, compulsive sexual behavior, or acting out sexually are not anomalies — they are reflexive responses shaped by trauma interacting with natural biological drives. They are common, not rare.

Some impulses surface in quieter ways: a compelled glance, a flash of anger that feels out of proportion, a sudden urge to withdraw. These reactions, even when socially uncomfortable, are rooted in the same old-brain wiring — the drive to survive, belong, protect oneself, and stay safe.

One of the most powerful moments in my work is when I help a client see that what they're experiencing is *normal*. The relief is visible — a deep exhale, a softening of posture, a sense that they are not broken or bad, just human. Using this understanding of our biology, clients can begin to respect what is normal, observe it, and respond without judgment. That same perspective is what I hope to offer you here.

As we move forward, remember this: the impulses, drives, and reflexes you experience are not *moral failures*. They are part of being human.

They've been with us for hundreds of thousands of years, long before smartphones and social media. Our old brain evolved to help us find food, attach to others, play, compete, reproduce, rest, and endure. Hunger, desire, fear, fatigue, ambition — these are signals, not defects. Respecting them doesn't mean surrendering to them. It means noticing, understanding, and learning to navigate modern life with awareness.

From the very beginning of our species, survival meant spotting a real bear before it spotted us. The problem now is that our nervous system often reacts as if bears are everywhere — even when today's threats are more likely to be words, rules, expectations, and social pressures. When that happens, stress doesn't just accumulate. It lies the groundwork for shame itself.

History matters here, too. From ancient tribal conflicts to modern politics and religion, the forces shaping human behavior are deeply rooted. Our old instincts still echo wherever we draw lines around belonging. When we ignore their origins, we judge ourselves and others harshly. When we begin to comprehend them, patterns emerge— and with them, the possibility of compassion, clarity, and a deep understanding.

My interest in this type of biology didn't come solely from textbooks. It came from trauma — from witnessing how automatic, deeply wired, and universal these responses are. Again and again, I watched what happened when someone realized they weren't broken — just human. That insight has guided every page of this book.

This is my invitation to you: to understand the tension between our ancient wiring and the modern world, to honor impulses without shame, and to begin seeing yourself — and others — with curiosity and respect. Because these struggles don't stop with us. They ripple outward.

Our collective nervous system is running hotter than evolution ever intended, and the consequences reach beyond individual well-being to the health of families, communities, and cultures.

From here, we begin with Part I: **Understanding the Old Brain** — exploring the anatomy, reflexes, and survival drives that have guided humanity for hundreds of thousands of years, and that continues to guide us today.

Primal Wiring Collides with Modern Circuitry

PART I

*Understanding the Old Brain.
Foundations of the Mind – Biology, Survival,
and the Roots of Shame*

Chapter 1: Anatomy of a Dual Mind

"The attempt to escape from pain is what creates more pain."
— *Gabor Maté*

As we begin a deeper dive into understanding the Old Brain, let's be clear—without being too repetitive—that the focus of this book is on biology, especially primitive biology. Understanding our own biology is key to many factors that impede people's lives. I will share a brief account of how I arrived at this place as a social worker, focusing on the primitive biology that shapes the challenges in our modern world.

Having been in private practice for over 20 years and in the mental health field for more than 30, I began to view this through a biological lens in the mid-1990s, when I started working as a psychiatric technician at a psychiatric hospital with no training or experience—my education was an associate's degree in law enforcement technology. (Yes, I wanted to be a cop for a long time, but that's another story.)

Once I started on the units, I became fascinated and perplexed by the clients hospitalized for PTSD. I remember thinking, when listening to them describe intrusive thoughts triggered by sounds or sights, "Why don't they just stop that?" (Oh, the wisdom I had!). Now, as a clinical social worker, I realize that was a very limited and ignorant perspective. They would have stopped those symptoms if they could. The problem is that they can't, and that's what makes it so challenging. That early confusion sparked my fascination with trauma.

Returning to school, delving into literature, journals, and conferences, and learning from experts such as Bessel van der Kolk, Peter Levine, Pat Ogden, Stephen Porges, and Gabor Maté, I began to understand the fight-or-flight system and the primitive biology underlying traumatic stress responses. Trauma started to make sense. The key realization was that when we look at trauma with a rational, logical lens, we appear dysfunctional—but through a lens of primitive biology, everything starts to make sense. I help my clients see themselves through that biological lens. It not only makes sense for them but also provides a sense of relief that they are not "crazy"; it's just biology.

This brings me to a broader point: we live in our heads. Sir Ken Robinson observed that point when he spoke of professors and said, "There's something curious about professors in my experience — not all of them, but typically, they live in their heads. They live up there, and slightly to one side. They're disembodied, you know, in a kind of literal way. They look upon their body as a form of transport for their head." (Robinson, 2006)

I believe many of us struggle with that theme; we just see our bodies as a way to get our heads around the world. The idea that we are disembodied holds true in my work with clients. We have lost sight of the importance of our bodies. We've become so focused on the smart part of our brain that we forget we are animals at our core. Understanding biology is respecting that we are, at our core, animals. Animals have drives and needs built into our DNA and physical body—but we've lost sight of them.

The challenge of modern life is that technology evolves far faster than our biology. In my own lifetime, I've gone from calling friends on a rotary phone (yes, you had to wait for the dial to spin back around—good luck if you misdialed) to being connected to six or seven devices simultaneously. Our nervous system wasn't built for that constant, rapid pace of change, and it shows in the prevalence of anxiety and stress today.

The Old Brain in Action

Let's break down the old brain. Think of your brain in two parts: the top part, with fancy names like the neocortex or frontal cortex, I call the new brain. This is where you pay bills, plan vacations, and do your thinking. The lower part at the base of the skull, sometimes called the limbic system, the reptilian brain, or the caveman brain, I call the old brain. Evolutionarily, this brain stem existed hundreds of thousands of years before the frontal cortex. Its focus? Survival. Period!

Quick note on language: *Throughout this book, I use the term* **old brain** *for simplicity. Technically, much of what I describe overlaps with what scientists call the* **autonomic nervous system** *and parts of the* **limbic system**. *In practice, the old brain and the nervous system are deeply intertwined—two ways of talking about the same survival machinery. I stick with the old brain because it's vivid, easy to remember, and keeps us focused on how ancient this system really is. As I often tell clients, "The full biology is more complex than this, but understanding the basic themes of the old brain is usually enough to make sense of what we're experiencing."*

Key structures include:
- **Thalamus:** sensory filter.
- **Amygdala:** fear and emotional response.
- **Hippocampus:** memory storage.
- **Hypothalamus:** master gland regulating homeostasis—balance in nutrients, hydration, temperature, and sleep.

All these functions are automatic, and the purpose is simple: keep us alive. Appetite, thirst, sleep, digestion, elimination, sex, attachment, play, and safety—these are all core survival drives, many of them involuntary, that ensure survival and reproduction.

It's important to understand that, when I talk about bodily functions like sleep and hydration, the old brain also involuntarily influences heart rate, breathing, digestion, and hormonal regulation. These changes aren't just physiological—they're tied to neurochemical stress responses. When stress hits, your old brain controls a symphony of body systems that impact how you feel, think, and react.

The stress response in the old brain operates like a stereo dial. Threats crank the dial up to 10; ideally, it resets to zero. But repeated stress, modern triggers, or poor self-care can leave it stuck at 3–4 (anxiety) or 8–10 (PTSD). The new brain can sometimes regulate these responses, but only to a point. This is where the concept of a "coping bucket" comes in: the quality of caregiving we received, plus basic biological maintenance—sleep, hydration, nutrition—determines our overall capacity to regulate primitive responses.

But here's the catch: even when your coping bucket is full, the old brain can still slam the override button. If it decides the threat is too big, survival takes priority, and you're launched into full-blown fight, flight, or freeze before you even realize what's happening. And honestly—that's a good thing. Because at the end of the day, the ultimate goal of the old brain isn't to keep you calm, it's to keep you alive.

Picture walking in the woods when a bear jumps out. Your sensory data—sight and sound—are processed by the thalamus and sent to the amygdala, which alerts the hippocampus. The hypothalamus activates the adrenal system: cortisol surges, your heart races, your muscles tense—you're ready to fight or flee.

Neuroscientist Joseph LeDoux has shown that the old brain has a fast track for danger—sometimes called the *low road*. Sensory data can travel directly from the thalamus to the amygdala and set off an alarm before the thinking brain is even aware (LeDoux, *The Emotional Brain,* 1996). Through repeated pairing, neutral sights, sounds, smells—even certain words—can become learned fear cues. That means a single charged word that's been linked to danger in the past can trigger a full fight-or-flight surge in a split second.

The amygdala **tags experiences with emotional significance**, linking them to bodily reactions rather than to verbal stories, while nearby regions, such as the hippocampus, record the context. When the five senses pick up those cues again, the amygdala can slam the alarm button before the frontal cortex has time to weigh in. These aren't abstract thoughts—they're *implicit emotional memories*: stored patterns of sensation and response that bypass language altogether. It's the same system that once kept our ancestors alive when a rustling bush might hide a predator, and it still fires today when something our senses associate with a past threat crosses our path. This is why the old brain can feel as if it "remembers" danger and reacts first, while the frontal cortex scrambles to catch up and explain what just happened.

This response is automatic. Appetite, sleep, digestion, and other homeostatic functions temporarily take a backseat. The goal is survival, and this system is powerful, precise, and fast. Evolution designed it for short-term threats, like a bear in the woods. As Peter Levine describes in *Waking the Tiger* (1997), when our nervous system is allowed to complete a full cycle of activation, the chemical surge of fight-or-flight typically lasts about **90 seconds** before the body begins to reset. But here's the problem: we were never meant to stay in that activated state for hours, days, weeks, or months. The old brain's emergency gear is designed for short, immediate survival—not the unending buzz of modern life. Repetitive, long-term stress and threat can leave a system that is built to reset **stuck on high alert**, keeping that internal stereo dial cranked far beyond what evolution intended.

Here is a modern-day example of this response: imagine walking into work, having made a mistake, and your boss rushes at you, red-faced, finger-pointing, yelling, maybe even spitting out of the sides of his mouth. Your old brain might perceive this as life-threatening and start to respond to the threat (And remember the deepest of imperatives of that old brain is to keep us alive). But a thought crosses your brain, "This is not a threat." Your new brain knows this rationally: "My boss doesn't eat people…as far as I know, at least he doesn't eat people." But if your coping bucket is low, your primitive system floods in, and you may panic, freeze, or snap at your boss. Reflexively, you might say something you regret, even if briefly satisfying. Suddenly, you feel guilt and shame—what a horrible person I am.

Four Responses to Threat

I want to talk about the four responses our old brain has when facing a threat. You've probably heard of fight-or-flight, but there's also freeze. These are all basic, simple responses to danger. In addition to fight, flight, and freeze, therapist Pete Walker (2013) describes a fourth trauma response he calls "fawn"—an appeasing, people-pleasing survival strategy. While not a formal diagnostic category, the idea complements Stephen Porges' polyvagal theory, which shows how our autonomic nervous system can shift into patterns of social engagement to defuse danger (Porges, 2009).

Freeze is an old standby from our cave-dwelling days. If we came across a predator or threat we couldn't run from or fight, we would freeze. We see this in the animal kingdom today—small animals will play dead.

Sometimes they play dead so well that they die. Guess that's where the phrase "scared to death" comes from.

Humans can lock up, pause in the face of danger, unable to escape or fight. When we experience freezing, it can be particularly impactful—many of my clients describe the "paralyzing feeling," sometimes worse than the threat itself. Freeze can also appear in subtler ways: dramatically slowed thinking or movement, loss of coordination, or even complete disconnection.

The point is, these basic responses were appropriate for the threats we faced thousands of years ago. But in our modern world? Not so much. Pretty sure your boss does not want to wrestle you because your timesheet was wrong last week. These responses are crude, simplistic, and society tells us to "get your you-know-what together and knock it off," yet much of this can be involuntary. With the correct perception, or not enough in your coping bucket, you're off and running—or freezing—without control.

The takeaway: the way our old brain responds to threats is simplistic, built for survival, and certainly never designed for our 24-hour news, TikTok, and constant notification world.

Bottom-Up and Top-Down Processing

The old brain is bottom-up: it responds automatically to sensory data. The new brain can do top-down regulation, modulating primitive impulses if the coping bucket is sufficiently full. But when stress, poor sleep, dehydration, or hunger deplete the bucket, we default to raw, primitive responses: anger, fear, attachment-seeking, and survival behaviors. This is not "wrong," it is biology doing its job.

It is important to know we have a sort of built-in radar that naturally leans a little toward "better safe than sorry." That bias helped our ancestors stay alive when a rustling bush might hide a predator, and it's still alive and well today. Under stress, this tilt toward danger can become even more pronounced: perception narrows, and the old brain decides first and fastest that what's happening could kill us—whether that's true or not.

We tend to overestimate the power of the frontal cortex—our 'smart brain'—believing it can always override our primitive responses. While it is incredibly capable and essential for higher reasoning, decision-making, and shaping our lives, it has limits, and relying on it exclusively can close our eyes to the unstoppable instincts of the old brain.

When it comes to PTSD or trauma triggers, the old brain stores implicit sensorial memories—sights, sounds, smells, or touches—that can flash unexpectedly. People often aren't cognitively aware of these triggers because they're stored in non-verbal, sensory memory circuits. When these cues are picked up again, the fight-or-flight system activates, sometimes leaving people feeling like they're "losing their mind." This is biology, not insanity. There are times when clients can tell a story about their triggers, what is known as explicit memories, but not always.

As Peter Levine writes in his book, *Waking the Tiger,* "Anxiety and despair can become a creative wellspring when we allow ourselves to experience bodily sensations, such as trembling, that stem from traumatic symptoms."

In other words, when we stop fighting those sensory fragments and instead lean into them with curiosity, they can become pathways toward healing rather than just reminders of pain.

Sensory Grounding Strategies

One of the exercises I ask my clients to do is identify what I call **Sensorial Soothing Strategies** to help provide sensory grounding. The idea is simple: reflect on your five senses—sight, sound, smell, taste, touch—and identify things that recall positive memories or feelings of safety and connection. For example:

- The scent of lavender.
- The sound of ocean waves.
- A visual memory of your childhood home.
- A blanket that feels warm and soft.
- A favorite snack from childhood.

Personally, I have one: when I was little, I would accompany my dad while he worked on the railroad. I loved skipping along the tracks (clearly illegal, but I was a kid, who knew?) while inhaling the smell of creosote from the ties I was hopping on. Today, when I smell creosote,

I'm instantly transported back to that positive memory—the sense of joy and playfulness I had in those moments—and it happens automatically.

Using these sensory cues intentionally can help the old brain dial down the stereo volume. It's not magic, but it works because the old brain's language is sensory. Intentional grounding—sounds, smells, textures—feeds safety signals to the old brain, helping it calm down. As Bessel van der Kolk puts it in *The Body Keeps the Score,*

"Trauma victims cannot recover until they become familiar with and befriend the sensations in their bodies."

That's precisely why I say the language of the old brain is sensory. It's not your thoughts—it's what you feel, smell, see, taste, or touch. When your body holds fear or shame, we need to speak back to it in that same sensory language.

Technology Overload

I absolutely love technology. I've been fascinated with it since I was a kid. In the early 1980s, I thought personal computers—think VIC-20—were the coolest thing ever. What I couldn't have anticipated was how rapidly technology would evolve. Now we're bombarded: emails, notifications, social media, instant messaging. Phones ding every few seconds. We're expected to respond immediately, and there's a subtle but persistent social pressure: "Why did it take you five minutes to respond?"

Our nervous system wasn't built for this constant, rapid pace. This mismatch between primitive wiring and modern life contributes to stress, anxiety, and that old stereo dial cranked way past zero. Technology also enables the instant dissemination of news worldwide. When I was a kid, and something big happened, you had to wait for the evening news. Today, we can witness horrific events unfold in real time, all from the comfort of our chairs and devices.

Remember: the old brain is primitive. When it starts taking in danger signals—even if the threat isn't directed at us but at other humans—it can still kick into gear. And now, unlike in the past, this happens weekly rather than occasionally. The old brain was never designed to process or defend against such a high and constant rate of perceived threats.

This activation from witnessing another human under threat is part of why scary movies work so well. There's a rush—a surge of hormones—because it taps into our number one desire: to stay alive. And make no mistake—corporations know this. Sex sells, indulgent food ads make us crave, and thrillers keep us glued to the screen for the same reason: they hijack our old brain. It's subtle, and we rarely realize it, but our system responds exactly as it was designed—with attention, desire, and action.

These same principles apply in other ways, too. Advertising scarcity, creating a fear of missing out, or dramatizing danger all stimulate the old brain's survival circuits. The result? We often walk away with lighter wallets, a sense of urgency, and a side order of lingering shame. Corporations don't have to trick us—they just present stimuli our biology can't ignore, and we respond predictably.

This is precisely why technology has become such a double-edged sword. With instant notifications, social media, and constant streams of information, our old brain is bombarded with stimuli that corporations, media, and apps have optimized to grab our attention—sometimes to sell us something, sometimes to keep us hooked, and sometimes to tell us what is *right or wrong*. The same primitive biology that once kept us alive is now constantly triggered, and our nervous system struggles to keep up.

Technology also gets in the way of *real play*. Our devices provide stimulation, but rarely the kind of play that restores or connects. The old brain knows the difference between swiping a screen and kicking a ball.

Sexuality, Reproduction, and Primitive Drives

Somehow, we all know that reproduction is necessary for our species, but even thinking about sexual desire can make people uncomfortable. At its core, sexual drive is just another primitive impulse—necessary for procreation but often clashing with societal constructs. Western culture often encourages us to ignore sexuality or feel shame about it. We are animals. Sex is part of survival. Without it, none of us would be here. Yet conflict with social rules, body image pressures, sexuality, and cultural norms can turn a natural drive into guilt, shame, or anxiety.

Safety, Connection, and Everyday Life

The old brain isn't just about threat—it's about balance. Safety, food, sleep, water, sex, play, attachment—these are essential for survival. Modern life often conflicts with these drives. As a clinician, I am fascinated by clients who neglect hydration, skip meals, or sacrifice sleep. Basic interventions—drink water, eat properly, rest—can improve focus, mood, energy, and sleep, because you're feeding your coping bucket. This drive for connection isn't a modern invention; it's etched into our species from the beginning of human history.

Anthropologists like Robin Dunbar observe that early humans lived in small hunter-gatherer bands—often described as our original human environment (Dunbar, 1996). These groups, usually 20–50 people, were not optional social clubs; they were life-support systems. The tribe supplied food, fire, defense against predators, and care for children and the sick.

The flip side was equally powerful: to be cut off from the group was often a death sentence. Dunbar and other anthropologists have shown that social exclusion or ostracism functioned as one of the harshest punishments because it removed protection, resources, and emotional connection.

Even in more recent traditional societies (for example, many Native American nations), temporary banishment— "you're out until the next full moon"—was a serious sanction, not a symbolic one. This deep dependence on the group is etched into our wiring. For most of human history, being excluded from the tribe wasn't just sad—it was life-threatening.

That's why our nervous system still reacts so strongly to anything that hints at separation or rejection. The old brain doesn't parse whether the threat comes from a prowling predator or a shift in social standing; it just reads danger.

We may no longer face wolves at the cave mouth, but the survival circuitry forged in those small bands is still at work today, scanning for anything that might mean you're out of the tribe. There's a new kind of "bear" now, and we'll get to that in the next chapter. And trust me—this modern bear can be even scarier and more dangerous than any black bear you might meet in the woods. You might even find yourself wishing for the old-fashioned bears; at least they were simpler to fight.

The key to this biological puzzle is play. It may not look as automatic as breathing or hunger, but it is nonetheless hard-wired. Neuroscientist Jaak Panksepp even identified play as one of the brain's core emotional systems (Panksepp, 1998). From wolf pups wrestling to children inventing games out of thin air, play strengthens social bonds, relieves stress, and teaches the brain to adapt. For adults, it can be as simple as shooting hoops, playing music, laughing with friends, or goofing around with a pet. In other words, play is nature's own regulator—another way the old brain helps us reset and return to balance. As Jaak Panksepp's work demonstrates, play teaches skills, builds social bonds, and—even in adults—relieves stress and sparks creativity. Your old brain sees play as practice for survival, not frivolity. In a world that often equates success with productivity, this basic need has been squeezed out— especially for children, who increasingly spend school days trading movement and recess for more desk time and standardized tests. When we cut out play, we're not just trimming "extra fun," we're depriving the old brain of one of its natural ways to regulate and restore balance.

We also know from Stephen Porges (Porges, 2011), who describes in his Polyvagal Theory, that our social engagement system is a biological regulator. A calm face, steady eye contact, and a gentle prosodic voice literally tell the old brain, *"You are safe."* This isn't metaphor—it's neurophysiology at work. Just think of the positive impact we can have with a kind, calm face and soft tone on the nervous system of people around us. It is simple yet incredibly powerful in helping us rebalance and find safety and connection.

In fact, this idea of a calm face and tone is exactly how I greet my clients. Some walk in already in tears—and what do they see first? My smile. That's not an accident. It's key to my work. Beyond the words I might say or the techniques I might use, they get a different face right from the start. And what does their old brain do when it sees my smile, even amid tears? It smiles back.

Clients often think it's just me being friendly or kind—which it is—but there's a deeper neurophysiological reason, as Stephen Porges describes in his Polyvagal Theory. It's the start of regulation. I count on my face and tone of voice in sessions more than any other "intervention," because it's biology. There's a part of the brain that can't help but respond with a smile. I've even had clients laugh through their tears and say, *"That smile—stop it! I'm trying to be depressed here."* They're joking, but their old brain has already gotten the message: *safe, calm, connected.*

Now, I'm not suggesting my grin will bring about world peace (not yet anyhow), but it is a fundamental, primitive intervention that is incredibly effective. Imagine if my clients arrived, and I greeted them with a smirk or a worried face. What would their old brain do? Instantly trigger concern: *Paul, are you okay? What's going on? You look upset.* And just like that, it's my therapy session, not theirs—not terribly effective.

This is why therapists must have a plan and a place to process our own stuff. (News flash: therapists are humans, and we don't have all our "stuff" figured out.) The concept of calm facial and vocal regulation is highly important, and it will come up again when we discuss later the biological imperatives, drives, and impulses we must respect.

Now imagine—knowing the science behind our faces and tone of voice—the quiet power of a single smile in everyday life. Your expression could shift a room, settle a friend, soften a stranger. In the words of John Lennon, *Imagine.*

Our Built-In Reset Button

One of the most overlooked marvels of our biology is its **relentless drive to return to balance**—what science calls *homeostasis.* The old brain isn't just a danger alarm; it's also a quiet, steady maintenance crew. Think of what happens when you cut your hand: white blood cells rush in, blood coagulates, and a scab forms—all without a single conscious thought. You don't have to schedule healing on your calendar. It just happens.

The same principle applies to our **emotional and psychological life**. Given time and the right conditions, the nervous system tends to return to equilibrium. I see it in therapy all the time: with support and regulation, people begin to mend in ways as natural as that closing scab.

But here's the catch—and it ties back to one of this chapter's main themes.

You **can't outthink biology.** Our culture loves to glorify the frontal cortex as if sheer willpower can override every need. We skip meals, shortchange sleep, chug coffee instead of water, and tell ourselves we can "power through." The old brain disagrees. Ignore hunger, thirst, or rest long enough, and it will force a correction—cranking the stereo dial with anxiety, irritability, or physical symptoms until you pay attention.

Knowing how the old brain functions under stress is more than an academic lesson. It's **a survival manual**. By respecting the built-in rhythms of recovery—hydration, nutrition, sleep, sensory grounding, social connection, and even play—you give the nervous system what it needs to reset. Support the biology, and the psychology follows.

When We Ignore Biology, the Body Pushes Back

Failing to listen to our biology doesn't just lead to mood issues like anxiety or depression—it can literally make us sick. Long-term stress keeps the old brain's danger system switched on, and that constant activation has measurable effects on the immune system. Research by Segerstrom and Miller (2004) showed that chronic stress lowers levels of **immunoglobulin A (IgA),** a key protein that acts as the body's first line of defense against infection.

Think of IgA as part of your personal security team: it patrols the mucous membranes in your gut, lungs, and mouth, neutralizing viruses and bacteria before they invade. When stress keeps the alarm blaring, IgA production drops, leaving the gates unguarded. Suddenly, you're more vulnerable to colds, flu, digestive problems, and even slower healing.

This is hard proof that **you can't outthink or outwork your old brain**. Ignoring hunger, thirst, sleep, and recovery isn't just a mental-health gamble—it's a direct hit on your immune system. The message is simple but not optional: biology always collects its bill.

The Challenge of the Smart Brain

Here lies the challenge: our new brain is brilliant, but sometimes it works against us. It interprets social constructs—those invisible rules about what's acceptable, desirable, or worthy—judges our primitive responses, and fuels shame. Flashes of anger, sexual drives, or body image concerns—biological impulses—are filtered through cultural beliefs. The old brain isn't wrong; it's responding to survival, safety, attachment, reproduction, and balance.

Key Takeaways So Far

- The old brain is primitive, automatic, and focused on survival: safety, food, water, sleep, play, attachment, and reproduction.

- Modern life often conflicts with these drives, producing stress, anxiety, and misinterpreted signals.

- The new brain is powerful but influenced by social constructs, leading to shame when it judges raw biological responses.

- Coping capacity (bucket) and self-care are critical for regulating primitive impulses.

- Sensory grounding strategies, social connection, and respect for bodily needs are essential tools for calming the old brain; our five senses are its language.

Exercise: Sensorial Soothing Strategies

Take some time to sit quietly and reflect on your life—especially moments when you felt safe, loved, playful, or happy. As you revisit those memories, notice if any of your five senses stand out. Was there a particular smell, sound, taste, or texture that anchored that feeling for you?

Now, play around with recreating that sensory input. Maybe it's the smell of lavender, the sound of ocean waves, or the feel of a soft blanket. Notice what happens in your body when you engage with it. Often, you'll find the same sense of safety or calm you felt back then begins to resurface.

Many of my clients already have these sensorial soothing strategies without realizing it. Once I explain the concept, they can usually rattle off a list from memory. Chances are, you've got some of your own—

you just haven't thought of them as tools. Now you know the science of why they help with regulation.

But here's an important note: some clients tell me they don't have many, or even any, memories of safety. They can't tie soothing experiences to their five senses. If that's you, no worries. This isn't about getting it "right," it's about experimenting. Go to one of those smelly candle shops in the mall. Try out different scents. Play around with different sounds or music: test textures or flavors. You might stumble across something that unexpectedly calms you, even if you don't have a memory tied to it. It may take more effort and playfulness, but the principle is the same. And honestly, the worst-case scenario is you end up with a house full of candles. (There are worse problems to have.)

The key is to write these down and intentionally incorporate them into your daily life. Play a recording of ocean waves during your commute. Hang a calming scent in your car. Keep a soft object nearby that connects you to a safe memory. The more you bombard your old brain with sensory cues tied to safety, love, and connection, the more likely you are to turn that stereo dial down.

It's not a magic cure or a guarantee, but here's the good news: there are no side effects, and the potential benefits are all positive.

Summary

So, now that we've given the old brain some love—hydration, snacks, soft blankets, and the occasional smelly candle—it's time to see how this biology collides with the world we live in. Because just like your fridge doesn't care about your diet plan, society doesn't always care about your primitive impulses.

Take a breath and notice what you've just explored: you've mapped the stereo dials of your body, understood how primitive impulses operate, and started collecting your personal sensory tools. Consider it stretching before the next mental marathon.

Next, we'll look at how culture and social rules try to hack those ancient circuits. From everyday words to unspoken expectations, social constructs quietly shape how we interpret our most basic drives—sex, food, play, attachment, even elimination. And when those rules crash into a brain that's still wired to keep you alive and hydrated, sparks fly.

If we step back from the individual and look at the planet as a whole, the pattern is hard to miss. Modern life is dysregulating the human nervous system at a species level. Every phone alert, every 24-hour news cycle, every relentless demand keeps that old stereo dial humming hotter than it was ever built to run. What I see in my office every day is not just personal stress; it's a collective biology pushed past its evolutionary design.

So, grab some popcorn (I make a mean popcorn) and get ready for Chapter 2—we'll pull back the curtain on social constructs, those invisible cultural agreements that tell us how to think and feel about our own biology, ourselves, and the world around us.

CHAPTER 2: The Modern Bear: How Culture Becomes a Biological Threat

Why the culture that shapes us can also shame and endanger us—body first, mind second.

"Your old brain doesn't care about rules—it cares about survival. Shame? That's just a social trick; it didn't evolve to handle."

—*Pinette, Field Notes, 2025*

Social Constructs

The last chapter explored those ancient circuits in detail so you could see the solid ground we stand on in old-brain biology. **That foundation matters now,** as we turn to a concept called *social constructs*. Most readers have never heard the term and have no idea how much power these invisible rules hold over us and our relationship to the world.

What are social constructs?

Social constructs—what academics might call **sociocultural constructs or socially constructed norms**—are just the unspoken cultural rules and shared agreements that shape how we think, feel, and behave.

They're the messages we absorb from every direction: social media, movies, books, family, religion, and peers. Sometimes they're direct and obvious; other times they come as *metamessages*—a kind of hidden code beneath the surface.

Either way, these signals shape how we see the world, what we believe, and how we move through daily life. And I've begun to realize they reach further than we ever imagined—quietly embedding themselves in the body, not just the mind.

Think of this as laying the foundation: once you start noticing these hidden codes, it's only a short step to the heavier, more enduring words and cultural rules—the ones that carry identity, history, **and deep weight and pain.**

And this is especially true today, when we're flooded with constant, overwhelming messaging through social media and instant connectivity. The sheer speed and volume mean that cultural pressure has never been stronger. Constant repetition—regardless of truth—has an impact: we begin to believe the messages as fact, without ever checking the facts.

Psychologists call this the *illusory truth effect*—repeat a statement often enough, and the brain begins to treat it as reality, even when the facts don't add up (Fazio et al., 2015).

History is full of examples. Joseph Goebbels, Hitler's propaganda minister, is often linked to the chilling idea that "a lie told often enough becomes the truth," though scholars debate the exact wording. What isn't in dispute is that Goebbels openly described and practiced the strategy of repeating big lies until they felt inevitable. Today, anyone with a social-media account, podcast, or YouTube channel can do something similar—broadcasting an opinion so relentlessly that it starts to feel like common sense. In the nervous system, constant repetition carries weight, whether the message is accurate or not; the body begins to register it as reality.

The trouble is most people—including many of my clients—aren't even aware these constructs exist. They treat them as truths carved in stone when they're not. And when those "rules" are left unexamined, they can quietly shape everything from mood and self-worth to anxiety and depression.

Part of my clinical work is helping people *see* these forces and their role in everyday life. Because once you notice how a single word, expectation, or hidden rule can bend the nervous system toward stress and shame, it becomes clear: culture can activate the same survival alarms as a charging bear.

Everyday Constructs: From Letters to Bananas to Holidays

Words have power. A lot of power. I know—that sounds so cliché. When was the last time your A, B, Cs hurt anyone, right?

I mean, everyone knows the old saying, "Sticks and stones may break my bones, but words will never hurt me." Well… buckle up. You're not going to look at Sesame Street's "letter of the day" the same way again.

To show how powerful social constructs really are, we'll move through this chapter like a funnel. We'll start with light, familiar, everyday examples of how society quietly teaches meaning—then narrow toward charged words and rules with serious emotional weight. By the time we reach messages about sex, food, ambition, or worthiness, you'll see how these aren't just cultural curiosities. They're woven into the body.

The truth is that language isn't just letters strung together. Words are carriers of culture. They tell us what is acceptable, what's desirable, what's shameful. And those cultural agreements—those "constructs"—quietly shape how we feel about our bodies, our drives, and our most basic biological needs long before we're aware of them.

Later, I'll show how certain words, looks, and expectations can set off the same survival circuitry that once protected us from predators—like a bear rustling in the bushes. Only now the "bear" may be repeated words, cultural beliefs, or judgments stored in the body as learned cues of danger.

Let's start simple and light, with a single word: house.
It's made of five letters—H-O-U-S-E.

When I say, "I'm heading to my house," most people instantly picture something similar: a structure with walls, a roof, a kitchen, and bathrooms.

You don't know my color scheme or how badly my 1940s kitchen needs an update, but we share a basic agreement about what *house* means. That's a harmless, even useful construct—it lets language work.

But what happens if I decide to call my house a "banana"? Imagine me saying, *I need to paint my banana* or *the lawn around my banana needs mowing.*

At first, people might laugh. After a while, they'd get irritated. Some might even get angry and snap, "Paul, it's not a banana—it's a house. Stop it!"

That's the discomfort of challenging a social construct. The pushback isn't about fruit. It's about the human need for shared meaning and predictability.

When those shared meanings wobble, people can feel threatened—like their own mental map of the world is under attack.

Now, most constructs aren't that silly. Many feel so natural that we barely notice them. Take colors and gender: today, "blue is for boys, pink is for girls" feels eternal, yet a century ago, it was reversed.

Or think of the old saying "boys don't cry," which quietly teaches that real men should be stoic and strong. Yet at other times, men are told they should be more open, softer, and more emotionally expressive. Any wonder why so many men feel confused about what they're "supposed" to be?

The same goes for play and toys. Advertisers still steer boys toward trucks and girls toward dolls—even though both are just bits of plastic and metal. Plastic and metal have no gender at all, yet culture assigns them one. And if toys and colors can carry that much hidden weight, imagine what happens when the stakes get higher.

Take the fashion police favorite, for example: no pajamas in public. It isn't a law, but walk into a grocery store at 2 p.m. in flannel bottoms, and you'll feel the stares (seriously—it's not illegal to shop in PJs). A few threads of cloth—labeled "sleepwear"—can trigger judgment, proving how deeply we tie meaning to simple fibers.

Or consider that once-practical greeting, the handshake. It started to show you weren't carrying a weapon and has now become a default sign of trust and confidence.

Age comes with its own quiet codes. Children often have little voice because they don't earn money; older adults can be dismissed for the same reason. It's as if our worth rises and falls with our economic output, a relic of the days when every tribe member had to carry their weight to survive.

And birthdays? We light candles on the cake without asking why. The practice is a mash-up of old European customs and modern marketing, reinforced by greeting-card aisles and bakery ads. The meaning—that aging deserves a ritual—feels natural because it's repeated.

Holidays are some of the most powerful examples. I can't count how many therapy sessions have revolved around a disastrous Thanksgiving when Uncle Johnny drank too much and "puked all over the turkey." People absorb glossy, Norman Rockwell expectations of togetherness, only to crash into messy reality. Even those who don't celebrate can feel pressure or exclusion, as if there's only one correct way to mark the season.

Take Mother's Day. Its ancient roots were about honoring goddesses and "mother churches. The U.S. version began in 1908 when Anna Jarvis organized a memorial for her mom. By 1914, Woodrow Wilson had signed it into law, making it a national holiday. Jarvis later fought the very commercialization she helped spark, angered by florists and greeting-card companies who turned a heartfelt tribute into big business. Father's Day lagged, only becoming official when Nixon signed it into law decades later.

Don't misunderstand me—I'm not anti-holiday. I have a mother too. But every year, I see clients in tears because they didn't buy the "right" gift or host the "perfect" dinner. The more profound message is that love must be proven on one specific date, when in truth, we could honor loved ones on any of the other 364 days.

These examples may seem light, even funny. But that's precisely the point. They show how seamlessly social constructs weave into life—

until breaking one can feel like breaking a law. Left unquestioned, the exact mechanism that enforces birthday candles or firm handshakes can harden around far heavier words and rules. Those are the ones we're heading toward next.

Why These Examples Matter

The trouble is, if you don't stop and examine social constructs, the consequences can be serious. Sure, some are harmless—like wearing pajamas to the store (though keep it up and the fashion police might try to outlaw it). But many others run much deeper. I'll often ask clients, "Who said this is the way it has to be?" They pause. "I don't know… other people, I guess." "And where did they get that idea?" Another long pause—cue the crickets. Almost every time the answer is, "I don't know."

Then I'll say, "So let me get this straight: you've built parts of your life on these so-called rules—rules that feel absolute and uncomfortable to break—yet you can't tell me where they come from or why they should govern you. Are you living your own life, or the one society wants you to live?"

Some constructs—like birthday candles or who pays the tab—aren't going to wreck your nervous system. But the deeper, more charged ones can. Left unexamined, they don't just shape thoughts; they can activate the old brain the way a sudden rustle once signaled a bear. And they ripple outward, affecting us both collectively and individually. That's why I challenge clients to question these "truths," even when it's scary. Because a life run on unexamined social constructs is a recipe for anxiety, depression, and, in my view, the most significant trauma of all: the struggle to live authentically.

So far, many of the examples have made you chuckle. They may not seem earth-shattering. But the very ordinariness is the point. These everyday rules—words, expectations, silent agreements—create patterns powerful enough to steer emotions and decisions without us noticing. Which brings me to my clinical hypothesis.

Social Constructs as Embodied Threats

Building on Stephen Porges' polyvagal theory (Porges, 2011)—which shows how social cues of safety or threat can shift the nervous system in real time—and on Joseph LeDoux's work on the brain's threat pathways, I propose that certain deeply ingrained cultural constructs act in much the same way. In today's relentless media and technology environment, it may not even take decades of repetition anymore; a shorter, high-intensity barrage can be enough to hardwire a message.

LeDoux demonstrated that the old brain has a low road for danger, where sensory information travels directly from the thalamus to the amygdala, allowing a learned cue—a sound, a smell, even a single word—to trigger fight-or-flight before the thinking brain catches up (LeDoux, 1996). Porges' work helps explain what happens next: how those cues are interpreted as signals of safety or threat, shaping physiology, behavior, and connection in real time.

This is where my clinical hypothesis takes root. Repeated social constructs don't just shape culture; they sink into the nervous system itself. They become embodied threats—what I call the **modern bear**.

This understanding is drawn from decades of sitting with clients and aligns with what trauma science already knows about implicit memory."

When Culture Becomes a Bear

Over the years, I've often told clients, *"Your body is reacting as if there's a bear about to eat you—but there is no bear."*

Lately I've come to realize that, in a very real sense, there is a bear—a modern bear. It isn't a grizzly in the woods; it's the barrage of cultural messages about worth, sexuality, success, gender—you name it—that have taken root in the nervous system.

Social constructs don't always stay abstract; some embed themselves in the old brain until they register as actual survival threats. So, when someone flinches at a slur, panics at disapproval, or feels terror at the thought of rejection, their biology isn't "overreacting." It's doing precisely what it was wired to do: defend against danger.

Only now the threat comes from words, expectations, and repeated judgments, rather than claws and teeth. Ordinary words get hijacked, twisted, and weaponized into shame.

The Modern Bear at Work

My insight is that repeated social messages—"you're not good enough," "you're not lovable," "real men don't cry"—can become learned danger cues, a modern bear. Sometimes it's years of exposure; sometimes a shorter, high intensity burst. Either way, these signals are stored in the body as implicit threats. When a familiar word, look, or tone of voice reappears, the old brain fires as if a predator were nearby.

It doesn't matter that the "predator" is cultural; the reaction is biological.

The modern bear isn't hiding in the woods—it's hiding in the meanings we've absorbed, biological bears carried inside the nervous system. And all this fosters deep shame.

Shame From Two Directions—One Loop

What makes shame so powerful is that it comes from two directions at once, which are really part of the same loop.

First, shame can arise when we struggle to manage the implicit threat posed by social constructs themselves. A loaded word, a disapproving look, or a cultural rule about who belongs and who can't feel as dangerous as the snap of a twig in the forest. That's the survival circuitry saying, *I might be out of the tribe.*

Second, many of these same constructs dictate how we're supposed to feel about the very drives that keep us alive—sex, appetite, ambition, competition, even the need for rest or play. When a culture shames desire, hunger, or sexuality, the old brain is caught in a double bind: the drive is natural, but the message says it's dangerous or dirty.

Shame, then, isn't the threat itself. It's the smoke after the fire—the conscious, painful feeling that follows the body's split-second survival response.

We may no longer face wolves at the cave mouth, but the survival circuitry forged in those early human tribes still scans for anything—social or physical—that might mean we're out of the group—or in danger. When these embedded cues light up the old brain, it reacts first and fastest, long before the neocortex can explain, soothe, or reframe what just happened.

These are two faces of one phenomenon. What begins as a cultural rule—how to eat, how to love, how to succeed—becomes a learned cue of danger in the nervous system. Whether you feel inadequate for "breaking the rule" or guilty for simply having the impulse, the old brain doesn't split hairs. If my hypothesis is correct, it fires the same survival alarm.

Shame may feel universal, but it isn't written in our biology. It's a cultural overlay on natural impulses.

Setting Up the Deep Dive

In the pages ahead, we'll unpack how society, religion, and history have shaped what we feel ashamed of—from food to sex to ambition—and how those forces *shape the way our nervous system responds to the world.*

Understanding these constructs will give you a framework to see the tension between natural drives and social rules before we dive deeper into each biological domain. With that lens in place, we can now look at some of the more charged words and cultural rules that prove the point—terms and expectations so soaked in repetition and history that they no longer merely describe; they can trigger.

Modern Bear Examples

Please be warned—we're heading into heavier territory. If certain words bring up pain or discomfort, pause and read in small blocks. Take breaks.

Before we go deeper, a quick reminder: humans evolved in tribes where carrying one's weight wasn't optional—it was survival. Belonging meant food, safety, and connection. Ostracism often meant death. These instincts haven't gone away. As you read about today's "modern bears," remember that your nervous system is still wired to respond to threats to belonging just as fiercely as it once did to prowling predators.

Why Words Can Still Bite

Some words and labels are soaked in generations of fear and judgment. Repeated often enough, they carry the weight of law. They don't just guide behavior; they shape identity and belonging.

These cultural "rules" can spark a nervous-system alarm as fast as a twig snapping in the dark—because years of repetition have literally embedded them in our biology.

So, as we explore these modern bears—emotionally loaded words— keep asking two simple, but life-changing questions:

"Who said?" and *"Does this construct still work for me?"*

It isn't just an academic exercise. It can change how you live, love, and understand yourself.

When a Word Becomes a Weapon

Take the word faggot. Most people assume it only means a slur toward gay men. Open a dictionary (if you can still find one!) and you'll see the original meaning: a bundle of sticks, or in British usage, even a type of meatball.

My point isn't to reclaim the word—it's to show how culture hijacks meaning. When enough people use a word a certain way, that usage becomes *truth*. The cultural meaning erases the original.

That's the power of social constructs: they turn language into shame and shame into reality.

Clinical vignette: When I worked with adolescent boys, none of them could give any definition of "faggot" beyond a gay slur. They were stunned when I showed them the dictionary definition and asked, *"How many other words do you accept as absolute truth without knowing where they came from?"* Silence. Crickets.

More Words That Shifted—and Cut Deep

Another example, in ancient Greece, the word idiot simply meant "a private citizen." No shame there—it just meant you weren't a politician. (Which, given the times, feels almost reassuring.) But over time, it morphed into an insult, something you call the guy who cuts you off in traffic. The meaning didn't come from biology—it came from culture deciding it did.

Or look at lunatic. Once upon a time, people thought the moon (luna) caused madness. It was more superstition than science, but the word stuck as a way to stigmatize people with psychiatric conditions. Again, culture created the shame, not the brain.

And then there's hysteria. Rooted in the Greek word for womb, "hysteria", it was the perfect label for dismissing women as "irrational." For centuries, women's voices, pain, and even illnesses were written off under this cultural stamp. By the late 1880s, Freud was popularizing hysteria in his work with women, using it to describe repressed trauma or unconscious conflicts—often sexual in nature. Somehow, this evolved into the idea that women were "too emotional" or "unstable." Feel free to blame Freud on this one—he played a big part in fostering the term, and, well, he kind of blamed your mother for everything anyway. A word became a social construct, and the construct became a cage.

The same thing happened with clinical terms like moron, imbecile, and retard. At first, these were actual psychological categories. But culture got its hands on them, stripped them of their scientific meaning, and turned them into everyday insults. Today, they carry nothing but shame. These were once clinical categories in psychology in the early 20th century; each was tied to IQ scores. They quickly leaked into everyday language as insults. The medical community abandoned them, but the shame lived on. Even "scientific" terms aren't immune to being turned into cultural weapons.

Another example: queer—once a simple word for "strange" or "odd"— was twisted into a slur. Only recently has the LGBTQ+ community begun reclaiming it as a badge of pride. That's how powerful words are: they don't just label us, they tell us what is acceptable, who is desirable, and who should feel ashamed.

And this is where it matters for us: shame doesn't live in the "old brain." The old brain is just trying to get us to eat, mate, play, bond, and—yes—poop in peace. (Elimination is a drive too, awkward but true.) What happens, though, is that culture builds entire social constructs around these basic urges. Sex isn't just biology—it's wrapped in taboos and double standards. Eating isn't just calories—it's tied to body image and worth. Attachment isn't just survival—it gets tangled with ideas of masculinity, femininity, independence, and weakness. Even elimination carries shame—ask a four-year-old who has an accident in preschool—or remember the childhood terror of bedwetting. Culture builds entire constructs around those basic urges, functions, and drives.

Words don't just describe reality; they create it, police it, and punish people who don't conform.

So, when someone shrugs and says, *"It's just a word,"* don't buy it. Words are the front lines where culture meets biology. They're the chisels with which society carves shame into needs that were never shameful to begin with. Imagine your old brain pleading: "Dude! I'm just trying to keep you alive. A little respect here, please!"

The Modern Bears I Hear Every Day

Now think about the other heavy hitters I hear all the time in therapy: fat, skinny, short, too big, ugly, stupid, loser, white trash, among so many others.

Words like *immigrant*, *foreigner*, DEI, woke, *disabled*, *unemployed*, or even *kindness* have been twisted until kindness itself is sometimes framed as weakness.

These are modern bears—predators made of syllables—capable of spiking the heart rate, tightening the gut, and hijacking the mind.

The 3 Big Ones

Some social constructs are so loud and constant that they almost deserve their own warning label. I hear these three all the time in my office—Success, Happiness, and Love—and they aren't just ideas. They're modern bears.

Success: "Enough" Is Never Enough

When I ask clients, *"What does success mean to you?"* eight out of ten reflexively say money. Almost as quickly, they add, *"I know that's not true... but—"* and here comes the pause, the sigh, the realization that their daily choices don't match their better wisdom.

That "but" is the tell. It signals a hidden rule running the show. They've absorbed the cultural script that more income, a bigger house, and a fancier car equal safety and worth.

Think about it through the lens of old biology. Our ancestors needed resources—wood, water, food, warm shelter—to survive winter or predators. Running out of resources wasn't inconvenient; it was deadly. Fast-forward to now: *resources* have been translated into money and stuff. George Carlin, an outstanding comedian, had a great skit around "stuff"; it's worth watching if you find the time. Not getting enough isn't just disappointing; deep in the nervous system, it can feel like a risk of death.

Corporations know this and exploit it. Every ad whispering *upgrade, buy, secure your future* is tickling the same circuitry that once told the tribe *hunt now or starve later*.

Clients rarely make this connection on their own, but once they see how money and "success" light up the survival system, they finally understand why the pressure feels life-or-death. It isn't greed. It's old wiring hijacked by modern marketing.

Happiness: The Moving Target

Happiness is supposed to be simple, right? Ask most people to define it, and they freeze.

Social media shows perfect vacations and smiling couples; ads say it lives in the next purchase or the next promotion. It's like chasing a mirage—you run and run, but the horizon keeps moving.

This too is tribal. Belonging once meant sharing food and warmth; now we measure it with likes, square footage, or how "Instagram-able" our weekend looks. When a neighbor upgrades their kitchen or a friend posts tropical selfies, some deep part of us still mutters *They have more, I have less*. Old brain translation: *they're safe in the tribe; I'm at risk of being left behind, or I don't have enough"*.

Clients arrive saying, *"I should be happy, but I'm not,"* as though unhappiness means they're broken. The truth is that the concept of a permanent, blissful "happiness" is itself a modern bear.

Our nervous system evolved for moments of satisfaction and long stretches of ordinary life—not a nonstop dopamine carnival. Seeing that frees people to build a steadier, more authentic contentment rather than an endless chase for dopamine.

Love: From Fairytale to Real Life

Then there's **love**, maybe the most myth-soaked construct of all. Movies and storybooks promise effortless magic and *happily ever after* in under two hours. Clients who've been married a few years often sit down and confess, *"The spark is gone. Maybe we fell out of love."* What they don't realize is that the flood of neurochemicals—dopamine, oxytocin—that powers early infatuation is supposed to fade. That's not failure; it's biology resetting from fireworks to the steadier burn of long-term bonding.

But culture rarely mentions the ordinary side of love: the work, the grief, the inevitable conflicts. Instead, it sells a fantasy of a forever honeymoon.

When real love starts to look less like a rom-com and more like Tuesday night dishes, shame creeps in. Clients think they picked the wrong partner when, in fact, they've just entered the next, more intentional stage of attachment.

Love, too, has its survival logic. Pair-bonding protected infants and stabilized tribes. Our brains still crave closeness, but the story we tell about what that should look like—always warm, never messy—can turn the most natural of drives into a source of anxiety.

Bringing It Together: When Rules Become Triggers

These three constructs—**success, happiness, love**—illustrate how words and cultural expectations can **sink into the nervous system** until they feel like life-or-death conditions. Break the "rule," or fear you might, and the old brain hears danger just as surely as shifting shadows once signaled threat.

I often see clients spiral into self-criticism—*"Why can't I just be happy?"* or *"What's wrong with me if I don't want a bigger house?"* The answer is: nothing. Their bodies are simply reacting to **learned cues of threat**, not to actual failure.

This is why I press people to ask, **"Who said?"** Who said more money equals success? Who said happiness means constant smiles? Who said true love never changes? The moment you start questioning those rules, you begin to loosen the biological grip they have on you.

How Social Constructs and Shame Play Out

The nervous system is disrupted—even when no bears are chasing us anymore. I mean, when was the last time you had a grizzly on your heels? (And no, Uncle Bob in the Halloween bear costume doesn't count.) For most of us, the number is a solid zero.

But here's the thing: modern bears are everywhere. They arrive by the hour, maybe the minute, every time you flick on a screen or glance at your phone. They hide in notifications, headlines, and "trending" topics. Each new ping can carry the subtle message *you're not enough*, or *you don't belong,* and the old brain reacts the way it always has—by turning on the fight-or-flight system. The result is a nervous system that lives in a state of high alert, marinated in long-term, repeated threats.

This is where social constructs and shame collide. Our culture is packed with invisible rules about worth and identity. They shape how we see ourselves, how we measure our value, and how we respond to life's demands. Left unexamined, they can make us doubt our worth and slowly internalize shame.

I see this every week in my clinical practice. Clients describe feeling "broken" or "overreacting," as if something inside them is defective. My job is to help them see the truth: it isn't them. It's often the social constructs—deeply imprinted in the body—that drive the anxiety, depression, and sense of never measuring up. When they finally see that, the relief is visible. They sit a little straighter. They breathe.

The Built-In Truth: Innate Worthiness

Humans are born with inherent value—both biological and social. You can see it in the way every culture protects and nurtures its infants; the survival of our species depends on that early care. Worthiness isn't something you earn. It's something you are—as fundamental as a heartbeat, as natural as breath.

But somewhere along the way, culture rewrote the rules. We started measuring worth in terms of productivity, appearance, success, money, and status—treating it as something to be won rather than something we already carry. That confusion is one of the modern bears we face: the illusion that we must *prove* our right to belong, when biology has said from the beginning—we already do.

The Learned Distortion: Doubt and Shame

Over time, **experience layers over biology.** Trauma, neglect, and constant cultural messaging can cloud that inborn worth. People start to feel unworthy or ashamed, not because it's true, but because they've absorbed signals that tell them so. This is a learned doubt. It's a psychological fog, not a biological flaw.

Restoring Perspective

Therapy and deep self-reflection are about **remembering what was never lost.**

Through the lens of biology and survival, people rediscover that their worth was there all along, waiting beneath the noise of culture's demands. And as powerful as that inner work is, the same forces that wound individuals don't stop at the personal level—they spill into the collective.

From Shame to Demonizing

Forces don't stop with the individual. When a society begins to attach danger and disgust to entire groups, the stakes rise dramatically. When shame moves from private experience to public policy, it becomes something even more corrosive: *demonization.*

Demonizing happens when a culture takes a group—by race, gender, class, religion, or politics—and loads it with fear and blame. The group becomes "other," a convenient repository for everything dangerous or unwanted.

History is full of examples: enslaved Africans dehumanized to justify brutality, immigrants branded as invaders, women labelled as hysterical or unfit for leadership, and entire faiths caricatured as threats.

Here's the twist: the same nervous system that once helped our ancestors spot danger is now hijacked to create certainty. A repeated story— *"They're dangerous", They're Lazy", They're immoral"*—doesn't just stoke fear; it offers the illusion of order. It tells the old brain who the threat is. Each retelling strengthens the association until the mere mention of a group sparks a visceral stress response—fear, anger, disgust—long before the rational brain can question the narrative.

This cycle feeds itself. The fear justifies harsher laws or violence, which in turn reinforces the story. Social media adds rocket fuel: a single post can ignite millions of nervous systems within hours. The result isn't just prejudice—it's a society living in chronic fight-or-flight, primed to see neighbors as enemies.

Recognizing this process isn't just moral; it's biological. Demonizing is shame turned outward and certainty mistaken for safety. If we don't disrupt it, it keeps the collective nervous system locked in survival mode—exactly the trap this book hopes to help us escape.

Seen this way, demonizing is the macro-scale version of what you've just read about on the personal level. The old brain's wiring to protect the tribe doesn't disappear—it simply shifts its focus to larger targets. We'll return to this danger later, but it belongs here as a reminder: when language becomes a weapon, the modern bear isn't just personal. It's tribal—and it lurks at scale.

We Can Reconstruct the Constructs

The good news? Social constructs are not destiny. We can examine them, choose which ones to keep, and rewrite the rest. But let's be honest—don't expect a parade when you start living on your own terms. Society defends its rules fiercely. Breaking them threatens the very glue that holds groups together. Some people will resist, shame, or even lash out to "keep you in line."

Technology amplifies this pressure. Anyone can start a YouTube channel, launch a podcast, or produce 100 TikTok clips without factchecking.

Food, sex, attachment, rest, play—each is wrapped in expectations that often deny or shame the very impulses that kept us alive. No wonder people feel torn. Their old brain is simply trying to do its job while society tells them to fight or hide those needs.

Bridging to What Comes Next

This is why the following chapters will go straight to the heart of those primal drives.

We'll explore how social constructs and shame have entangled themselves with:

- **Touch, Impulse, Desire, Shame, and Connection** – how dependence, attraction, and sexuality became shamed instead of celebrated.

- **Food and the Body** – how nourishment turned into anxiety, comparison, and endless cycles of control.

- **Safety, Faith, Politics, and Fear** – how our search for certainty can replace genuine security with rigid belief.

- **Rest, Play, and Joy** – how culture dismissed them as lazy or childish, equating busyness with worth.

- **Status and Competition** – how our ancient instincts for belonging and hierarchy morphed into modern status anxiety.

These are not side issues; they are the very biology of being human. My aim isn't to shock but to help us feel at home in our own skin, so that understanding ourselves also increases our capacity to understand one another.

By the time we reach the deepest layers of these constructs—those tied to our most basic drives—the gap between primitive reality and cultural story will be wide enough to split families, communities, even nations. If we can't make peace with our own biology, how can we hope to make peace with each other?

Because what we call *culture* doesn't just live in history books or social media feeds. It lives in our nervous system. And that's where the modern bear prowls next.

Chapter 2 Recap and Key Takeaways

This chapter began with light examples—houses, pajamas, toy aisles—and moved steadily toward the heavyweights. By now, you can see how a social construct can **jump from culture into biology**, how a word can become a modern bear, and how shame grows when survival wiring meets impossible expectations.

In the chapters ahead, we'll travel deeper into the **biological drives themselves—sex, attachment, food, rest, play, and status.** We'll see how social constructs around appetite, desire, competition, and even bathroom habits tangle with the old brain's survival agenda. Each drive will show another face of the same truth: **if we don't make peace with our own biology, we can't fully make peace with each other.**

Key Takeaways

- **Social constructs are invisible agreements that feel like facts.**
  From colors and toys to "success," "love," or "real men don't cry,"
  these rules are learned, not biological. Yet your nervous system
  responds to them as if they're real survival threats.

- **Words can act like predators.**
  Through constant repetition, a word, look, or expectation can light
  up the same low-road circuitry (thalamus → amygdala) that once
  saved us from an actual bear. The "modern bear" is built from
  meaning, not claws.

- **Shame is the smoke, not the fire.**
  First comes the biological alarm ("I might be out of the tribe"),
  then the conscious pain of shame. Culture overlays shame on
  natural drives—sex, food, attachment, play—until even basic
  biology can feel dangerous.

- **Repetition and speed intensify the effect.**
  In the age of social media, a message doesn't need decades to take
  root. A short, high-intensity barrage can become embodied as
  quickly as years of slow repetition.

- **You can question and re-author your own rules.**
  Social constructs are powerful but not permanent. Seeing them
  clearly is the first step to deciding which ones you'll keep,
  rewrite, or drop.

We've seen how culture rewrites biology, turning survival reflexes into
social rules. Now it's time to feel that story in the body.
The first and most powerful language of connection isn't words or
ideas—it's touch and sexuality.

Exercise: Spot and Rebuild Your Own Constructs

Grab a notebook (or your phone if you must) and try this three-step practice:

1. **Identify**
   List key social constructs that shape you.

   - What does it *mean* to be a man or a woman?

   - How do you define success, happiness, love, or grief?

   - Which words about body image, sex, food, ambition, or rest echo in your mind?

     Jot down the phrases, rules, or "should" you grew up with.

2. **Investigate**
   For each item, ask two questions repeatedly:

   - *Who said this had to be true?*

   - *Where did that person or group get it?*
     Don't be surprised if the trail disappears into "I don't know." That's the point—it shows how deeply cultural repetition, not truth, sets the rule.

3. **Re-author**
   Decide which definitions you want to keep, revise, or release.

   - What *does* success mean for you—time with loved ones, creative work, something else?

   - How do *you* define love or happiness outside of social-media highlight reels?

   - Which biological needs (food, rest, sexuality, play) deserve more respect and less shame?

   Reality check: Society will not throw you a parade for rewriting the rules. People may push back—sometimes harshly—because when one person lives freely, it threatens the shared script. Online echo chambers and algorithm-driven feeds can magnify that pressure by repeating the old rules until they feel like absolute truths.

Remember, your old brain isn't the enemy here. It's simply trying to keep you alive. The goal is to use your new brain—your frontal cortex—to question and choose the constructs you live by, instead of letting inherited rules or viral memes do it for you.

Part II

Domains of Desire, Impulse, and Shame

Chapter 3 – Naked Truths: Shame, Touch, and the Need to Connect

Sex, Reproduction, Touch, and Intimacy

"Shame is a soul-eating emotion."
— *Carl Jung*

Setting the Stage

Now we're going to get into hot, passionate sex. *(I know what you're thinking—finally this book is about to get good! Cue the funky background music and dim the lights.)*

Oh wait…no, no. What I really mean is that sex, gender, and reproduction are hot topics, and people are passionate about them all (insert wink emoji here).

Sex and intimacy have always stirred strong feelings. Still, in today's world, they're among the most charged arenas for social constructs, sparking tension on every level—within individuals, inside relationships and families, and across entire cultures. My aim here is to help you see where deep biological drives meet learned cultural rules, and how those rules can tangle us in shame and create havoc in our relationships.

No Political Camp—Just Human

Before we wade deeper, I want to be clear: I don't write for any political side or identity group.

At different points in this chapter, you might think, "Oh, he leans left, I mean right or maybe middle," or "He's defending men," or "He must be speaking for same-sex couples."

None of that is true.
This chapter—and really this whole book—stands for one class only: humankind.

Yes, I've supported women escaping domestic violence, coached gay men exploring their identity, and counseled heterosexual couples and people of many faiths and ethnicities. But my purpose is education and understanding, not partisanship. The themes I present are based on patterns I've witnessed in decades of clinical work—themes that cut across race, gender, and culture. There will always be exceptions and outliers, and I don't claim to speak in absolutes. What I do claim is that shame and social constructs are universal dance partners, showing up in remarkably similar ways across very different lives.

True or False

Being naked comes with an inherent shame response.
Careful how you answer.

Most people raised in Western-influenced cultures will instinctively say *true*. But watch an infant or toddler, and you'll see the flaw. They dash, bare-bottomed, through sprinklers or streak from bath to bedroom with pure delight. There's no blush, no urge to hide, no "oops."

Shame only enters when someone says, *Cover yourself,* or T*hat's not proper!* That is the moment a social construct takes root, and from there it can shape how a person thinks and feels about their body for decades.

This isn't just a quirk of childhood development. Across the world, there are still Indigenous and traditional societies where daily life is carried out in minimal or no clothing—places where nudity isn't sexualized and doesn't carry an automatic sense of indecency. Among the Mbuti of Congo, for example, everyday forest life unfolds with very little clothing and without the moral freight Western cultures attach to bare skin (Turnbull, 1961).

Similar patterns appear among the Trobriand Islanders of Papua New Guinea, where ethnographers have long documented open courtship rituals and relaxed dress norms, especially before the influence of colonial and missionary forces (Malinowski, 1929).

Even today, Hadza hunter-gatherers of Tanzania live with minimal clothing, especially children, without any evidence of "built-in" embarrassment (Marlowe, 2010). If shame around nakedness were truly biological, we'd expect every culture to display the same reaction. They don't. The difference isn't in our DNA. It's in the cultural message.

Enter Shame—Culture's Fastest Learner

Researcher Brené Brown defines shame as *"the intensely painful feeling or experience of believing that we are flawed and therefore unworthy of love and belonging"* (Brown, 2012).

Notice the loop:

- **Construct** – a rule arrives: *Cover up. Hide. Be modest.*

- **Shame** – the rule lands in the nervous system.

- **Self-policing** – we start enforcing the rule on ourselves.

- **Deeper construct** – the cycle tightens.

It's construct → shame → self-policing → stronger construct.
Soon, we won't need anyone to scold us; the shame runs on autopilot.

When We Can't Even Say the Words

The power of this conditioning shows up in something as basic as language.

In therapy, I've watched countless people hesitate to utter simple anatomical words like *penis* or *vagina*. Faces tighten; eyes dart away. Instead, they say things like *the wahoo, the ying-yang, down there,* or *you know what I mean.*

We don't nickname our hands *the ding-dong* or our heads *the whatchamacallit.* Why do we rename sexual anatomy? Because social constructs have wrapped those parts—and even the words for them—in embarrassment.

Over the years, many clients have told me they were taught these body parts were "dirty," "gross," or "disgusting." Even everyday functions like elimination become the butt of nervous jokes (No pun intended). But biologically, these are simply typical structures and processes—nothing more, nothing less. That we can barely say the words out loud is itself evidence of how shame and culture intertwine.

A Personal Lens

This isn't just clinical observation; I lived it. Growing up in a religious environment, I was taught that even thinking about sex was a sin. By early adolescence, with normal hormones surging, I was sure I was already bound for hell. Imagine trying to police 60,000 or 70,000 thoughts a day. It was an impossible—and shaming—task.

Many of my clients have described similar experiences, and not just in adolescence. I've sat with people in their sixties and seventies who still struggle with deep-seated sexual shame planted half a century earlier.

These early lessons don't evaporate; they embed in the nervous system, consistent with what neuroscience calls the "low road" of emotional processing, where sensory information can move directly from the thalamus to the amygdala before the thinking brain can respond (LeDoux, 1996). And I hear stories over and over again that validate that "low road"; it just sticks.

Where Biology and Culture Collide

Everything we're talking about—desire, arousal, the surge of adolescent hormones—is normal biology. The shame isn't. Yet religious teachings, cultural taboos, and unspoken family rules can convince us otherwise. The result is a conflict between ancient drives and modern constructs:

- The old brain says *this is natural*.
- The learned narrative says *this is dirty, dangerous, or sinful*.

This collision is the heart of the chapter ahead. We'll see how all of these aspects—sex, reproduction, touch, and intimacy (not necessarily in that order; they're deeply connected)—essential for our survival as a species—get wrapped in prohibitions and double standards, shaping us relationships, our identities, and even the simple comfort of living in our own skin.

All these observations—how we learn to cover ourselves, rename our body parts, and fear our own impulses—are not random cultural oddities. They're signals that our collective nervous system is being rewired by social constructs, just as a single person's nervous system can be reshaped by trauma.

Touch as Nervous-System Medicine

When people hear the word *touch* today, many automatically think, *"Yeah, I've got a touch screen."* But that's not the touch I'm talking about.

Touch is a primal survival input—a built-in biological requirement. When social norms restrict it or sexualize it, the old brain reads that deprivation as a chronic threat—a modern bear in slow motion.

We often think of touch as mere comfort or bonding, but it also has measurable, systemic effects on the body's stress and immune systems. The nervous system knows what it needs, and the benefits are striking.

Recognizing those benefits helps us see the flip side: lack of touch is a detriment, not just a missing luxury. And when screens become the primary way, we "touch each other," (think COVID) that's a huge hit to an old brain wired for skin-to-skin contact. The nervous system cannot be fooled by pixels.

And in case you were wondering, yes—touch is required for procreation. Good luck reproducing, or even bonding with a partner, without some kind of physical contact. Biology is unapologetic about that.

These aren't metaphors. They're physiological facts.

In one study, couples who spent 10 minutes holding hands and sharing a brief hug before a stressful public-speaking task had lower increases in systolic and diastolic blood pressure and heart rate compared to couples who did nothing (Grewen et al., 2003).

More broadly, a review of "Touch interventions" concluded that regular physical touch is consistently linked to reduced blood pressure (Field, 2010) and to improved sleep and lower fatigue (Mueller, 2023). Even very brief contact matters: in a small preliminary study, 30 seconds of gentle wrist touch lowered heart rate compared to a no-touch control (Eckstein et al., 2020).

Gentle massage or slow, soothing stroking shows similar power. Small trials demonstrate that touch raises oxytocin—the bonding hormone—and reduces physiological stress markers such as cortisol (Uvnäs-Moberg et al., 2015; Light et al., 2005). This isn't just a "nice idea"; it literally changes our chemistry. For example, a brief therapeutic touch intervention in healthy adults led to measurable hormonal shifts consistent with lower stress(Morhenn, Beavin, & Zak, 2012).

A recent meta-analysis found these benefits across multiple mental-health outcomes and physical stress metrics — and found little difference whether the touch came from a loved one or from a trained clinician (Packheiser et al., 2024).

Touch also supports the immune system. Repeated massage therapy across multiple sessions has been shown to increase circulating lymphocytes and reduce inflammatory cytokines—measurable biological effects that, if replicated, may have implications for managing inflammatory and autoimmune conditions (Rapaport et al., 2012).

Animal research complements these findings: in mice, massage-like stroking improved T-cell counts and reduced stress-induced immunosuppression (Major et al., 2015). And in aging adults, more frequent physical touch predicts lower inflammation years later, based on biomarker studies (Thomas & Kim, 2021).

What ties all this together is the way touch shifts the autonomic balance. Reviews covering humans, animals, and even robotic simulations show that simple static touch lowers heart rate and blood pressure, reduces skin conductance (a proxy for arousal), and tilts the body toward parasympathetic — rest-and-digest — dominance (Eckstein et al., 2020). Even a single minute of gentle touch can measurably quiet the sympathetic "fight-or-flight" system.

Put simply: human touch, eye contact, and soothing physical presence are not luxuries. They are life-sustaining inputs—every bit as critical as food or clean water.

Can't Live Without

The truth is that touch is the one sense we literally cannot live without.

We might imagine we need sight or hearing more, but touch is biologically primary: if it's absent, survival itself is threatened.

No one disputes the importance of touch for infants, and the evidence is clear. Pioneers like Tiffany Field (University of Miami) and Michael Lamb have shown that affectionate physical contact—holding, cuddling, gentle massage—is not optional but foundational. Field's work demonstrates that early touch supports emotional bonding and physiological regulation, including stress reduction and even immune-system effects (Field, 2010; Field, 2014). Lamb's attachment research shows that consistent caregiver touch is a core ingredient of early social and emotional development (Lamb, 1977).

Their research also documents subtle cultural patterns—for example, parents often hold, cuddle, and talk to baby girls more than to baby boys, shaping the emotional worlds those babies grow up in. Field captures these early differences in affectionate touch, and Lamb's work shows something just as striking: mothers tend to hold infants in the rhythm of caretaking, while fathers more often scoop them up to play. From the very beginning, babies are learning two different languages of connection—both shaping how they come to understand comfort, attention, and relationship (Field, 2014; Lamb, 1977). And Field's decades of work on infant massage have since become standard reading in developmental psychology and pediatrics.

If this science weren't convincing enough, history offers a haunting case study that underscores the biological necessity of touch.

The Hospitalism Studies

In the 1940s, René Spitz, a psychoanalyst, published groundbreaking observations on what he called *hospitalism* (Spitz, 1945).
He compared two groups of infants:

- **Group 1:** Babies in a foundling home (orphanage) who were well fed and kept clean but received almost no physical affection.

- **Group 2:** Babies born to incarcerated mothers but cared for in prison nurseries where daily holding, eye contact, and interaction were the norm.

The results were stark. Infants in the orphanage suffered stunted growth, profound developmental delays, and strikingly high mortality rates—yes, some babies died—up to 37% in some reports—despite adequate nutrition and medical care (Spitz, 1945). By contrast, the prison-nursery infants, though their mothers were incarcerated, developed normally.

Spitz's conclusion was revolutionary for its time: *It was not food, safety, or medicine that the foundling infants lacked. It was a consistent human touch and relational presence.* Later, John Bowlby and Mary Ainsworth built on these insights, showing that secure attachment—built largely through physical and emotional contact—is a biological requirement for healthy psychological development (Bowlby, 1969; Ainsworth, 1978).

Biology Confirms It

Modern neuroscience dovetails with these classic findings. And again, Porges reminds us that safe, nurturing touch activates the parasympathetic— "rest and digest"—branch of the nervous system, promoting growth and restoration rather than fight-or-flight survival (Porges, 2011). Touch literally cues the body to feel safe enough to thrive.

Put simply: human touch, eye contact, and soothing presence are not luxuries. They are as vital as food or water—inputs our biology requires to feel safe enough to thrive. Yet many of us, especially men, grow up in cultures where expressing the need for touch is quietly shamed. The construct whispers that craving affection signals weakness.

But biology doesn't stop with touch. Later in this chapter, we'll look more closely at the neurochemistry of desire—how testosterone, ovulation cycles, and the biology of reproduction create different patterns of drive, and how culture takes those natural rhythms and turns them into rules, blame, and shame. For now, let's look at how these early lessons about touch unfold differently for boys and girls, and how those differences ripple into adulthood.

Biologically, men's nervous systems are no different from women's or children's; the need for safe, regulating contact is universal. Yet from boyhood, many men absorb the message that wanting touch is a failure, something to "man up" and outgrow. When the desire for connection naturally arises, they suppress it, haunted by stereotypes—like men are pigs. At the same time, other rules demand they be tender enough to prove they're "good men," but not so tender that they appear weak.

It's the Goldilocks trap: don't be too soft, don't be too hard—be "just right," even though no one can define what "just right" is. The result is confusion and chronic tension. A fundamental biological need is recast as dangerous territory, forcing the old brain to wrestle with mixed messages that keep the modern bear—shame and fear of judgment—alive and well.

Men and Touch: The Rules Are Different

The old brain is wired to seek safe touch for regulation and bonding. But when a boy grows up hearing *"don't cry,"* *"man up,"* and *"don't hug like that,"* his survival wiring and social wiring collide.

Think about what that means: if touch signals safety, then lack of touch signals danger. And the old brain is not a fan of danger—it treats it as a real threat to survival.

So, from the very start, many boys receive a confusing double message:

Your biology needs touch to feel safe and thrive... but don't show that need.

That's not just a mixed signal. It's an ongoing stressor that the nervous system reads as *unsafe*—a slow-motion modern bear that follows men into adolescence and adulthood.

As noted earlier, developmental work by Michael Lamb and Tiffany Field shows that infant boys are typically picked up, held, and cuddled differently—and often less—than girls (Lamb, 1977; Lamb, 2012; Field, 2010). Even subtle early differences in touch and handling can shape how children later learn to regulate emotion and tolerate stress.

This matters when we talk about men's higher rates of touch deprivation and how it can distort adult intimacy and sexual expression.

I believe that for many boys who grow up with little physical affection, the culture teaches them—silently—that the only place they're allowed to seek touch and closeness is through sex. Our social constructs reinforce this narrow pathway. And it may explain—at least in part— why some men seem oversexualized or why so many interactions with women get filtered through a sexual lens. This isn't an excuse for harmful behavior—it's an attempt to understand where the patterns begin.

In many ways, I think our boys—who later become men—are often starving for affection. And that idea, while bold, carries some powerful implications if you sit with it for a moment. Understanding this is not the same as excusing harm; it simply helps us see the forces that shape people long before they make their choices.

A society that tells men they must be tough and self-contained is at odds with what we know about human biology. And nowhere is this more obvious than in how men touch each other.

Two-by-Four Hugs and the Fear of Tenderness

Most heterosexual men reading this will know exactly what I mean. Women generally have social permission to hug, hold hands, or rest a hand on a shoulder in conversation—simple gestures of human connection.

Now watch two men hug. Often it looks like a collision of two pieces of 2x4 lumber: a quick chest bump and a few hard thumps on the back, as if to signal, *don't worry, we're still manly here*—meanwhile, their biology longs for something gentler.

Why the stiffness? Because for many heterosexual men, the worst fear is to be perceived as gay. The social construct says tenderness equals weakness—or worse. As a result, men self-police and starve themselves of the very thing their nervous systems crave.

It's striking to notice the difference when hugging gay male friends or relatives: men who already know and accept their orientation often give warmer, longer hugs. They don't carry the same fear of "what will people think?"—and that freedom shows.

The Double Standard in Caregiving

This double standard shows up starkly in professional life, too. Early in my mental health career, I worked on an inpatient unit where staff were warned not to initiate physical touch—a rule made especially clear for men.

Meanwhile, a small, compassionate RN on the same unit would sometimes approach very large male patients and gently ask, *"Do you need a hug?"* I watched men melt into her embrace, tears streaming— pure human connection, nothing sexual. Everyone else looked on with appreciation, sometimes even relief.

Could I, as a male staff member, have done the same? No way. The standing rule was NO TOUCH—no matter how therapeutic a brief, consensual hug might have been. Yet somehow, it seemed more acceptable when a woman did it. Even looking back, nothing about those hugs felt inappropriate; at the time, it just seemed normal when a female staff member offered them.

The concern about trauma triggers and boundaries is real and necessary. But some of that caution is a cultural construct—the assumption that if a man offers a hug, it must have an ulterior motive. The result is that many men are systematically deprived of affectionate touch. Not because they don't want it, but because society has decided they do not need it.

This isn't about men as victims; it's about recognizing how culture creates dynamics that shape relationships and drive behavior.

Why It Matters

When boys and men grow up hungry for nonsexual affection, it can play out in confusing, even destructive ways. Early deprivation shapes how intimacy is approached later in life. Many men learn to equate closeness with sexuality—not because they want to, but because it becomes the only socially acceptable place to seek the connection their bodies still crave. It can distort how men approach women, sometimes fueling objectification or the belief that sexual contact is the only route to closeness.

Again, this is not an excuse for harm. It's an attempt to understand the biology beneath the behavior so we can interrupt the cycle rather than simply demonize men and repeat it.

And here's the deeper truth: adult touch deprivation is not benign. We already saw how touch lowers stress hormones, supports immune function, eases depressive symptoms, and signals safety to the nervous system. When boys grow up without those signals—and men continue living without them—the absence leaves a physiological and emotional mark.

Even brief, gentle contact can calm the body, slow the heart rate, and nudge the system into the parasympathetic "rest and digest" state. Without these cues of safety, many men carry a nervous system calibrated more for vigilance than connection.

Taken together, all of this suggests that men (and anyone) raised under conditions of touch deprivation may carry that deficit into adulthood:

- a nervous system less habituated to safety,
- a body less primed for healing, and
- a mind more susceptible to shame, disconnection, and relational distortions.

When a culture punishes or denies men the need for nonsexual touch, the result is not strength. The old brain reads chronic danger and stays in a low-level fight-or-flight state—chronic unease. That is exactly how a modern bear prowls: quiet, constant, invisible.

Touching Base

I want to stop here for a moment and literally touch base with you, the reader.

Remember back at the start of this chapter when I said I'm not writing for the left or the right, for men or women, or for any particular class or camp? I meant that. My lens is humankind.

I say that again because—up to this point—we've been talking a lot about men: how lack of touch and affection leaves boys and men biologically undernourished, how that hunger can shape adult intimacy and relationships. It would be easy to think, *See? I knew he was for men.*

But here's the truth: this chapter has been the hardest one to write, and not just because it's charged out there in the culture. It's charged in me.

Last time I checked, I'm still part of the human group (at least until the next Close Encounter). And while writing about nakedness, touch, and the mixed signals we give men, I could literally feel it in my body—tightness in the chest, little zings of discomfort, that gut-level hum.

Friends, that is the modern bear.

If, while reading, you've felt something in *your* body—an uneasy flutter in the stomach, a heaviness in the chest, a tension in the shoulders—you just met one of your bears, too.

This is exactly the clue I watch for in therapy. When a client describes a painful word, a family rule, or a cultural "should," I'm not only listening to the story. I'm watching their body. Does the breath change? Does the posture shift? That's how I know we're not just talking about an idea.

We're touching something deeper than the new brain—something that has dropped into the nervous system as a lived threat.

As Bessel van der Kolk so famously put it, "the body keeps the score."

So, as we move forward, I invite you to pay attention to your own body. Notice if your heart rate picks up, or your stomach clenches, or you just feel "off" for a moment. Don't push it away. Be curious.

Because from here on out, we are quite literally going on a bear hunt. The bears may be cultural messages about touch, desire, gender roles, or intimacy. But your old brain doesn't care that they're cultural; it only registers danger.

This practice—tracking your inner reactions—is one of the most powerful tools I use in trauma work. In Eye Movement Desensitization and Reprocessing (EMDR), when someone feels stuck, I often ask, *"Tell me what you notice in your body."* That single question can open an unprocessed channel of stored trauma. We can't change what we don't first bring into awareness.

So, as we turn to Women and Touch (see, I told you it wasn't just for men), keep that inner radar on. Notice. Feel. Get curious about what stirs inside you. That awareness is the first step in mapping the modern bears that quietly shape our relationships—and our lives.

Women and Touch: Beyond the Caretaker Script

Setting the Stage: Women's Touch Beyond Sex

Women, like men, have deep biological needs for touch, but the way those needs are expressed—and permitted—differs. In my practice, I hear repeatedly from women who say what they long for is not just sexual contact, but closeness: cuddling, being held, hair stroking, resting together. These are not whims or indulgences; they're rooted in physiology. Touch stimulates oxytocin release, lowers cortisol, and helps regulate stress (Uvnäs-Moberg, 2003; Ditzen et al., 2007).

Here's the rub: many women tell me their partners assume that any form of touch is a prelude to sex. A hand on the shoulder, a back rub, a hug— often interpreted by men as foreplay rather than connection. This mismatch leaves women feeling unseen in their biological needs, while reinforcing the idea that their role is to provide access rather than to receive nourishment themselves.

Cultural Scripts and Invisible Labor

This isn't just about biology; it's also about centuries of cultural messaging. Women have long been assigned roles as caretakers:

- The 19th-century "angel in the house," an idealized woman who sacrifices her needs for husband and children.

- Religious and cultural teachings that frame sexual availability as a "wifely duty."

- Modern echoes in media portrayals of the "perfect mom," or the low-maintenance wife who never "needs too much."

These constructs, described in sociological work on emotional labor (Hochschild, 1983; Allen & Hawkins, 1999), have trained women to prioritize the emotional and physical needs of others, while suppressing their own. In this script, women are the givers of touch and care—not the receivers.

I often sit with mothers after their children are grown who confess, sometimes in tears: *"I don't feel needed anymore. Who am I now?"* Their sense of worth has been so entwined with caregiving that when the tribe no longer "needs" them in the same way, the nervous system reads this as danger. If belonging equals survival, then not being needed feels like exile. That's the modern bear—quiet but devastating.

Biology Meets the Modern Bear

Women's neurobiology and socialization patterns support higher levels of affectionate, non-sexual touch and emotional attunement—patterns linked to bonding and relational maintenance (Uvnäs-Moberg, 2003; Taylor et al., 2000; Floyd, 2006).

Yet social constructs distort this truth.

- Biology says: touch is mutual nourishment.

- Culture says: your role is to meet others' needs first.

The result is a chronic conflict. Women may suppress their need for nurturing touch, fearing they'll be seen as "needy," while also internalizing shame for wanting sexual fulfillment outside of a caretaking role. Over time, these messages embed in the nervous system: *If I ask for what I need, I'll be rejected. If I don't give, I won't be loved.*

That loop—need colliding with shame—is how a modern bear prowls the female nervous system. It doesn't roar; it paces quietly in the background, whispering *don't ask too much, don't be too much, don't need too much.* The old brain hears those whispers as survival rules. And when culture repeats them often enough, they get coded into the body like instinct. To truly understand how these constructs get embedded, we have to trace the thread from early touch in childhood to adulthood—where trauma, desire, and culture all collide in the nervous system.

Women and Touch: The Other Side of the Coin

To grasp how deeply these patterns become embodied, we have to walk further into the cave. Up ahead, another bear waits—the one that shadows women's relationship with touch. From childhood through adulthood, biology tugs one way while cultural scripts pull another. And when those messages collide in the nervous system, what should be a source of safety and bonding can instead become a source of shame, silence, or survival.

Remember that developmental research shows boys are held and cuddled less often than girls (Field, 2010; Lamb, 2012). That difference cuts both ways. On one hand, many women grow up with more permission to connect physically with others—a hug from a friend, holding hands, stroking hair. This freedom carries into adulthood as a relational resource that men often lack.

But layered beneath that is another message, one that grows louder with age: a woman's value lies in her body. As girls become teens, touches that once signified affection and connection begin to be sexualized. The construct shifts: her worth is tied not only to being nurturing but also to being desirable.

In my office, I hear this again and again: women who long for affectionate, nonsexual touch—cuddling, holding hands, resting together—yet feel trapped by the belief that to keep a partner, sex is non-negotiable. They don't always say it out loud, but it surfaces between the lines: *if I don't engage sexually, I won't have a relationship.* Talk about a modern bear embedded in the nervous system: *no sex = no belonging.* For the old brain, that equation is terrifying.

Trauma and the Biology of Repetition

And then there's trauma. When female clients describe themselves as "promiscuous," often with shame in their voices, almost always there's a history of early sexual trauma behind it. This isn't about a "high sex drive" or moral weakness. It's neurobiology. As Peter Levine (1997), Bessel van der Kolk (2014), and Pat Ogden (2006) explain, the nervous system seeks resolution after trauma—the old brain pushes the body to re-create the situation in hopes of a different outcome.

That's why many survivors find themselves in repeated high-risk situations. The biology is trying to repair the wound, and the culture piles shame on top. Society labels women "loose," "immoral," or "damaged"—negative constructs that reinforce the trauma rather than heal it. So, the modern bear doesn't just lurk; it stalks openly in their nervous system, doubled by the cultural ridicule that follows them.

I spend a lot of time educating my male clients about this. When they dismiss a woman as "oversexualized," I tell them: "What you're seeing is probably trauma, not desire." Many are stunned. For the first time, they look at these women with empathy instead of judgment.

The Double Standard

Men, of course, can also reenact trauma through sexual risk-taking. But here the construct is flipped. Male promiscuity is often rewarded—seen as a sign of manliness or conquest—even when it, too, may stem from trauma or touch deprivation. Women are shamed; men are celebrated. One construct punishes, the other praises. Both obscure the underlying biology.

This double standard creates a perfect storm:
- Women reliving trauma, seeking safety through repetition, but drowning in shame.

- Men starving for nonsexual touch, validated only when they pursue sexual conquest.

Put those forces together in relationships, and you can see why so many couples sit in my office in pain.

Modern Bears in the Nervous System

For women, the bears often take these forms:

- If I'm not needed as a mother, who am I?
- If I don't give sexually, I'll be rejected.
- If I ask for what I need, I'll be shamed.

These are not logical thoughts; they're survival cues, embedded in the body. Trauma wires them in. Culture reinforces them. And shame keeps them running on autopilot.

One of the most profound shifts I witness is when a female client begins to see her history not as a moral failing but as her nervous system trying to survive. When they understand the "biology of repetition," the shame starts to loosen. They sit taller, breathe easier, and sometimes cry in relief. They begin to build a sense of self-respect—empathy for themselves—instead of living under society's condemnation.

As we've seen, touch is never neutral—it carries layers of biology and cultural meaning. For men, deprivation often drives hunger and confusion. For women, oversexualization or suppression often warps the natural desire for affectionate connection. Both carry their own modern bears. But before we move into the neurochemistry of desire, it's important to pause and look directly at touch itself—how it can heal, and how it can harm. Because not all touch is created equal. Safe, nurturing touch regulates the nervous system and fosters connection; unsafe or coercive touch embeds trauma and shame deep into the body. That distinction—between good touch and bad touch—is the next cave we have to enter.

Good Touch, Bad Touch

Let's pause for a moment and look at a touch that almost everyone experiences but almost no one talks about openly: masturbation. It's one of the clearest examples of how a basic biological need has been distorted into shame through cultural constructs.

From a purely biological standpoint, masturbation would seem to be as normal as scratching an itch or massaging a sore muscle. Many mammals do it—including domestic species like cats, dogs, and horses (Sommer et al., 2022). And over 40 primate species have been observed engaging in masturbation, often as a way to regulate stress or maintain reproductive health (Dixson, 2012). If so, many other mammals engage in it, how is it that humans have turned it into something "gross," "dirty," or morally suspect?

Here's a personal example that proves the point (I know what you were thinking when I said personal). When I dictated this section into my word-processing program, every time I said the word masturbation, the software replaced it with asterisks— "************." I had to go back and manually type it in. Think about that. A neutral biological word, just a string of letters, was flagged as too shameful to even appear. As I discussed in Chapter 2, words themselves are constructs, yet they hold tremendous power in shaping how our nervous system interprets reality. A simple word can be turned into a modern bear. And here's the irony: masturbation would actually be a great Scrabble word—if you could just get away with putting it on the board without everyone blushing.

And it isn't just computers that censor themselves. Many of my clients struggle even to say the word out loud. They'll lower their voices, trail off into euphemisms, or avoid it altogether. Some have reported literally feeling a wave of nausea or disgust when touching themselves—an embodied signal that shame has settled into the nervous system. In those moments, I point out the biology: masturbation is natural, even healthy. It releases oxytocin, calms the body, and helps regulate the old brain. But still, for many, the modern bear roars louder than the facts. They sit in silence, their bodies tense, as though the act itself proves they are "bad" or "dirty."

The Physiology of "Good Touch": Yes, Actual Science

When stripped of stigma, masturbation is a form of "good touch." It is a biological regulator that calms the body and supports health. Research documents a wide range of benefits:

- **Stress regulation:** Orgasms release oxytocin and endorphins, promoting relaxation and stress relief. Research also shows that partnered intercourse, in particular, supports nervous-system regulation (Carmichael et al., 1994; Levin, 2007).

- **Immune function:** Frequent ejaculation has been linked to reduced risk of prostate cancer in men, likely due to reduced buildup of carcinogenic compounds in the prostate (Leitzmann et al., 2004).

- **Cardiovascular effects:** Sexual activity produces short-term cardiovascular changes like moderate exercise—raising heart rate and blood pressure during arousal and orgasm, followed by recovery. In men with erectile dysfunction, higher sexual frequency has been associated with better endothelial function and healthier vascular profiles (Corona et al., 2013). In broader populations, sexual activity shows mixed cardiovascular associations that vary by age and gender (Liu & Waite, 2016). Overall, evidence suggests that regular sexual activity can act as a form of mild cardiovascular exertion, though long-term heart-disease protection remains unproven (Frappier et al., 2013).

- **Sleep:** After orgasm, many people experience a surge of relaxing neurochemicals like oxytocin and prolactin, which appear to improve sleep onset and, for some, enhance overall sleep quality — especially after partnered sex (Oesterling et al., 2023; Lastella et al., 2025).

- **Pain modulation:** Orgasm — whether through masturbation or partnered sex — activates endogenous opioid pathways and appears to raise pain thresholds in many people, suggesting it may ease discomfort. Some small studies and case reports indicate this may include relief from menstrual cramps or migraine attacks (Whipple & Komisaruk, 1985; Hambach et al., 2013). However, effects vary considerably between individuals and are not reliably consistent across studies.

If any of these benefits were available in pill form, the medical community would prescribe them freely. Instead, society has buried them under piles of shame and secrecy.

Imagine for a moment if we treated drinking water the same way. If someone said, "I'm thirsty," and the response was: "Ew, disgusting. Do you drink water? You should be ashamed." Absurd, right? But culturally, we've done exactly that with masturbation. A normal biological function becomes the butt of jokes, whispers, or condemnation—another modern bear crouched in silence, waiting to pounce whenever the subject arises.

The Other Side: "Bad Touch"

Of course, not all touch is good touch. At the opposite end of the spectrum is violence—touch that harms, intimidates, or degrades. Domestic violence is a prime example. While women can and do commit acts of violence, men are statistically the greater perpetrators. In the U.S., men account for about 93% of the sentenced state and federal prison population (Carson, 2023). (That's a whole other topic.) Globally, men also make up the vast majority of persons imprisoned and of violent crime perpetrators, underscoring a consistent gender disparity in serious offending and incarceration.

According to the CDC's National Intimate Partner and Sexual Violence Survey, approximately 41% of women and 26% of men in the U.S. have experienced contact sexual violence, physical violence, or stalking by an intimate partner in their lifetime (CDC, 2024).

But even here, cultural scripts muddy the waters. Men who women strike often feel they "shouldn't" respond, because "real men don't hit women." In sessions, I've had men recount sitting frozen while being struck, torn between anger and shame, unsure if defending themselves would make them a "monster." Others describe the silent humiliation of being laughed at or dismissed when they admit their partner has hit them. Police-report studies consistently show gender disparities in domestic-violence arrests — men are more likely than women to be arrested, even when both partners report violence or when women initiate the call for help. Many men hesitate to report abuse at all, fearing ridicule or even arrest. And for those who do reach out, the response is often discouraging. Men frequently report being treated dismissively by officers and encountering reluctance to charge female offenders (Hamilton, 2010; Dim & Lysova, 2022). And in same-sex relationships, law enforcement often struggles to identify who is the "real perpetrator," showing how much gendered constructs distort our perception of violence (Hirschel, 2008; Hirschel & McCormack, 2021).

Clients who've lived through this often describe the modern bear in their nervous systems not as words but as bodily states: a clenched stomach, a pounding heart, a buzzing in their skin. They know the danger is real, even if society insists on minimizing it.

This is why I propose a simple, universal rule: nobody gets to hit anybody. Period. Bad touch is bad touch, no matter who delivers it. When we strip away the social constructs, it becomes obvious: the nervous system doesn't care about gender, size, or social rules. It only knows safety or danger.

Why sort "good" from "bad" touch at all?

Because the old brain is literal, gentle, consensual touch (including self-touch) is a safety cue; it lowers arousal and supports recovery. Assaultive touch is a danger cue; it conditions hypervigilance and shame. When culture swaps those labels—shaming the safe thing, excusing the dangerous thing—we embed contradictions in the nervous system. That's how a modern bear keeps quietly pacing in the background: we fear what's harmless and minimize what harms.

When Touch Turns into Bears

When we strip away the cultural scripts, the nervous system makes it simple. Good touch—whether affectionate, sexual, or solitary—regulates us. It calms the old brain, signals safety, strengthens immunity, and restores balance. Bad touch—whether violent, coercive, or shaming—dysregulates us. It spikes cortisol, fuels vigilance, and wires fear into the body.

The tragedy is that culture has twisted both ends of the spectrum. Masturbation, a healthy form of regulation, is wrapped in shame and secrecy until the body itself recoils from it. Violence, which should be universally condemned, is excused, minimized, or filtered through double standards that keep people confused and unsafe.

This is where the modern bear prowls most effectively—not in obvious roars, but in the subtle distortions that make us question our needs, mistrust our biology, or doubt our right to safety. Some of my clients feel the bear as nausea when they touch themselves, others as pounding fear when they're struck and told to endure it, and still others as silence, frozen in shame. Different bodies, same message: *you are not safe to be what you are.*

If we want to tame these bears, we must learn to see touch for what it truly is—biology first, construct second. Only then can we reclaim the simple truth the nervous system has been telling us all along: safety is not optional, and regulation is not shameful.

From Touch to Neurochemistry

We've looked at touch from many angles—comforting, nourishing, distorted, or violent. But to really understand why it matters so much, we have to look under the hood. Touch isn't just skin-deep; it runs on chemistry. Our bodies are wired with cycles of oxytocin, testosterone, dopamine, and cortisol that set the stage for bonding, desire, and regulation. The old brain doesn't separate "biology" from "meaning"— it simply reacts. And when culture mislabels those reactions, the result is confusion, shame, and bears that prowl unseen.

Here's the irony: most of us were never taught any of this. Men often don't know how women's arousal or ovulation cycles shape their impulses. Women often don't know how testosterone levels pull men toward a near-constant readiness. And almost no one learns how same-sex desire runs on the very same biology, only to be burdened with extra layers of stigma. That lack of education is its own modern bear—leaving couples, families, and individuals stumbling in the dark, misreading their own nervous systems.

So, before we step into the cave of "what this looks like in relationships," let's pause to shine a light on the chemistry itself.

Neurobiology isn't the whole story, but it's a foundation. And when we ignore it, we let culture fill the gaps with rules, blame, and shame.

Neurochemistry and Desire: What We Don't Know About Ourselves

For all our cultural obsession with sex, most people know remarkably little about the biology that drives it. When I sit with couples, I often find their understanding of each other's bodies and neurochemistry isn't much more profound than what they learned in a high school sex-ed class. In my case, that class was taught by a man named Mr. Dick—no, I'm not kidding. And what we learned were the mechanics: sperm, egg, contraception. What we didn't learn was the messy, fascinating, and sometimes uncomfortable reality of how hormones and neurochemistry drive desire, connection, and conflict. No wonder so many of us feel like we're living without a user manual.

The Chemistry Beneath Desire

At its core, sexuality is biological. Testosterone, present in both men and women but at much higher levels in men, fuels sexual desire, visual sensitivity to erotic cues, and readiness for intercourse. It's one reason men, on average, report more frequent sexual thoughts and greater baseline interest in sex (Bancroft, 2005; Cunningham et al., 2016). Women, by contrast, experience cyclical shifts. Estrogen and luteinizing hormone peak around ovulation, often increasing desire during the few days when conception is possible (Regan, 1996). From an evolutionary standpoint, this division makes sense: if women were fertile only two or three days a month, and men also had a narrow fertile window, the odds of survival for early humans would have been slim. Instead, men's near-constant readiness functioned as an insurance policy for the species.

But here's where biology meets misunderstanding. Many women complain in my office that their partners "are always ready." Men, on the other hand, are shamed for this drive—treated as pigs, animals, or morally weak. What often gets missed is that the old brain isn't flawed; it's doing what evolution designed it to do. That doesn't excuse harmful behavior. We still have the capacity to regulate impulses with our "coping bucket." But understanding the biology can reframe the shame.

Meanwhile, other neurochemicals are working in the background:

- **Oxytocin** — sometimes called the "bonding hormone" — surges during key life and intimate moments (childbirth, breastfeeding, and, in many people, orgasm), helping to reinforce attachment, calm, and emotional connection (Uvnäs-Moberg, 1998).

- **Dopamine** — the brain's primary reward and motivation chemical — rises in anticipation of sexual activity and even in response to erotic cues, driving desire, pursuit, and approach behaviors (Pfaus, 2009).

- **Orgasm**— triggers a release of calming neurochemicals — including prolactin, oxytocin, and endogenous opioids — which may help promote relaxation and, for some people, facilitate easier sleep onset (Bartlik, Goldstein, & Meston, 2018).

These are not "optional extras." They are survival mechanisms—ways the nervous system rewards behaviors that keep us bonded, reproducing, and safe in groups.

The Shame of Not Knowing

Here's the problem: most of us never learn any of this. Instead, we inherit jokes, stigma, and silence. Women are told their menstrual cycles are "gross," or that pregnancy mood swings are just "drama," as if deep hormonal shifts could be willed away. Men are ridiculed for being too visual, too interested, or for noticing others at all.

Even the basics get twisted. The vagina maintains its own healthy microbiome and is easily disrupted by washes, douches, and sprays— yet billions are spent marketing these products as though genitals are inherently dirty (Fashemi et al., 2013).

I've spent a lot of time providing information on sexual health, biology, and neurochemistry to show how complex this all is. The truth is that all humans—men and women—are a constantly shifting mix of chemistry, hormones, and neural patterns that drive emotions, impulses, and needs. Yet in our culture, we don't always respect that men are shaped by this chemistry, too.

Most people are sympathetic when a woman is experiencing PMS, pregnancy, or postpartum changes. We understand the hormonal surges and physiological shifts that influence her feelings and behavior. But we often expect men to simply "override" their own biology—as if the complex neurochemistry we readily acknowledge in women somehow doesn't apply to them.

I've said before: there's a persistent belief that we can override nature with sheer willpower. And while regulation is possible—and essential—it must begin from understanding, not denial. That's one of the reasons I've spent so much time exploring this topic: to help all of us understand each other a little better.

And hopefully you can see how social constructs take neutral biology and twist it into shame—modern bears embedded in the nervous system.

That same confusion extends beyond anatomy. Our not knowing doesn't stop at how the body works; it reaches into what the body *feels*. Few places reveal the shame of not knowing more deeply than sexuality itself.

In my many years of sitting with clients—and with colleagues and friends who are gay or lesbian, particularly gay men—I can't count the number of conversations that began in heartbreak and ended in relief.

"Paul, I tried so hard not to be gay." "I dated women. I even tried to watch straight porn. I thought maybe if I got over the abuse, I'd become straight again."

I've heard those sentences, or ones like them, dozens of times in twenty-plus years of practice. They were often said through tears—grief and shame tangled together in the desperate effort to be "normal." What they were really describing was the terror of exile, the fear of being cast out of the tribe. Once they realized they couldn't change who they were, the relief that followed was immense—but so was the courage required to live authentically in a world that still shames sexual identity.

That's how strong the old brain's bears can be: they can make us deny even our own biology. The sliding spectrum of orientation unsettles the old brain because it loves predictability—yes or no, black or white, male or female. But biology has never been that simple.

Same-Sex Biology and the Sliding Spectrum of Orientation

If misunderstanding between men and women is one source of conflict, misunderstanding same-sex orientation is another. Decades of research show that same-sex attraction is not a "lifestyle choice" but deeply rooted in biology. Twin studies consistently show moderate heritability for same-sex attraction — often around 30–40% — indicating a meaningful genetic component (Bailey, Dunne, & Martin, 2000; Långström, Rahman, Carlström, & Lichtenstein, 2010). Prenatal hormonal influences—particularly variations in androgen exposure—are also linked to later same-sex attraction (Hines, 2011). Neuroscience studies may have identified measurable structural and connectivity differences between heterosexual and homosexual individuals, suggesting that sexual orientation is linked to underlying neurodevelopmental factors rather than being simply a matter of learning or choice (Savic & Lindström, 2008).

And it's not just a human phenomenon. Same-sex behavior has been observed in more than 1,500 animal species, including dolphins and bonobos, penguins, and rams (Bagemihl, 1999). Across ancient civilizations—Greek, Roman, and numerous Indigenous cultures—same-sex relationships were acknowledged as part of the natural fabric of life (Crompton, 2003). The reality is apparent: this isn't new, deviant, or rare. It's part of nature's blueprint.

In truth, sexuality itself may be best understood not as a fixed category but as a fluid continuum. Most heterosexual men can tell when another man is handsome; most women can recognize female beauty. Recognition doesn't mean desire—it simply shows that our nervous systems are wired to notice others. We are designed to perceive attraction, connection, and belonging.

When I was younger, the doctor's office had a balance scale—the kind with sliding metal weights (yes, I know, old-fashioned) that moved left or right until the beam found equilibrium. It's a perfect metaphor for sexual orientation. Some people's weight is firmly settled at one end—deeply heterosexual. Others rest near the opposite side—clearly same-sex oriented. But for many, the weight moves somewhere in between.

It's not flipping or indecision—it's the subtle variability of being human.

If the scale metaphor feels dated, think of a dimmer switch instead of a light switch. It's not on or off—it slides through infinite gradations of brightness. Orientation, too, isn't binary. It's a sliding scale, a spectrum of intensity and direction. Some people's settings glow brightly at one end and dim at the other; others hover somewhere in the middle. Most people live along that continuum, not at its edges.

After more than twenty years of clinical work and thousands of conversations, I've found that human attraction rarely fits neatly into the categories we're taught. Some clients identify as straight but admit to occasional attraction toward the same sex. Others who identify as gay or lesbian describe moments of appreciation—or even emotional attraction—toward someone of the opposite sex. These aren't contradictions; they're reflections of a flexible, living system. Biology allows nuance; culture demands certainty.

And here's the truth: this very fluidity—the lack of a clear "either/or"— is what awakens the bears. The old brain doesn't like uncertainty; it craves categories, predictability, and control. When biology refuses to fit into tidy boxes, the nervous system grows uneasy, and culture rushes in to restore order through judgment. That discomfort—born of ambiguity—fuels the same fears that drive our politics, our religions, and our need to define what should have remained as wonder.

More on that in the next chapters, where we'll explore how uncertainty itself becomes a threat to safety—and how the bears learn to feed on it.

If sexual orientation were truly fixed, heterosexual people wouldn't even be able to see same-sex beauty, and gay individuals wouldn't recognize opposite-sex appeal—but we all do. That ability to notice, without necessarily desire, reflects something universal: we're wired for connection and perception, not for rigid boxes.

And yet, for many people, even acknowledging that variability triggers discomfort. It shakes the illusion of certainty that culture has built around identity. The shame and fear that follow are classic signs of a modern bear—a social construct turned threat in the nervous system. What if this means I'm not who I think I am? The old brain whispers. But this unease doesn't come from biology—it comes from the message that biology must fit into a **binary system.**

Nature doesn't make sharp corners; it makes gradients. The sliding scale isn't chaos—it's coherence. As evolutionary biologist Joan Roughgarden (2004) reminds us, sexual diversity across species isn't a flaw in nature's design—it is nature's design.

Why This Matters

When people lack this basic biological education (sorry, Mr. Dick), culture rushes in to fill the void—with blame, jokes, shame, or silence. Men get condemned for their testosterone-driven readiness. Women are shamed for cycles and odors that are nothing more than biology. Same-sex people are told their desires are unnatural, despite overwhelming evidence to the contrary.

These distortions don't just live in the mind. They settle in the body as modern bears—silent, chronic threats that whisper: "Something is wrong with me." Understanding the neurochemistry of desire doesn't erase the complexity of relationships, but it does give us a foundation of respect. Biology isn't destiny, but it is the ground we stand on. And the more clearly we see it, the less power shame (and that modern bear) has to stalk us from the shadows.

Notes — Take a Breath

Some readers like to pause here — to reflect, annotate, or simply breathe. Others may wish to continue on.

From Biology to the Room Between Us

Now that we've explored the chemistry running beneath our skin—the testosterone, oxytocin, dopamine, and all the old-brain messengers that shape desire—it's time to look at how those forces collide in real life. Biology doesn't live in a vacuum; it plays out in kitchens, bedrooms, therapy offices, and the long silences between partners who love each other but can't seem to reach each other.

This is where the modern bears start to roar.

What begins as biology—a surge of hormones, a craving for connection—meets the social constructs that tell us what's "appropriate," "masculine," or "feminine." When those collide, the friction doesn't just confuse the mind; it activates the body. In my office, this is where the real work begins: helping people recognize how their old-brain wiring and cultural conditioning have been dancing—and sometimes wrestling—with each other all along.

So, let's step into the next cave together: the one between people. This is where we'll see how these forces look in relationships—the misunderstandings, the rejections, the longing—and where we'll meet the biggest grizzly of them all: the fear of being alone. It's the one bear that never truly sleeps, and the one that drives more of our behavior than most of us care to admit.

What It Looks Like in Relationships: How These Scripts Collide in the Room

By now, we've traced how shame, language, nakedness, touch deprivation, and mismatched social rules all embed themselves into the nervous system. You've seen how men and women are taught different touch rules, how we misunderstand our bodies and biology, and how those misunderstandings become modern bears pacing beneath our relationships.

So, what does that actually look like in the therapy room?

In the Room

You can feel it before anyone says a word—the air gets heavier, the body language folds in. One person looks down, the other crosses their arms. Somewhere between them, the bear is already awake.

"My husband doesn't look at me anymore. We haven't had sex in years. I don't think he loves me."

"My girlfriend doesn't want to have sex anymore—no matter what I do. I chase her around, I compliment her, I touch her. I think she doesn't find me attractive."

"He's masturbating again. It must mean I'm not enough." "I saw her looking at another man. He was built, confident. I think she wants him, not me."

"Men are always gawking at me. I don't like it—but if they stop, I wonder if I'm still attractive."

"I don't think he loves me anymore. I've gained weight." "We don't touch each other anymore. It's like living with a roommate."

Different words, same bear: *Am I still wanted? Am I still safe*

Beneath the Surface

What begins as a fight about sex, affection, or attention is rarely about those things alone. Beneath the conflict lies the biology of attachment— what Stephen Porges (2011) calls the **social engagement system**. Eye contact, tone of voice, and touch tell the nervous system whether we are safe or in danger. When those cues disappear, the old brain panics.

Research supports what I see daily: affectionate, nonsexual touch lowers cortisol, increases oxytocin, and enhances relationship satisfaction (Gulledge et al., 2003; Floyd et al., 2006). When that touch fades, the body literally moves into a threat state. What partners interpret as "rejection" is often the nervous system screaming, *I'm not safe.*

Men and women experience this mismatch differently but with the same pain. Men, starved for nonsexual touch, often reach for sex as the only culturally permitted form of closeness. Women, socialized to be caregivers and not ask for what they need, often interpret that reach as objectification rather than longing. Both end up feeling unseen.

The Dance of Shame

When couples lose physical or emotional connection, shame rushes in to fill the silence. Men wonder, "A*m I too much?"* Women wonder, *"Am I not enough?"* Both retreat.

These cycles mirror what trauma theorists like Bessel van der Kolk (2014) and Pat Ogden (2006) describe as the body's attempts to regulate threat. The nervous system toggles between fight, flight, and freeze. For many, withdrawal isn't indifference—it's a survival reflex.

I spend time in session educating clients about biology: that sexual desire, affection, and touch are not moral choices but physiological expressions of safety and connection. When people start to understand this, shame softens. They begin to see each other not as adversaries but as two nervous systems seeking safety together.

The Modern Bear Between Them

Every story, beneath the words, carries the same quiet terror—the fear that love might not find them again. That's the grizzly I see most often in the room: the fear of rejection, of being alone. It's the same one that's been stalking humans since the first tribe gathered around a fire.

When people are disconnected, their old brains don't whisper—they roar. One client once said, "It feels like my whole body's bracing for impact, like something bad's coming if I can't fix this." That's not a metaphor. Neuroscience shows that social rejection activates the same brain regions as physical pain (Eisenberger, 2012).

These fears don't reside in the mind; they reside in muscle tension, shallow breathing, and tears that come from nowhere. The modern bear prowls between partners, feeding on silence, misunderstanding, and the lack of a shared biological language.

The Takeaway

When you strip away the shame and the stories, what's left is biology trying to connect—two nervous systems trying to sync, two people trying to feel safe enough to be touched, seen, and loved.

The modern bear doesn't want to destroy intimacy—it just wants safety. And until we can name it, it keeps prowling between us, unseen.

The Biggest Grizzly: Fear of Rejection and Being Alone

I want to pause here and name what may be the biggest grizzly of them all—the 600-pounder that lives in nearly every nervous system: the fear of rejection and being alone.

As I've mentioned before, belonging to a tribe is not optional; it's a survival imperative. For our ancestors, exclusion meant vulnerability and death. Remember, neuroscience confirms that this isn't metaphorical—social rejection activates the same pain circuits in the brain as physical injury (Eisenberger, 2012). That's why loneliness feels visceral rather than abstract.

When early attachment is disrupted, this fear becomes magnified. Without consistent caregiving and attunement, the "coping bucket" stays small, and the old brain registers even mild relational distance as catastrophic. These clients don't just fear being alone; their nervous systems expect it, scanning constantly for signs of abandonment. The grizzly never sleeps.

This fear doesn't discriminate. I hear it from men who say, *"If I don't pursue her sexually, she'll stop loving me,"* and from women who whisper, *"If I don't give him what he wants, he'll leave."* Different expressions, same biology. The fear of being cast out of connection— the tribe—is universal.

Research continues to affirm that attachment drives nearly every aspect of relational functioning. Securely attached adults report higher relationship satisfaction, lower cortisol levels, and better emotional regulation (Mikulincer & Shaver, 2016). Chronic loneliness, by contrast, is linked to inflammation, cardiovascular risk, and premature mortality (Hawkley & Cacioppo, 2010). And the data goes even further: social isolation itself is a stronger predictor of mortality (yes, you are reading that correctly) than smoking or obesity. An extensive meta-analytic review found that poor social relationships increase the risk of death by roughly 50%—a magnitude comparable to quitting smoking and exceeding many traditional risk factors such as obesity or physical inactivity (Holt-Lunstad et al., 2010). The cost of the grizzly is not only emotional—it's biological.

And when these primal fears collide with the social constructs of gender, the modern bears grow larger. Men are told their desire makes them "pigs." Women are told that withholding makes them "cold." Both internalize shame; both feel unseen. It's a collision of two nervous systems, each wired to seek connection but each carrying embedded threat cues that whisper, *If I reach, I'll be hurt. If I don't reach, I'll be alone.*

When the fear of being alone reaches its peak, it's not just a bear—it's a **Clash of the Grizzlies.**

(Yes, it sounds like a pay-per-view wrestling event, but in this ring, the blows are real.)

Both partners are fighting for safety, yet both feel unsafe. Biology pulls them toward closeness; social constructs push them apart. The result is a perfect storm of longing, confusion, and misread intentions—two nervous systems circling, each afraid the other might bite.

Clash of the Grizzlies

If the old brain had a soundtrack, it would be the sound of two grizzlies pacing opposite sides of the same cave—each growling not out of hatred, but fear. That's what I see in my office every single week: two nervous systems trying to connect but braced for danger.

Each client's bear is different, but the instincts are the same. One roars, *Don't leave me.* The other growls, *don't trap me.* The same biological need drives both—to stay connected and survive—but their strategies collide like tectonic plates.

Attachment theory has long shown that when our need for closeness meets fear of rejection, we move into patterns of protest, pursuit, or withdrawal (Johnson, 2004; Mikulincer & Shaver, 2016). The anxious partner reaches out, sometimes frantically, scanning for signs of love or rejection. The avoidant partner pulls away, trying to preserve safety by minimizing threat. Each one's nervous system is fighting for survival, not logic.

Here's how it often looks: A woman sits on the edge of my couch, tears in her eyes, saying, "I just wish he'd hold me." Moments later, a man in another session says, "Every time I try to touch her, she seems annoyed. I don't know what she wants anymore." Two bears in one cave—both starving, both afraid.

Neuroscience confirms what we feel in those moments. When we detect relational threat—an eye roll, a sigh, a turned-away phone—the brain shifts instantly. The amygdala activates in response to perceived social danger (Eisenberger, 2012), cortisol rises as the body enters a stress-response pattern (Dickerson et al., 2008), and prefrontal regulatory regions temporarily downshift, reducing our capacity to stay calm and think clearly (Siegle et al., 2007). In that instant, partners stop hearing words and start reading danger. The body says, *run or fight,* even when all the person really wants is to be seen.

So many couples I see are not broken—they are dysregulated. They are trying to speak love languages from within alarm states. I remind them that this is not a character weakness; it's the old brain doing its job too well. It's scanning for bears in the modern world and finding them everywhere: in a sigh, a turned back, or a cold bed.

The irony is that both partners' bears are trying to protect the same thing—the connection. But without awareness, protection turns into pursuit or withdrawal, and the cave becomes louder and colder. When I help clients name their grizzlies— "This is the part of me that fears being left," or "This is the part that feels unsafe when closeness comes too fast"—the growling starts to quiet. Curiosity replaces accusation. The body begins to settle.

That's the heart of this work: helping people recognize that their grizzlies are not enemies. They are frightened guardians of love, wired in biology, shaped by history, and amplified by modern social constructs. When partners can name the bears rather than become them, connection—real, embodied connection—finally becomes possible.

Relearning Safe Touch

In this space of awareness, safe touch becomes possible again. Couples begin to rediscover that touch doesn't have to lead anywhere—it can simply be. A hand resting on a shoulder, fingers brushing in passing, two bodies sharing the same quiet space on the couch. These small gestures start to re-educate the nervous system. Research shows that affectionate, nonsexual touch increases oxytocin, reduces physiological stress, and supports healthier relationship functioning (Light et al., 2005; Gulledge et al., 2003). Biology, once feared as the source of conflict or shame, becomes an ally again.

When there has been sexual trauma, the process is slower, more deliberate. I often begin by teaching clients about the primitive system itself—how fight, flight, and freeze responses live in the body; how the old brain stores not just the memory of what happened, but the feeling of it. Once the bear has been named, we begin retraining it.

Clients practice small moments of safe touch under their full control. They decide where touch happens, how long it lasts, and when it stops. The partner's task is to listen—to stop immediately when told, to start only when invited. Over time, these micro-moments teach the body a new lesson: that touch can be safe again, even good, even healing.

It takes patience. The old brain is cautious, scanning for the danger it once knew. But as trust grows, the body starts to exhale. Muscles soften, heart rates sync, breath evens out. What was once a threat becomes a bridge. Each touch is a message to the nervous system: *You're safe now.* And that, perhaps more than words, is where healing begins.

Taming the Modern Bear

When touch becomes safe again, the modern bear finally starts to quiet. What once prowled in the shadows—shame, fear, vigilance—begins to lose its power. The nervous system learns that closeness doesn't have to mean danger. It can mean home.

Every time a couple practices safe, intentional touch, they are not just repairing a relationship; they are rewiring biology. They are teaching the old brain a new story—one where connection doesn't come with a cost. In trauma work, we call this *corrective experience,* but really, it's the art of taming what once terrified us.

The bear doesn't disappear. It still watches from the cave's edge, doing its job—protecting, scanning, warning. But it no longer rules the body. It becomes what it was always meant to be: a guardian, not a predator. And when couples reach that point—when they can touch, hold, and be held without flinching—the bear finally lies down to rest.

Chapter 3 — Key Takeaways: Sex, Shame, and the Body's Long Memory

- **Touch and Attachment:**
  Touch is our first language of safety. The body learns trust and connection long before the mind forms words. Adult intimacy reactivates those early attachment patterns.

- **Shame as a Body Reflex:**
  Shame isn't a thought — it's a contraction in muscle, breath, and gaze. It's the nervous system bracing against rejection, not a moral failing.

- **Different Rules, Same Fear:**
  Cultural scripts train men and women differently — men toward control and performance, women toward caretaking and compliance — yet both protect against the same fear: **being alone or unwanted.**

- **Biology vs. Culture:**
  The body seeks closeness; society teaches containment. This mismatch fuels confusion, guilt, and distance around desire.

- **Repair Through Safety:**
  Healing shame happens through safe, attuned connection — steady touch, trust, and rest — not through logic or moral effort.

Bridge to Chapter 4 — Food, Body, and Belonging

Our old brain doesn't separate hunger from safety any more than it separates touch from love. In tribal life, food was both *nourishment and belonging*—to be fed was to be *included.* To go without was to risk *exile.* Scarcity wasn't only about calories; it was about *connection.*

In the modern world, food is no longer scarce—but foo*d safety still is.* We live surrounded by abundance yet haunted by the old brain's memory of lack. That primitive fear whispers that we must earn our place at the table—through control, thinness, discipline, or moral purity. What once was about survival has been rewritten as *body image, self-worth, and social belonging.*

Just as Chapter 3 explored how shame and intimacy intertwine, Chapter 4 turns to how *hunger, fullness, and the body itself* have become moralized extensions of our attachment needs. Food becomes another language through which the old brain asks, *"Am I safe? Am I loved? Do I belong?"*

Before moving on, let's take a moment to pause. The next pages invite you to notice how your own body has carried these stories of safety, shame, and touch. The following exercise will help you trace where those old Bears live and begin the slow work of taming them.

How's the Bear Hunt Going?

A field guide for tracking shame, touch, and intimacy in your body

Before you begin:

Chapter 3 can stir a lot. Give yourself 2–7 days off after finishing it. Then come back and skim (don't deep-dive) with a pen in hand.

Step 1: Notice the "Zings"

As you skim, put a ★ in the margin whenever you feel a zing—a jolt, flinch, heat, clench, or sudden urge to look away. Common zing spots readers report:

- Nakedness/body exposure
- Masturbation
- Same-sex desire/identity themes
- Touch and consent in couples' vignettes
- Words like "need," "want," "too much," and "not enough."

Write down *2–3 zing words* that kept echoing. These are your *Bears* for this exercise.

Example: "nakedness," "masturbation," "being left," "performing," "same sex," "touch = danger."

Step 2: Map It in the Body (2–3 minutes per Bear)

For each Bear, quickly note:

- **Where** do you feel it? (jaw, chest, throat, stomach, pelvis, hands)

- **Sensation** words: tight / hot / numb / fluttery / heavy / prickly

- **Intensity (0–10)** right now

- **Action impulse**: hide? please? push away? perform? go still?

(THIS IS DATA, NOT A JUDGMENT.)

Step 3: First Sighting — When Did This Bear Leave the Cave?

Gently recall early memories connected to this Bear. No over-digging—just headlines:

- **When** did you first notice this feeling or rule?

- **Who** was around (family, friends, peers, faith community, media)?

- **What** message did you absorb? (e.g., "good girls don't…," "real men must…," "desire is dangerous," "my body is wrong," "I'll be alone if…")

Step 4: Name the Social Construct (Chapter 2 tie-in)

Identify the **rule,** culture, gender scripts, or family handed you:

- What were **men** "supposed" to do/feel?
- What were **women** "supposed" to do/feel?
- What happened to people who didn't follow the script?
- Did this rule **keep you safe then**? Does it **serve you now**?

Reminder: Constructs are **repeated ideas**, not universal truths.
Your **new brain** can reassign meaning.

Step 5: Keep the Bear, Change Its Job

We don't evict Bears; we reassign them. Complete these sentences for
each Bear:

- **Old job:** "This Bear has been trying to protect me from ____
  (rejection, shame, abandonment, failure)."
- **New job:** "This Bear now helps me notice I need ____
  (slowness, reassurance, clearer consent, privacy, warmth)."
- **New brain statement:** "My body's alarm is about safety, not
  my worth."

Step 6: Taming Tools (choose 1–2, 3 minutes total)

Use these as quick resets while you sit with a Bear. They don't erase
the feeling; they help your nervous system **remember safety** while
you stay curious.

- **Hand-on-heart + slow exhale:** 4–6 breaths, making the exhale
  longer than the inhale.
- **Grounding touch:** Press feet into the floor or gently press
  palms together.
- **Orienting:** Look around and name five neutral objects in the
  room.
- **Warmth cue:** Wrap in a blanket or hold a warm mug near your
  chest.

- **Sensorial Soothing Strategies (from Chapter 1):** Return to one or two of your earlier identified "sensory anchors."
    - SIGHT: Soft lighting, candle flame, or watching trees move outside.
    - SOUND: Low music, white-noise track, hum, or quiet, steady rhythm.
    - SMELL: Favorite lotion, tea, or essential oil on a wrist.
    - TASTE: Sip something warm or cool, notice the first three seconds of flavor.
    - TOUCH: Weighted blanket, soft fabric, pet your dog or cat.
    - MOVEMENT: Sway, stretch, or step outside for a few breaths of air.

(If your intensity rises above 7/10, pause, stand up, get water, and look out a window. Come back later when your body feels ready.)

Step 7: Micro-Experiments (optional)

Choose **one** low-stakes experiment for the next week:

- **Language:** Say "I want to go slower" or "I like this, not that" once with someone safe.
- **Boundary:** Keep a towel/robe nearby after showering; choose **when** you reveal your body to yourself or a partner.
- **Self-contact:** Place a hand on your own forearm and breathe for 60 seconds. Notice what shifts.
- **Consent practice (partners):** Ask, "Green/yellow/red?" once during touch; stop or adjust based on the answer.

Step 8: Make a "Bear Card" (index-card quick sheet)

For each Bear, create a card you can revisit:

- **Name:** "The Performance Bear," "The Alone Bear," "The Nakedness Bear"
- **Trigger(s):** words, scenes, contexts
- **Body cues:** where/sensation/0–10
- **New job:** what it reminds you to ask for

- **Helps:** breath, phrase, boundary, person
- **Support plan:** who you'd talk to if it spikes (friend/therapist)

Step 9: Close the Loop (2 minutes)

Re-rate intensity (0–10). Write one line of *self-credit:*

"I stayed curious with a hard thing. That's regulation."

Gentle Cautions & Care

- *This is not exposure therapy.* It is *relationship-building* with your nervous system.

- Trying to *purge* or "fix" Bears often makes them louder. We *recognize, befriend, and retrain* them.

- If this work spikes panic, dissociation, or persistent shame, *pause* and consider doing it with a *therapist.* Courage is also knowing when to get a co-regulating other.

Optional Journal Prompts

- "When I felt the zing at *(Nakedness/masturbation/same sex/tough)*

- my body believed _____ would happen."

- "The rule I learned was _____. Today, I am allowed to believe _____."

- "If my Bear could talk kindly, it would ask for _____."

Privacy & Consent Notes

- Keep your notes in a *private place.*

- If doing partner experiments, agree on *opt-outs and after-care* (e.g., hug, tea, space).

Chapter 4 — Feeding the Bear: Food and the Modern Body

Safety, Control, and Nourishment

"It's not what you are eating, it's what eating you."

—*Pinette, Field Notes 2025*

Feeding Shame

Fat. He's too fat. She's too fat. They're too fat. *I'm* too fat. Too big. Too much. (Notice any bears stirring as you read those words?)

In Chapter 3, I talked about the biggest grizzly roaming through our nervous system — the fear of being alone, of rejection. But a close second, one that often walks paw-in-paw with connection, touch, and belonging, is the bear of *body image*.

I know what you're thinking — *Paul, isn't this chapter about food?* It is. But food and body are so intertwined that you can't talk about one without the other. Food is one of the oldest, most primal functions our nervous system monitors. The old brain's constant question is, *"Do we have enough to survive?"* — enough calories, enough energy, enough safety. But today, that question has been hijacked by another: *"Am I enough?"*

I hear the word *fat* hundreds of times a week in my sessions — whispered, joked about, or confessed like a sin. The look on people's faces when they reveal this "second grizzly" — the one that growls, *I'm too big, too unattractive, too unworthy* — it's heartbreaking. People starve themselves, chase bizarre diets, and scroll through endless social media feeds comparing their bodies to curated images of others. It's one of the deepest pains I see in my office, second only to that primal fear of rejection. And of course, they're linked.

Because when culture tells us that being "too big" means being *unlovable*, *lazy*, or *disgusting*, our old brain hears something much simpler and far more terrifying: *If I'm unlovable, I'll be alone. If I'm alone, I won't survive.*

This is the old brain at work — the tribal part of us that knows survival depends on connection. Long ago, being cast out of the tribe wasn't a metaphorical fear; it was a death sentence. Today, that same circuitry still fires when we feel excluded, criticized, or shamed for how our bodies look. So, the word *fat* becomes a kind of social weapon — one that triggers deep biological panic.

The Word "Fat": From Fuel to Fear

Let's start with something simple: the dictionary.

Fat: a natural oily or greasy substance occurring in animal bodies, especially when deposited as a layer under the skin or around certain organs.
Example: "Body fat helps insulate against the cold."

Fat: a substance composed mainly of triglycerides, used as a source of energy in the body and found in food such as butter, oils, and meats.
Example: "Dietary fat is essential for vitamin absorption." (Merriam-Webster, 2024)

So how did this perfectly neutral biological term — *a survival resource* — become a social slur? Historically, *fat* was associated with **abundance**. In the 1600s, to be fat was to be fortunate — well-fed, wealthy, secure. The term *fat cat* originally meant someone prosperous enough to eat well. It was a compliment. But by the late 1800s, as industrialization reshaped social hierarchies and "self-control" became a moral virtue, *fathead* became an insult. By the 1940s, *fatso* had entered the language, dripping with contempt.

Then came the mid-20th century, when America's postwar obsession with health and image collided. In March 1954, *Life Magazine* ran an article titled *"The Plague of Overweight"*, calling obesity "the most serious health problem today." At that time, only about 3% of Americans were classified as obese (Life Magazine, 1954). But fear spreads faster than fact — soon, diet fads exploded: the grapefruit diet, the cabbage soup diet, even the absurd Domino Sugar Diet (yes, that was real, look it up if you want).

From there, the narrative took hold. The message wasn't just "eat healthy," it was "control yourself." Fat was no longer a descriptor; it became a moral category.

When I ask clients to define the word '*fat*,' their voices drop and their faces tighten. Words like *lazy*, *gross*, *weak*, or *unlovable* tumble out. They've been taught that body size says something about their character — that weight equals worth. And these aren't fringe beliefs. They're woven into our cultural nervous system through advertising, fitness trends, and a billion- dollar industry built on the fear of being too much.

What's striking is how quickly children absorb it. Many of my past youngest clients talked about "good foods" and "bad foods." This binary — broccoli good, donuts bad — seems harmless until you realize the psychological math underneath:

"If I eat bad food, I am bad."
"If I eat too much, I'm out of control."
"If I'm out of control, I'll be judged, rejected, alone."

The tribal wiring still hums: *Stay small to stay safe.*

Food, Trauma, and the ACEs Connection

If you've been around psychology in the past decade, you've likely heard of the Adverse Childhood Experiences (ACE) Study — a massive research project launched in the 1990s by Dr. Vincent Felitti and Dr. Robert Anda through the CDC (Felitti et al., 1998). The study found that the more adverse experiences a person endured — things like neglect, abuse, or household dysfunction — the higher their risk for everything from heart disease to depression, substance abuse, and obesity.

But here's the story that led to that study — and it's worth pausing on.

In the early 1980s, Dr. Felitti ran an obesity treatment clinic in San Diego. Patients were losing significant amounts of weight, but mysteriously, many began dropping out — even those who were succeeding. When he interviewed them, he discovered a painful pattern: many had histories of childhood trauma, especially sexual abuse. For them, weight wasn't the *problem* — it was the *protection.* Obesity had become a buffer against threat, a way to feel safe in a dangerous world.

That insight reframed everything. Overeating, in many cases, was not gluttony or laziness; it was an adaptive strategy— the body's way of coping with unbearable emotion or threat. Food was comfort, safety, armor. In short, the old brain was doing its job.

The ACEs findings echoed what trauma therapists already knew intuitively — that the body keeps the score, and eating behaviors are often an unconscious attempt to regulate a dysregulated system (van der Kolk, 2014). Unfortunately, society's narrative didn't catch up. Instead of compassion, people got condemnation. The culture said, *"Your body is the problem,"* when in truth, the body was often the solution that helped them survive.

The Old Brain and the Biology of Enough

Let's revisit the old brain. Remember, this part of our nervous system evolved hundreds of thousands of years ago — in a world of scarcity and danger. Our ancestors were tribal hunters and gatherers, roaming across uncertain terrain. If they stumbled upon a patch of berries or a successful hunt, they ate until they couldn't eat another bite. Why? Because they didn't know when the next opportunity would come.

This wasn't gluttony; it was survival intelligence.

The old brain doesn't have a built-in "off" switch for abundance. It evolved in scarcity. So, when food was available, it sent a clear directive: *Eat now. Store energy. Live another day.* That's why it still takes our modern brains about 20 minutes to register fullness — the lag is a remnant of that evolutionary design.

Now picture that same survival brain in a modern grocery store — aisles of abundance, food on demand, 24-hour drive-thru. To the old brain, this isn't luxury; it's chaos. A tribal organism dropped into overstimulation.

A friend of mine who immigrated from Cuba once told me that his first trip to an American grocery store left him in awe. "In Cuba," he said, "you'd go to the store, and maybe there was one box of cereal. You'd grab it fast because you didn't know when more would come." In the U.S., he walked for hours, mouth agape, stunned by the endless rows of options. His body couldn't compute *so much plenty.*

The old brain was built to seek food in a world where scarcity was the rule. Now, it's forced to resist food in a world of constant supply — and that's an impossible biological contradiction.

And just to make things harder, our modern environment is full of triggers designed to hijack that circuitry. Advertisers know that food imagery activates the same neural pathways as hunger. Every "melty cheese" commercial or close-up of chocolate lava cake — *and that one's hard for me; it's one of my favorites—pokes at that ancient bear, whispering, eat, you might not get another chance.*

So, when clients tell me, "I have no willpower," I remind them — it's not a moral failing. It's a mismatch between an ancient survival brain and a hyper-stimulating world. The old brain is trying to save us. The new world keeps offering dessert.

Breaking Bread: The Tribal Nature of Eating

Food has always been more than fuel — it's a ritual. It's how tribes bond, how families connect, how belonging is signaled. Anthropologists have long noted that eating together is one of the oldest social contracts; sharing food is a way of saying, *"You are safe with us"* (Fischler, 1988).

In traditional societies, meals were communal and sacred. To break bread was to reaffirm trust. Even today, every culture uses food to mark rites of passage — birthdays, weddings, funerals. We don't just eat; we *belong* through eating.

But in modern Western culture, something has twisted. The act that once connected us now often isolates us. If you live in a body that culture deems "too big," even the act of eating in public can feel like exposure, like proof of failure. Imagine the contradiction: the very behavior that. Once *signaled* safety and belonging, it now threatens to bring shame and rejection.

That's the second grizzly: *I eat; therefore, I am bad.* And yet, I have to eat.

Food is both a source of safety and a trigger for shame. In therapy, I often see this conflict play out: the nervous system seeks regulation through food—the dopamine that rewards, the oxytocin that emerges in moments of comfort or shared connection, the soothing rhythm of chewing and tasting—while the mind overlays judgment and fear.

We have to eat. But we can forget that eating is how tribes survived together. When that communal safety breaks down, food becomes both comfort and punishment, feast and exile.

Control as Safety

What happens when we live inside this tug-of-war — needing to eat to survive, yet fearing that the very act of eating will make us unworthy of belonging?

We try to control it. Control becomes safety.

Calorie counting, fasting, moralizing foods into *good* and *bad* — these aren't just health habits; they're rituals of containment. They soothe the same fear that once drove our ancestors to sharpen spears and guard the cave entrance.

In an unpredictable, overstimulating world, control is our modern shelter. I see it daily in my practice: clients who starve themselves, track every bite, or label hunger as weakness. And when I ask, "What did you eat today?" the answer is often heartbreaking — an apple, maybe a lettuce leaf. The logic goes like this: *If I can control my body, I can control the chaos around me.*

But the body doesn't read calorie charts; it reads survival cues. The brain can't run on lettuce. When I gently remind them — because it is well documented — that the brain consumes about 20% of the body's total energy and quite literally runs on glucose, they nod — and then still whisper, "But I can't eat more; I'll gain weight."

This is the modern bear trap: *Thin means safe. Full means shame.*

And yet, biologically speaking, restriction is a signal of famine. The old brain doesn't know you're trying to "fit into jeans." It thinks the tribe is running out of food. It slows metabolism, heightens cravings, and doubles down on the impulse to eat later — all while the new brain scolds you for "failing again."

Women, in particular, have carried the cultural weight of this double bind. Control over food has become coded safety behavior, a way to demonstrate worth in a system that equates thinness with discipline and desirability. Men aren't immune — but the scripts differ. For men, the "fit" body becomes proof of dominance or self-mastery. For women, it's proof of acceptability. Both are cages built from the same ancestral fear: *If I lose control, I'll lose belonging.*

Or, as some clients have said softly, "I wasn't counting calories — the food was my friend. It never judged me."

Most people can cognitively tell me they know they need to eat enough, but they struggle to know the difference between eating to nourish themselves versus regulating emotion or anxiety.

Because of the dopamine and endorphins that get released when we eat, there's this physiological overlap — food will calm the nervous system but can also mask unmet emotional safety needs. That overlap often creates binge–purge cycles.

And yet, the same dynamic applies not just to food, but to all of our basic biological cues. The modern bear doesn't only shape what we eat — it shapes what we ignore.

Ignoring the Body's Alarms

One of the strangest signs of how disconnected we've become from our own biology is how often people ignore hunger and thirst cues. The old brain sends these signals as simple alarms — *you need fuel, you need hydration, you need safety* — but the modern brain often overrides them with social constructs. Hunger gets rebranded as "discipline." Thirst becomes "optional." I've had clients look genuinely surprised when I suggest that much of their fatigue, irritability, and fog might be dehydration. They'll say, "It can't be that simple," and yet after a week of eating regularly and drinking water, they return saying, *"I can't believe how much better I feel."*

But that's how far the modern bear has taken us. In a culture that glorifies restriction, productivity, and image, we've learned to treat our most basic biological cues as weaknesses. Dehydration alone can reduce focus, mood, and cognitive performance (Armstrong et al., 2012; Popkin et al., 2010). and under physical or heat stress, dehydration has been linked to elevated cortisol and stress-hormone responses (Maresh et al., 2007). Hunger cues, too, are ignored or moralized — as if the need for food were a flaw of willpower instead of the body's wisdom.

Instead of water, many people reach for caffeine — the socially sanctioned substitute for rest. Caffeine keeps us alert, awake longer, and temporarily sharper, so we tell ourselves it's productive. But then we can't sleep because of all the caffeine, and we start the next day even more fatigued. The cycle becomes its own form of survival: push, deplete, repeat. We drink more coffee to stay up, then alcohol to come down, mistaking this rollercoaster for normal life. The modern bear loves this pattern — the illusion of control, the rush of doing more, the avoidance of stopping long enough to feel what the body is asking for.

What's also interesting — and profoundly simple — is how this shows up in times of acute trauma. After a sudden loss, accident, or crisis, one of the first things I often encourage clients to do is to drink water. They look at me like I'm missing the point: *"Paul, I just lost someone — I'm shaking, I can't think straight."* And I'll say, *"Yes, and your body is working hard to flush out stress hormones. Water helps."* It's not a magic cure, but it's a start. Hydration supports the body's natural stress recovery system. When we're dehydrated, our cortisol response to stress tends to be more pronounced; when we're hydrated, the body shows a more regulated stress hormone reaction (Kashi et al., 2025).

And that's the bigger picture here — we need both food and water to maintain homeostasis. The old brain is constantly working to maintain that delicate balance. Every time we override hunger or thirst, we disrupt that system. The result isn't just physical fatigue; it's emotional dysregulation. I sometimes wonder how much of what we call anxiety or depression is really the body's way of saying, *"You've ignored me too long."* In that sense, our fear of the modern bear — the drive to be thinner, faster, busier — becomes its own kind of starvation. And when that starvation becomes the norm, our bodies start speaking for us — carrying the message our culture keeps sending back.

The Body as a Social Mirror

The human body has become a billboard for identity, morality, and value — a kind of social mirror reflecting both personal control and tribal worth.

Our old brains evolved to scan the environment for safety signals: *Who's healthy enough to hunt? Who looks strong enough to survive? Who looks sick, weak, or unreliable?* Appearance was survival shorthand. But now, the new brain layers morality and status on top of that wiring. The result? A world where the shape of your body feels like a moral report card.

Social media amplifies this to absurdity. We've gone from communal fires to digital mirrors, each of us both hunter and hunted in an endless loop of comparison. The "fit body" becomes not just desirable but *aspirational*. The "flawed" body becomes something to fix, cleanse, or atone for.

Anthropologists would call this a tribal signaling system (Henrich, 2015). In small societies, visible cues — tattoos, adornments, or ritual markings — showed who belonged to whom. In ours, it's diet culture, workout routines, wellness regimens. Body and belonging are still intertwined; only the symbols have changed.

And so, the body, once a vessel for living, becomes an anxious performance. A currency. A plea: *Am I still in the tribe?*

The Skinny Truth on Fat

Let's pause for a moment and talk about the real truth of being fat — or, more accurately, the truth of being human in a body that carries weight.

In our culture, "skinny" has become the moral currency of worthiness. We're told that being thin is the golden ticket — the way to be desirable, accepted, and loved. But the reality is far more complicated, and frankly, the "skinny ideal" is one of the biggest cultural lies we've ever swallowed (Bordo, 2003).

If we look through the lens of biology, the story shifts completely. The impulse to eat, to store energy, to survive — that's not vanity; that's evolution. The old brain doesn't care what size jeans you wear. It doesn't care about your BMI, your mirror selfie, or how many influencers tell you, "Strong is the new skinny." Its only job is to keep you alive. And one of the main ways it does that is by driving you to seek food and conserve energy.

So, let me be clear: obesity or being heavy is not a moral failure. It's the outcome of a complex interplay of biological, genetic, neurochemical, and psychological factors — the vast majority of which have nothing to do with willpower (Loos & Yeo, 2022).

A simple example? Body type.

Biologists have long recognized natural somatotypes — ectomorphs, mesomorphs, and endomorphs — roughly corresponding to small-boned, medium-boned, and large-boned frames (Sheldon, 1940). These differences are genetic. Yet I can't tell you how many of my female clients, 5'8" or 5'9", with broad bone structure and strong builds, punish themselves for not fitting into a size 2 — as if biology itself were a moral failing.

That's the tragedy of this bear: people are fighting a losing battle not with their bodies, but with a cultural illusion. The shame runs deep because the social message is clear — if you can't control your body, you can't control yourself. It's the same illusion we've explored before — that our new brain, our proud frontal cortex, should be able to override every old-brain impulse simply through thought or discipline.

But the truth is that biology still drives the bus most of the time. The new brain gets to hold the map — not the wheel.

And yet, this is what makes the shame so potent. Society moralizes what is biology and adaptation. The body becomes a billboard of supposed virtue or failure when, in fact, it's simply doing its job — surviving in the context it's been placed in.

And this isn't just theory — you can see it in the stories we tell about bodies. Take the late, beloved actor John Candy, adored not for chiselled abs but for the warmth and humanity he brought into every room. In the recent documentary *John Candy: I Like Me* (Director Colin Hanks, Prime Video), he said he saw the world through *"thin eyes"* — he didn't care what someone looked like, only who they were.

Years later, another reporter brought up his size again — a theme he endured throughout his life — asking, *"Does anybody pressure you about your weight... about slimming down?"* Candy smiled and replied, *"No... I think it bothers other people more than it bothers me. But does it bother you?"* When the reporter insisted it didn't, Candy chuckled: *"Oh good... because you brought it up."*

He wasn't the punchline — he was revealing the joke. What if the weight we fear isn't the size of our body, but the heaviness of judgment placed upon it by others? The shame we think is ours is often just someone else's fear echoing off our skin.

It's made worse, of course, by centuries of conditioning that link physical form to moral worth. As Dr. Martin Luther King Jr. once said, he longed for the day when people would not be judged by the color of their skin but by the content of their character (King, 1963).

If I may humbly extend that wish, I long for the day when we are not judged by any external marker: not by color, race, poverty, intelligence, sexual orientation, gender, size, or symmetry, but by the content of our character.

That's the real skinny truth about fat: What determines belonging, love, and worth isn't body shape, but integrity — the depth of kindness, the courage of empathy, and the ability to live aligned with values rather than appearances.

When clients start to understand this — to see the "fat" bear not as an enemy but as a messenger of unmet safety needs — something shifts. They stop asking, "How can I fix my body?" and start asking, "How can I make peace with it?"

And that's the work that truly changes lives — and tribes.

Inherited Bears: How Family Messaging Shapes the Body Story

Many of the fears and hungers we struggle with aren't new — they're inherited stories about safety, control, and belonging that our old brains keep replaying. When we talk about food, body image, and shame, we're not just talking about the present moment. We're talking about *inheritance.*

The belief that being heavy is a "problem" isn't new; it's been echoing through generations ever since the social meaning of fat shifted from abundance to moral failure. The stigma has had centuries to root itself in our collective nervous system — and families have been its most effective messengers.

We don't just inherit genes. We inherit coping codes. How our parents talked about food, their bodies, and their worth becomes the template for how we talk to ourselves. If they dieted, counted calories, moralized "good" and "bad" foods, or measured self-control by waistlines, those cues didn't just teach us how to eat — they taught us how to *feel* about eating.

I've sat with countless clients who can still recall the moment a parent or relative pointed to a body part — a stomach, a thigh, a face — and said it was "too big." That single comment often burrowed deeper than anyone realized. The unspoken message wasn't just about size; it was about *love that felt conditional.*

"I love you when you're smaller. I love you when you fit the image."

Few things injure attachment more than the idea that acceptance must be earned by shrinking yourself. And tragically, most parents who said those words weren't cruel — they were repeating the same pain that was once handed to them. They were trying, in their own anxious way, to protect their children from the very rejection they once endured.

That's how shame travels — not through intention, but through imitation. These messages about "control," "discipline," and "appearance" ripple through families like epigenetic code, shaping generations of nervous systems to associate food and body with safety and belonging. It's the familial version of the bear — *protective but misdirected.*

This isn't about blaming our parents. They, too, were victims of the same cultural conditioning. But bringing this to awareness allows us to see how the past lives in the present — and how every time we shame ourselves for eating, or teach a child to mistrust their body, we feed that same bear again.

The work involves interrupting the transmission. To remember that biology isn't betrayal. To offer our children what most of us never fully received — the simple, unshakable message:

"You are loved as you are. Your body isn't a problem to solve."

Only when we begin to re-parent those internalized voices can the collective nervous system start to heal.

Guess what, these are not just my observations; decades of research show how stigma, family messages, and cultural pressures shape body shame across generations. (Puhl & Latner, 2007; Neumark-Sztainer et al., 2010; Rodgers & Chabrol, 2009; Tiggemann, 2006).

Nourishment vs. Regulation

One of the most healing shifts I see in clients — and often one of the hardest — is learning to distinguish between nourishment and regulation.

Nourishment is about fueling the body. Regulation is about calming the nervous system. The two often blur. When we're overwhelmed, anxious, or lonely, food becomes one of the most effective — and socially sanctioned — tools for emotional regulation. After all, eating releases dopamine and endorphins. It soothes. Nature wired us this way to ensure survival.

But in modern life, where emotional safety is often scarce and stimulation constant, we use food not to *nourish* but to *stabilize.* We eat not because we're hungry but because we're dysregulated. Then, when the new brain sees the "bad" food choice, it adds guilt — layering shame on top of stress, creating a perfect cycle of binge, restrict, and guilt.

It's important to understand this isn't a character flaw. It's the old brain trying to self-soothe with the tools it knows best. For our ancestors, a successful meal meant a brief pause in vigilance — safety restored, if only for a moment. Today, a cookie or a bowl of mac and cheese can serve the same neurochemical purpose.

But because we moralize food, that momentary relief is followed by punishment. "I was bad." "I lost control." "I shouldn't have." And there it is again — shame, the social predator that keeps us running even when the threat is imagined.

As a therapist, I often invite clients to pause before the bite and ask, *"What is my body really asking for right now?"* Is it food — or is it comfort, connection, rest, permission? Sometimes the answer isn't fewer calories; it's more kindness.

Elimination: The Forgotten End of Nourishment

Okay, stay with me — this might sound like a tangent, but I promise it's not.

We've talked about eating as a biological function tied to safety, but what about the other end of that process?

Elimination — urinating, defecating, releasing — is the natural counterbalance to nourishment. It's literally how the body completes the cycle of intake and release. Yet, like eating, it's another primal function that modern culture has managed to shame, constrain, and schedule into submission.

Our ancestors didn't need permission to relieve themselves. They followed their body's cues naturally, often communally, and without moral weight. But today, we've turned elimination into something that must be justified, squeezed in between productivity metrics and lesson plans.

Let's start with schools, since they're the earliest social training grounds for this mindset. In many American schools, students have only three to five minutes between classes, and lunch periods as short as fifteen minutes — time that includes waiting in line, grabbing food, and finding a seat. Teachers, meanwhile, often go hours without drinking water or using the restroom because the schedule simply doesn't allow it; supervision demands and curricular pacing take priority.

What we're really teaching — both implicitly and explicitly — is that the body's signals are interruptions to achievement. Hunger and elimination are treated as inconveniences to "learning." But let's be honest: a child whose stomach is growling, or bladder is full, is not learning algebra; they're trying to survive the next ten minutes.

This pattern doesn't stop at school doors. It extends across entire professions—teachers, police officers, nurses, warehouse workers, truck drivers, factory staff—people whose jobs routinely force them to override their body's basic needs in the name of efficiency. A 2019 study found that more than three-quarters of nurses routinely delay urination and many restrict fluid intake to keep up with workload demands. Over time, this increases the risk of urinary tract infections, kidney problems, and pelvic floor issues (Pierce et al., 2019). If this is happening in nursing—a field that knows better than most what the body requires—it isn't a stretch to imagine similar patterns in other professions where bathroom access is limited or discouraged. Clients tell me stories of how long they "hold it," almost as if endurance itself has become a quiet badge of professionalism.

We call this *dedication*. But really, it's a biological disconnection.

When you hold urine, and the bladder inflates, stretch receptors trigger growing urgency and discomfort. In healthy adults, this "urge to void" has been shown to impair working memory and attention, reducing focus and likely increasing irritability (Lewis et al., 2011). And honestly, as one human to another, do I really have to provide research for this? Most of us already know exactly what it feels like.

When delayed voiding becomes habitual, the bladder is repeatedly stretched—sending stronger and more frequent urgency signals. Research shows that women who routinely "hold it," avoid bathrooms, or delay voiding have significantly higher rates of urinary symptoms, including urgency, frequency, and discomfort (Berry et al., 2025). In simple terms, when we ignore our elimination cues—our body's basic request for balance—we end up punishing ourselves for being animals.

It's not just a medical issue; it's a moral one. By prioritizing productivity, curriculum pacing, and corporate timelines over biology, we reinforce the illusion that the body is an inconvenience — something to be managed, minimized, or postponed.

If education and workplaces truly cared about "resilience" and "performance," they'd start by respecting biology instead of resisting it. Allowing adequate time for eating, resting, and elimination isn't indulgence — it's alignment with how the human nervous system was designed to function.

When we teach children—and model for adults—that bodily needs can wait, we teach them to ignore the very signals that keep them safe and regulated. The bear asks for release, and we tell it to hold it until the meeting's over.

Collective Hunger

Our culture is starving — but not for food. We are full of calories and empty of comfort. Fed by abundance yet malnourished by disconnection.

Anthropologists and sociologists describe this as a **collective hunger** — a society overfed and undernourished in every other way (Bauman, 2007). We hunger for authenticity, rest, and belonging. We hunger for pace, silence, touch. And because we no longer share meals as often, the social glue that once fed our nervous systems — eye contact, laughter, chewing in rhythm with others — has thinned.

So, we eat more, but feel less fed.

Meanwhile, marketing pours fuel on the fire. Every advertisement whispers both *indulgence* and *control*. "You deserve this burger" is followed by "But you'd better hit the gym." Our old brain is being played like a drum, bombarded with scarcity messages disguised as choice.

And so, we swing between feast and famine, abundance and shame. A world of overstimulation has left the collective nervous system buzzing — full and starving at once.

Food has become both anesthetic and ritual: it dulls the ache of disconnection while momentarily recreating the safety of togetherness. But until we name the hunger underneath — for rest, kindness, and shared safety — the bear stays restless.

Integrating the Bear

So how do we feed the bear without letting it run the show? We start by understanding that the bear isn't bad. It's ancient, loyal, and deeply confused.

The old brain still believes that food equals safety, that control equals survival, that rejection equals death. It's doing exactly what it was designed to do — just in an environment it was never designed for.

To integrate the bear means to listen to it without blindly obeying it. It means asking: What is my old brain trying to protect me from? What does it fear will happen if I stop counting, restricting, or shaming? What does it need to feel safe enough to rest?

Compassion becomes the bridge between the old brain and the new one—and later, you'll see just how significant that bridge truly is. When we meet our appetites — and our shame — with curiosity instead of contempt, the nervous system begins to soften.

Because feeding the bear was never about silencing it, it was about understanding what it's really hungry for. Not more food.

Not more control. But more safety. More belonging. More gentle permission to be human.

And as we'll explore in the next chapter, the bear also hungers for rest, for play, and for the simple, ancient relief of feeling safe in our own bodies again.

But there's one more bear we need to meet before we can truly feel safe—one that hides not in hunger, but in the fear of losing what we have.

The Abundance Bear

Not all bears growl.
Some purr softly while they nibble from our endless table —
streaming screens, 24-hour groceries, dopamine hits on demand.

This is the Abundance Bear: the one that doesn't chase us through the forest but sits politely beside us, whispering, *"Just one more."*

Our old brain never evolved for this. It was shaped by scarcity and trained to celebrate each discovery of food, warmth, or companionship as a victory. That burst of pleasure — dopamine, endorphins, oxytocin — said, *"You survived. Rest now."* But in the modern world, there is no end to the berry patch. The berries scroll—the notifications flash. The buffet never closes.

Even in plenty, the bear whispers scarcity. It keeps asking us to pick sides — disciplined or indulgent, pure or corrupt — as if survival depended on choosing correctly.

Neurochemistry of Endless Plenty

Dopamine isn't a chemical of happiness; it's a chemical of *pursuit.* It spikes in anticipation, not satisfaction (Berridge & Robinson, 2016). When the stream of reward cues never stops, the brain never receives the signal that the hunt is over. Instead of calm, we feel a kind of anxious hum — restlessness disguised as hunger. Cortisol, the stress hormone, joins the party, keeping us alert "just in case" there's a better berry around the next corner (Sapolsky, 2004).

This is why abundance can feel like pressure. The body senses the same uncertainty it would in famine: *When do I stop? What if I miss something important?*
The old brain hears "too much" as instability, and instability equals threat.

Resonance and Collective Overload

The Abundance Bear doesn't just live inside individuals; it prowls our collective nervous system. Tribes used to synchronize through rhythm — hunt, eat, sing, play, sleep. Now, we resonate through consumption. One person's urgency becomes another's FOMO.

Neuroscientists studying social contagion note that emotional arousal spreads through neural resonance—processes involving mirror systems and limbic attunement (Siegel, 2012). In other words, stress is contagious. When everyone is overstimulated, everyone else's body interprets that as danger, too.

So, we check again. Refresh again. Buy again. Eat again. Abundance turns into collective vigilance — a herd perpetually scanning the horizon of its own excess.

The Paradox of Plenty

From a biological perspective, abundance equals unpredictability. The homeostatic systems that evolved for cycles of feast and rest lose their rhythm when the feast never ends. The body's predictive machinery — its elegant system for balancing input and output — spins without closure. The old brain keeps asking, *"Is it safe to stop?"* and the modern world keeps answering, *"Not yet."*

That's the paradox of plenty: the safer and fuller life becomes, the less secure we sometimes feel. Abundance makes us anxious not because we're ungrateful, but because our ancient circuitry mistakes *limitlessness* for *instability*.

Making Peace with the Bear

The work is not to fight the Abundance Bear but to learn its language. It is the part of us that still believes safety must be earned through vigilance, consumption, or achievement. What it really needs is rhythm — the reassurance that pauses are allowed, that fullness can coexist with stillness.

Maybe abundance itself isn't the threat. Perhaps it's the absence of endings.

And that, more than anything, is why rest — real rest — feels revolutionary.

Perhaps the bravest thing we can do now isn't to gather more, but to stop — to let the bear sleep and trust that the world will still be there when we wake.

We've learned to silence hunger, ignore thirst, and chase productivity as proof of worth. But soon, the body finds other ways to protest. Safety, fatigue, sleeplessness, and burnout become the next generation of bears—the ones that roar when we refuse to rest. Even play starts to feel unsafe, like a waste of time.

These, too, are old instincts twisted by the new world: the drive to move, to laugh, to recover—turned into guilt. For most of human history, food was not a prize for the worthy; it was a birthright of the tribe—shared because survival demanded it, given because withholding it would have felt like violence against the group itself. Somewhere along the way, abundance was privatized. We began to build paywalls around nourishment, confusing deservedness with dignity.

The old brain never agreed to this arrangement; it still equates feeding with safety. To share food is to reassure the nervous system that the world is not ending. To deny it is to whisper danger back into the collective body. That truth hasn't changed, even if our systems have. Every hungry child, every food-insecure household, lives with the body's ancient alarm still sounding: *You are not safe.* We have enough for everyone, yet the fear of scarcity remains—an echo from a time when withholding food meant power. Perhaps the Abundance Bear isn't gluttony at all, but grief: our biology mourning the loss of communal safety.

The Birthright of Food

At first, food was not earned. It was shared. The hunt, the harvest, the fire — all belonged to everyone because survival depended on everyone. To feed another was not charity; it was instinct.

Anthropological studies of foraging societies, from the! Kung San of the Kalahari to the Hadza of Tanzania show that food sharing was the moral center of life, not a gesture of generosity (Lee, 1979; Sahlins, 1972). To hoard was to endanger the group; to share was to live another day. Evolutionary biologists later confirmed what the old brain already knew: altruism is adaptive (Hrdy, 2009; Gurven & Hill, 2009).

Only much later did we build walls around nourishment — charging admission to the table, measuring worthiness by labor, status, or luck. We began to confuse deservedness with dignity. The old brain never signed off on that. It still believes food is a universal right, a biological covenant older than money or merit.

When we withhold it — from children, from people with low incomes, from anyone — we re-enact the oldest fear: that safety must be earned. But the truth is more straightforward, older, steadier. A full stomach is not a reward. It is a signal to the body and the tribe alike: *you are safe here.* A tribe that charges its children to eat has forgotten what kept the fire burning in the first place. And yet, here we are — still arguing over who deserves a meal. Our modern systems speak in budgets and policies, but the old brain hears only one question: *Am I safe? Are my children safe?* We may call it economics or education, but underneath it all, the same ancient circuitry decides whether a society can truly rest.

Feeding the Tribe: Modern Proof of an Ancient Truth

Current research continues to affirm what our ancestors already practiced: feeding the young sustains the whole. (Please tell me I'm not the only one who sees the common sense in this… Bueller? Bueller…?) Research shows that universal free-meal programs are often associated with improved attendance, better behavior, and—in some cases— modest academic gains, across income levels. (Spill et al., 2024; Schwartz & Rothbart, 2020; U.S. Department of Agriculture, 2024) Food insecurity, on the other hand, raises cortisol and impairs attention and memory in children, keeping their bodies in a state of quiet alarm (Shankar et al., 2017).

School districts that adopt no-cost meal policies consistently report fewer nurse visits (Spill et al., 2024) and lower rates of disciplinary incidents (Prothero, 2024). Remember earlier when I said that if you want to build resilience in schools, you start with the basics—feed them. Fed children are safe children, and safe children are calmer. And get this: they can actually access their frontal cortex more effectively. That's how you improve test scores—not through elaborate reward systems, but through nervous systems that feel secure enough to learn.

The data confirm what the tribe always knew without a single statistic: when every child eats, the collective body steadies. The lesson is older than agriculture itself—a fed child calms the tribe.

Impression

The Abundance Bear was never the enemy. It was the old brain's confused guardian — pacing in circles around the fire, convinced that more food, more work, more vigilance would finally quiet the fear of hunger. But abundance was never meant to be hoarded; it was meant to be shared.

We have forgotten that the body relaxes not at the sight of plenty, but at the sight of generosity. When the tribe eats together, the nervous system exhales. A fed child, a neighbor invited to the table, a moment of rest after the harvest — these are the signals that tell the body, *you are safe now.*

Fed kids are safe kids, and safe kids can learn. That's how the brain works: the frontal cortex — the part that imagines, reasons, and creates — only opens when the old brain believes it's safe. Our ancestors knew this without a single MRI. They fed the children first and then told the stories that built the world.

Our biology does not care about profit margins or worthiness tests. It still believes what it learned beside the first fire: food is a covenant, not a commodity. The lesson remains as old as hunger itself — the only absolute abundance is shared safety. Maybe that's where the real work begins — not in feeding the body, but in learning what it means to feel safe once it's full. The plate is only the beginning. The deeper hunger is for safety itself. If you want to begin noticing your own bears — the ones that whisper, scold, or seduce you into believing safety must be earned — here's a simple way to start. This isn't about fixing anything. It's about seeing the lies clearly enough to remember the truth.

Key Takeaways – Chapter 4

- **Abundance and anxiety are twins.** The old brain still fears famine, so even in plenty it hoards, driven by the reflex that more equals safe.

- **The "Abundance Bear" is a survival mechanism, not a flaw.** It prowls when we confuse productivity, vigilance, and consumption with protection.

- **True abundance is shared safety.** In early tribes, food was communal—a biological covenant that kept everybody alive.

- **Modern scarcity is often artificial.** When nourishment is gated by money or "deservedness," the body reads it as danger, reigniting ancient fear.

- **Generosity regulates the nervous system.** Feeding others, resting, and allowing enoughness are biological acts of safety, not moral indulgences.

- **A fed child calms the tribe.** The health of any culture can be measured by how easily it feeds its young.

- **To let the Bear rest** is to trust that the world will still be there when we wake—and that safety grows stronger when it's shared.

Exercise: Those Lying Bears

By now, you've probably spotted a few of your own bears wandering through this chapter. The ones that murmur:
"You'd be more lovable if you were smaller."
"You can eat, but not too much."

"You'll be safe once you have control." "Those thighs are getting big."

Take a minute to name them. Write them down. The Body Image Bear. The Food Shame Bear. The Control Bear. Whatever names fit. See them clearly. Now say — out loud, even if it feels ridiculous —

THESE ARE ALL LIES!!

They are echoes, not prophecies — old survival messages that once protected you and now only keep you small. They were designed to help you survive, not to help you belong.

Now, think of a few people you genuinely admire. A parent, teacher, mentor, friend, or someone from history. What qualities draw you to them? Courage? Kindness? Humor? Integrity? Grit? Notice something: none of those qualities has anything to do with body size, weight, or shape. You admire the *content of their character*, not the circumference of their waist.

Now, find a few of those same qualities inside yourself — even the faintest flickers. Compassion. Perseverance. Empathy. Humor. They've been there all along. When you spot them, say this one out loud too:

THOSE ARE THE TRUTHS!!

That's the beginning of reclaiming your relationship with your body and your biology — not through control, but through connection.

Small Practices to Expose the Lies

1. The Pause Before the Bite

When the urge to eat hits, pause. Ask: *What is my body really asking for right now?* Sometimes it's food. Sometimes it's soothing. Sometimes it's the company.

You're not judging the answer — just learning the bear's language.

2. Water as Medicine

Try a one-week experiment. Each morning and mid-afternoon, drink a full glass of water before reaching for caffeine.

Notice your focus, energy, and irritability across the week. Hydration doesn't fix life, but it steadies the system that has to live it.

3. The Rhythm Reset

Create one small rhythm that honors your body's cycles — a real lunch break, a short walk, a quiet minute before bed.

Rhythm teaches the bear that safety isn't something to chase; it's something you return to.

4. The 20-Minute Fullness Rule

Your old brain evolved to eat fast when food was scarce. Give it time to catch up.
When you eat, pause after about twenty minutes and check in: *Am I still hungry, or just not full yet?*
Over time, this retrains the bear to trust abundance without fear.

5. Listening to the Quiet Bear

End by sitting in silence for a minute. Ask gently: *What does my body need — not what does it fear?* Listen without judgment. The quiet bear always tells the truth; it just speaks softly.

These practices may seem simple, almost laughably so. But they are **radical acts of biological loyalty.** Each one teaches your nervous system that safety isn't earned through perfection or deprivation — it's restored through rhythm, nourishment, hydration, and awareness.

Because every lie the bears tell is ultimately about fear. And every truth you reclaim is about love — the kind that starts by feeding, watering, and trusting the life that's already yours.

Chapter 5 — The Architecture of Safety: Faith, Fear, Flag, and the Old Brain's Search for Certainty

"Fear is the oldest architect. It builds the walls first, then calls them holy."
— *Anonymous*

Safety is supposed to be simple. But for most of us, it isn't.

The old brain doesn't recognize safety through logic or evidence—it recognizes through *pattern*. Familiarity feels safe, even when it's painful. Stillness can feel dangerous because movement once meant survival. And play—though essential to growth and connection—can feel reckless to a nervous system that equates vigilance with protection.

We say we want peace, yet the moment life quiets down, something inside us stirs. The bears wake up. The mind scans for what's missing or what might go wrong. The irony is painful: the same instincts that once kept us alive now keep us from resting, trusting, or laughing freely.

What if rest and play aren't indulgences, but *biological languages of safety* we've forgotten how to speak? What if the work is not to earn stillness, but to remember that the body already knows what safety feels like—if only we stop mistaking certainty for it.

Safety starts in the body long before it becomes a belief. When the old brain feels threatened, it reaches for certainty—at school, at work, on the playground, in religion, and in politics. The more afraid we are, the more we sort and judge. The healing arc is learning to feel safe without needing an enemy. To many readers, this idea of *not needing an enemy* may feel foreign. So much of our social fabric is built on the myth of good versus evil. We grow up on stories that promise clear villains and heroes—someone to defeat, someone to blame. "There has to be a bad person," we say, as if the nervous system itself demands it. But the truth is more complex: through the social bears we've created, we've turned each other into the enemy. The tribe no longer faces a common predator; we've become the predators to one another. And that doesn't bode well for a tribe.

That's what this chapter is about—understanding how safety is shaped, how it's lost, and how it can be reclaimed.

In the pages ahead, I'll draw not only from psychology and biology but also from some of the oldest human records of fear and safety: our scriptures. These weren't just religious documents— they were early attempts by the human nervous system to make sense of chaos, to calm the old brain's fear of uncertainty. I grew up within the language of Christianity, so those stories are the ones I know most intimately. But what I've come to see—both through study and through the lives of my clients—is that nearly every tradition carries the same biological truth in a different dialect: that love regulates fear, that belonging steadies the body, and that judgment—though it may promise order—often awakens the bears we were trying to soothe.

These same lessons show up not just in sacred texts, but in our earliest memories of belonging and exclusion—the first places our bodies learned what safety felt like, and what it didn't.

The Body Remembers the Playground

When I ask clients—or even educators—what the word *safety* means, their first thought is almost always *physical* safety. So that's where we'll start. The idea of not being injured or hurt is primal and obvious; it's written into the body's oldest code. Keeping ourselves physically safe is paramount to survival. As I've said many times, the old brain's first and only job is to keep us alive.

Most people agree on that. Physical safety is easy to name and almost universally accepted as a baseline expectation. Many of our rules— especially in schools—exist to prevent or respond to physical violence, and that's a good thing. But here's where we often stop short: most of what threatens the nervous system isn't visible. The body can be untouched and still unsafe. The bruises that don't show psychological humiliation, emotional neglect, and social exclusion can leave deeper marks than broken bones. These are the forms of danger the old brain still registers as life-threatening, even when no one has laid a hand on us.

For many of us, the earliest imprints of safety and danger appear on the playground—where belonging, fairness, and kindness first meet hierarchy, teasing, and shame. Long before we learn the language for it, our bodies start keeping score of what feels safe and what doesn't.

Alongside my private practice, I spent years consulting with schools on climate and culture—helping educators reduce bullying and harassment so that children could feel safe enough to learn. One of the most influential figures in that journey was Stan Davis, LCSW, an internationally known expert in bullying prevention and author of *Schools Where Everyone Belongs*. I was fortunate to be trained by Stan and to receive brief mentoring from him during my work.

What I admired most about his approach was its blend of research and empathy. He understood how damaging bullying and exclusion can be to a child's developing nervous system—and how the absence of safety impairs learning. I often remind schools that fed kids are safe kids—and safe kids are the ones whose frontal cortex can come online to learn, regulate, and grow. That's why safety isn't just a moral issue; it's a biological one.

Stan's title, *Schools Where Everyone Belongs*, captures something essential. Belonging is not just emotional—it's survival. To the old brain, exile feels like death. When a child is ostracized, the body reads it as a threat, not a metaphor. And unless something interrupts that experience, that same child will carry the modern bear of rejection into adulthood.

The Three Categories

One of the most valuable lessons I learned from Stan was his profound yet straightforward framework on relationships in schools. He described three categories: friends, classmates, and enemies.

- Friends play together, help each other, and share trust and kindness.

- Classmates may not be close, but they work together, respect each other's space, and help in an emergency. We don't have to like each other.

- Enemies mock, hurt, or exclude others—emotionally or physically.

The goal of a safe school climate isn't to make everyone friends—that's not realistic—but to eliminate the *enemy* category altogether.

That middle space—*classmate*—is crucial. It teaches children how to coexist with people they don't particularly like without dehumanizing them. In tribal terms, it's learning to live among members who aren't kin but are still part of the group. It's emotional maturity in miniature.

Yet many children never internalize that lesson, and many schools don't intentionally teach it. I've heard teachers tell harassed students, "Oh, just go get along." Ironically, those same adults often complain about their own struggles with coworkers. I've sometimes said, "Wait—you tell your students just to get along, but you admit that's hard for *you* to do, and you're an adult. How do you expect the kids to get it?" (No answers, just perplexed looks.)

The challenge is that many kids grow up seeing only two categories: friend or enemy. When that binary view of belonging becomes the template for adulthood, the results are everywhere— in workplaces, politics, social media, and, well, the whole world.

We like to believe those divisions are moral or cultural, but they're really biological. The bear doesn't care whether it's a schoolyard or a Senate floor—it only wants to know who's safe and who's not. The bear keeps asking us to choose sides. And the more frightened we are, the more certain our answers become.

Because the truth is this: safety begins in hallways and lunchrooms long before it's debated in sanctuaries or parliaments.

When a child learns that the tribe itself is dangerous, they grow into an adult who scans every room for an exit. Humiliation, unpredictability, and exclusion become internal alarms, hardwired into the threat-detection loop of the nervous system. The body keeps checking: *Am I safe here? Am I still part of the tribe?*

The Long Shadow of the Playground

The myths surrounding bullying run deep. We tell children, "Everyone goes through it," or "It'll make you stronger."

But there is nothing natural about being humiliated as a rite of passage. Nothing is strengthening about learning that your pain is normal or deserved. (In fact, research shows that children exposed to chronic bullying can develop symptoms consistent with PTSD—and that's not the kind of education anyone benefits from.)

These early betrayals of safety carve grooves in the nervous system that persist long after the bruises fade.

In my clinical work, I estimate that 80–90 percent of clients struggling with anxiety or depression can trace part of their pain back to school years marked by rejection, bullying, or ostracization.

Their memories surface decades later, often with tears: "I can still hear them laughing." "I sat alone at lunch for years." "The bruise healed—but the words didn't."

And even as they tell me these stories, I sometimes watch their bodies shift — a tightening of the shoulders, a shallow breath, eyes flicking to the side as if still scanning for danger. The child never really left the cafeteria; the nervous system never got the memo that it's safe now.

The old brain doesn't differentiate between the playground and adulthood—it only registers threat. Shame, rejection, and mockery wire themselves into vigilance. The child who once feared classmates grows into the adult who fears colleagues, supervisors, neighbors, and even strangers online.

That's why understanding physical and emotional safety early on is so critical. Without intentional structures—school climates that value inclusion, empathy, and belonging—the bears of threat and shame are born early and multiply. The expectation becomes: *This is what the world is like.*

From Playground to Workplace

Fast-forward twenty or thirty years, and the same patterns replay—just with new costumes.

Clients often tell me they're shocked to discover that the behaviors they faced in school— exclusion, gossip, humiliation—still exist in professional settings. We assume adulthood brings maturity, but hierarchy, power dynamics, and fear of rejection still run the show. Only now the stakes include mortgages, reputations, and paychecks.

Workplace bears come in many forms: subtle microaggressions, favoritism, sarcasm, power hoarding, and social exclusion. They thrive on the same primitive wiring: *If I'm not in, I might be out.* The nervous system doesn't care if you're on the playground or in a staff meeting—it reads tone, not titles.

Borrowing from Stan's framework again, the workplace might be seen through three similar categories:

- **Friends:** those we connect with personally and with whom we share trust or support.

- **Professionals:** those we work with respectfully, even without affection, and who help each other in times of crisis.

- **Unprofessional:** those who practice exclusion, harassment, or other subtle forms of harm.

These categories appear elsewhere, too—like among neighbors. The same dynamic plays out:

- **Friends:** we share meals, visit each other's homes, and maybe even vacation together.
- **Neighbors:** we coexist peacefully; we don't have to be close, but we know if one of us were on fire, the other would help put it out.
- **Malicious:** those who spread rumors, harbor resentment, or engage in subtle harassment.

The problem is that many people believe proximity should automatically equal harmony—that living near someone means we must "get along." But coexistence isn't the same as friendship, and disliking someone doesn't make them the enemy. The middle ground—mutual respect without intimacy—is a skill we rarely teach.

Many adults, however, still operate in a binary: friend or threat, ally or adversary. The inability to inhabit that middle space fuels the same polarization that begins in childhood. And what begins in one body inevitably scales into the body of the tribe.

From Personal to Collective

When enough dysregulated individuals fill a room—or a society—
what emerges is collective hypervigilance.
Every stick in the woods starts to look like a snake.
The reality, of course, is that most are just sticks.

A traumatized society mistakes difference for danger.
We're not merely witnessing frightened *people*; we're witnessing a frightened *organism*.

History gave us a language for fear long before it gave us tools to calm it. Until we remember how to regulate collectively, we'll keep mistaking tension for truth, and certainty for safety. And maybe that's why this part of the book feels quieter — because the work of safety isn't dramatic. It's the soft, steady re-teaching of the body that not every silence is rejection, not every difference is danger. That's where real peace begins to hum again — beneath the noise of the bears.

It makes sense, then, that humans eventually tried to legislate safety—to make it predictable, enforceable, even sacred. When the body couldn't find peace through instinct, we sought it through structure.

Across centuries, fear was formalized in story and scripture, woven into codes meant to keep the tribe intact. What began as biology became theology: rules designed to protect us from danger, sin, and chaos.

But the old brain doesn't distinguish between *divine law* and *survival law*—it only knows what feels safe and what feels like exile. In that confusion, fear became moralized. Safety became synonymous with obedience. And certainty—once just a reflex of the nervous system—was elevated to virtue.

Fear Bear in Scripture: When Safety Was Law

When our ancestors couldn't find peace within the body, they sought to create it outside of it. Safety became something to *enforce* rather than felt. Laws, rituals, and doctrines emerged not only to protect life but to give form to fear—to make the unpredictable world predictable.

This was, in many ways, a brilliant adaptation. The old brain wanted stability, and so the tribe built it: commandments, codes, covenants. Each rule became a kind of fence, an external nervous system meant to keep danger out and belonging in. But over time, those same fences began to define who was *inside* the tribe and who was not. What started as a quest for safety became a sorting system.

Across centuries, the stories we told about the divine were attempts to calm the old brain's anxiety. If lightning struck or harvests failed, we sought order: there must be a reason. If we obey the rules, maybe the gods will be pleased. Certainty became salvation. And in that bargain, fear quietly took the throne.

Yet, at their essence, the world's great religions were never about fear—they were about *returning home to safety through compassion*. When you strip away the centuries of dogma, the political scaffolding, and the human urge to control, each tradition begins in the same nervous-system truth: **love regulates, judgment divides.**

The Four Traditions: A Shared Nervous System of Compassion

- **Judaism** began with a covenant of care—a people bound not only by law but by responsibility to one another. "Love your neighbor as yourself" (Leviticus 19:18) wasn't a social suggestion; it was a survival instruction for the tribe. Justice, mercy, and compassion were the heartbeat of Torah law—rest, Sabbath, forgiveness of debts—each one a rhythm of regulation built into sacred time.

- **Christianity** carried that thread forward. Jesus didn't dismantle the law; he reframed it. "Love one another as I have loved you." "Judge not, lest you be judged." These weren't abstract ideals—they were invitations to downshift the old brain's vigilance. Every parable of forgiveness was a neural reprogramming exercise: to replace the reflex of defense with the practice of grace.

- **Islam** means "surrender," not in defeat but in peace. The Quran's teachings emphasize mercy, community, and balance—"God is with those who are patient," "Kindness is a mark of faith." The five daily prayers create a rhythm of grounding, a ritual return to regulation. The greeting *As-salamu alaykum*—"Peace be upon you"—isn't just polite; it's somatic, an invocation of safety between bodies.

- **Buddhism** turns inward to the same principle: to end suffering by loosening the grip of fear and craving. The Noble Eightfold Path—right view, right speech, right action—is a manual for nervous system alignment. Compassion (*karuṇā*) and loving-kindness (*mettā*) are the antidotes to the old brain's clinging and aversion. "Do not judge others, lest you too be trapped in delusion," the Buddha taught.

Seen together, these faiths form a single map of the human nervous system, seeking peace. Each one teaches, in its own language, the opposite of fear: belonging, compassion, surrender, and forgiveness. None of the great teachers asked us to sort one another out. They asked us to love one another.

If these traditions were nervous systems, love would be their parasympathetic state—the exhale after millennia of vigilance. Their rules were never meant to divide but to help regulate the collective—to create predictability, rhythm, and rest. Sabbath, prayer, meditation, fasting, service—all of these were early tools for calming the *Fear Bear*.

And yet, over centuries, the rules hardened. The fences grew higher. Fear crept back in, dressed now in sacred robes. Certainty began to matter more than compassion, obedience more than understanding. The old brain had found its way into the temple. The same biology that drives faith also drives fear. It's not evil—it's human. Both are the old brain's way of saying, "I want to survive."

What began as an invitation to rest in love became a demand to perform safety through conformity. Those who questioned were labeled heretics. Those who differed were cast out. The body of the tribe—once bound by belonging—began to turn on itself.

And that is the tragedy of the Fear Bear in Scripture: the moment when safety, once rooted in compassion, became confused with control.

In the end, *Fear Bear in Scripture* is about how the old brain first felt the fear—the rush of uncertainty, chaos, and the unknown—and how the new brain responded by trying to explain it. Religion became our earliest form of regulation, the frontal cortex's attempt to make sense of what the body could not control. The commandments and rituals were humanity's first effort to calm the bears through structure, to make life predictable, and protect the tribe from chaos. But the old brain doesn't know the difference between obedience and safety. What began as comfort for the nervous system became a cage for the spirit, teaching us to fear disobedience more than disconnection. And the bears we trapped in scripture would soon wake up inside the temple.

Before moving forward, it's worth pausing to say this clearly: none of what follows is meant to question the truth or sacredness of scripture. The Bible—and other holy texts—carry wisdom that has guided humanity for millennia. My intention isn't to challenge their divinity but to explore how biology may have shaped the way we've interpreted them. The old brain's longing for safety, order, and certainty may have influenced how those truths were received, recorded, and practiced.

Understanding that doesn't diminish faith—it deepens it. It reminds us that the same nervous system that once sought protection through law is still seeking peace through love.

And now, inside the temple, we'll watch what happens when that longing for safety meets power.

Fear Bear in the Temple

By the time we reach the temple, fear has become architecture. What began as stories told around the fire to comfort frightened bodies is now carved into stone and sung in ritual. The old brain's raw need for safety has been sanctified. The same instinct that once scanned the horizon for predators now scans theology for certainty.

Religion, at its core, was an attempt to soothe the chaos—the old brain's trembling need to make sense of what it could not control. When lightning split the sky, when famine struck, when children died, the nervous system cried out for order. The new brain—the storyteller—answered. It offered meaning where there was none. In trauma terms, this was brilliant: naming the danger makes you feel less helpless.

Even believing something incorrect can feel safer than believing nothing at all—because **not knowing** is the scariest bear of them all. The unknown cannot be predicted or avoided, and the old brain equates unpredictability with danger, even death. My clients voice this daily: uncertainty is often the hardest part of trauma to endure.

Many end up blaming themselves for what happened to "make sense" of something that doesn't make sense. Emotionally, we humans struggle to tolerate the idea that there may never be an apparent reason why. I hear it in session after session: *"I should have known better." "I didn't say no." "I should have spoken up."* The list goes on—each statement an attempt to wrestle chaos into order.

I tell them gently that self-blame is really the nervous system's way of trying to regain control. When the truth feels too unpredictable to bear, blame offers a counterfeit sense of safety—an illusion that at least someone, even ourselves, could have prevented the pain. But it's a false kind of order, and often the harshest judgment we ever face is the one we turn inward.

In that same way, humanity-built systems of belief not merely to worship, but to regulate. We built temples to make sense of thunder. We wrote scripture to make meaning out of loss. We formed rituals to anchor our bodies in rhythm and to convince our hearts that the world had a pattern. Religion gave the illusion of control, and control gave the feeling of safety. The body calmed—at least for a while.

But as with all trauma adaptations, what once protected us began to confine us. When safety becomes tied to certainty, curiosity feels dangerous. Doubt feels like sin. The very structure that once soothed the frightened body now punishes it for asking questions. The bears that once circled outside the campfire have moved inside the sanctuary.

I see this same tension every week in my office. Clients come in carrying deep faith and deep fear—often from the very systems meant to offer comfort. They describe trying to worship while simultaneously feeling judged, sorted, and found wanting. "I can't get it right," one client said through tears. "If I mess up, it's not disappointment—it's hell." For them, salvation feels conditional, and safety feels fragile.

The old brain doesn't hear theology; it hears threat. It hears: *"Be perfect, or you'll be cast out."*

And that's the heartbreaking paradox: judgment was never supposed to be ours. Across nearly every tradition, the texts are clear—God, not humans, is the judge. "Vengeance is mine," says the Hebrew scriptures. "Judge not, lest you be judged," says the Gospels. The Qur'an reminds believers that only God knows the hearts of men. The Dhammapada cautions,

"Do not judge others by what you see." The message was never ambiguous: humility belongs to us; judgment belongs to the divine.

But fear twists even the holiest messages. The old brain craves hierarchy and control, and so we grasp at authority that was never ours to hold. In doing so, we make ourselves godlike, deciding who belongs, who is pure, who is damned. Instead of being judged by one loving entity, we are judged by all. The result is a nervous system perpetually on trial. We live in fear not of divine wrath, but of human rejection cloaked in sacred language. In this way, the temple still sorts.

There's little room for being human—little flexibility for imperfection, error, or need. The nervous system of religion, once designed to calm, now keeps many in a constant state of activation. The message that was supposed to soothe the fear of death has instead created a fear of eternal punishment. And while faith can still bring hope and belonging, judgment often rides in beside it, wearing the same robes. Maybe that's why this whole section feels heavier to read than to write — because fear, once sanctified, doesn't just live in temples. It lives in us.

Notes — Take a Breath

Some readers like to pause here—to reflect, annotate, or simply breathe. Others may wish to continue on.

Spotted Bear (A Pause in the Pews)

I want to take a little break in the middle of this chapter, if you'll allow me.

While editing this section, I noticed something you might have noticed: the chapter feels heavier, slower, and perhaps a bit dense. At first, I told myself, *well, of course it does* — we're talking a lot about religion, one of the most sacred and personal topics there is. Of course, it's weighty. Of course it's loaded.

But then it hit me. Oh my. I found another one of my bears.

It showed up only after I'd finished writing, while rereading. I suddenly remembered what it was like growing up in church — those strict rules about how to behave during Mass. Sit up straight. Face forward. No talking. Certainly no laughter. No play.

I can still see my parents giving me *the look* when I so much as whispered to my sisters. I'm old enough (go ahead, tease the old guy) to remember when the priest still gave sermons in Latin. Even though it's fuzzy now, I distinctly remember my mother whispering to me in French to stop squirming and pay attention. (Did I mention my first language was French — and I was four?)

And then I thought, "wait a second, the whole next chapter is about the importance of play. I even describe laughter as a biological signal of safety. So why is this chapter so serious?"

That's when I started to imagine that all the prophets must have laughed. They had to. I can't picture Jesus traveling with twelve guys for years and never cracking a joke. Maybe one night around the fire, he poured Paul a cup of vinegar instead of wine and waited for the spit-take. Maybe he came back from the market saying, "You'll never believe this one — how many disciples does it take to light a candle?"

I know, I know — I'm speculating. But humor is biology. Laughter is regulation. Joy is proof of being alive.

So, the real bear here was the message I learned long ago: that holiness meant seriousness. That laughter and reverence couldn't share the same pew. (And can you see how that simple bear is so opposite to our biology?)

It's funny now to realize how deeply that bear was hiding in me. I didn't even notice it while I was writing. Only afterward, weeks later, did it dawn on me that the old fear—*behave or something bad will happen*—was still shaping my tone.

Before we continue, let's take a collective breath together. Relax your shoulders. Maybe even smirk a little. Then — alright, that's enough — sit up straight, wipe that grin off your face, and let's finish the chapter.

Faith, Fear, and the Search for Safety

Faith at its best regulates the nervous system—it quiets the need to control and reminds us that judgment belongs to something larger. It offers a collective sigh, the sense that we are held in something greater than ourselves. But when fear seeps in, the sacred can be twisted into armor. Every tradition has its version of this confusion, when safety and certainty blur until the message of peace becomes a manual for division. It's not that faith fails; it's that the old brain hijacks it. The same circuitry that once scanned the dark for predators now scans belief systems for threats.

When Fear Misreads Faith: Islam and the Illusion of Violence

One of the clearest examples of how fear distorts meaning is the way some people have misread Islam. To claim that Islam is a violent religion, one must cherry-pick a few battle-time verses from the Qur'an, remove them from their historical context, and ignore the hundreds of passages that focus on mercy, justice, and peace. The very word *Islam* comes from the Arabic root *s-l-m*—peace, wholeness, surrender to the divine. Its greeting, *As-salāmu 'alaykum*, means *"Peace be upon you."*

Yet when the nervous system is caught in threat mode, even sacred language gets hijacked. The old brain scans for danger and clings to anything that sounds protective. In that state, verses about defense in seventh-century Arabia can be misread as timeless commands for aggression. Fear edits scripture to match its own need for control.

This is not unique to Islam. Christians have done it with the Old Testament, Jews with Torah, Hindus and Buddhists with their own texts. Every tradition has moments when the *Fear Bear* dresses itself in holy words. But beneath the distortion, the original current remains the same: **peace, compassion, restraint, humility before judgment.**

The misreading isn't about the faith; it's about the physiology of fear. When our bodies crave safety, we can twist even the language of peace into the weapon of certainty.

Fear pretending to be faith is one of humanity's oldest patterns. It's the nervous system's attempt to find safety by drawing lines in sacred sand: us versus them, pure versus impure, saved versus lost. The more frightened we become, the more certain we insist on being. From temples to parliaments, the same bear keeps whispering the same promise—*if you choose sides, you'll be safe.*

We build temples of certainty because they feel safer than wilderness. But in doing so, we forget that every true revelation in human history began not in the temple, but in the unknown.

Fear Bear Meets Compassion

If the temple was built on fear, compassion was the quiet revolution that began to loosen its stones—by the time of Jesus, the old brain's system of control—law, hierarchy, obedience—had run its full course. It had brought order, yes, but also rigidity. The commandments had been meant to guide, not to imprison. Law was supposed to protect the vulnerable, to give the tribe structure so that belonging could thrive. But fear had rewritten the code. The same scriptures that once offered safety now carried punishment. The bears that guarded the edges of chaos had begun guarding the temple's doors.

Before I go further, I want to be clear about why I speak of Jesus here. It's not to preach or privilege Christianity over other faiths. It's simply the story I know best—the spiritual language I grew up around. My familiarity with Christian tradition makes it the lens through which I can most naturally explore these ideas. But through my research, study, and the voices of my clients, I've come to see how *every* major faith carries the same nervous-system wisdom at its core: that love regulates, that compassion soothes, that judgment divides.

The Buddha, Muhammad, and the prophets of Judaism all offered their own versions of this message. The languages differ, but the biology is the same.

Jesus entered that world not as an outsider trying to destroy the law, but as someone trying to re-regulate it—to restore the nervous system of faith. "I did not come to abolish the law, but to fulfill it." In trauma language, that's the work of integration. He was saying: the structure itself isn't the problem; the fear driving it is.

Every word he spoke about love, forgiveness, or mercy was a countersignal to the old brain's alarms. When he said, *"Judge not,"* he was addressing the reflex we now call hypervigilance. When he said, *"Love your enemies,"* he wasn't promoting naïveté—he was teaching down-regulation. He was inviting the tribe to rest, to feel safe enough to connect again.

This was more than theology; it was biology turned sacred. Compassion is what happens when the frontal cortex begins to soothe the amygdala—when understanding interrupts the reflex to strike or exclude.

From a trauma perspective, Jesus was introducing the nervous system to a new language: *You are safe enough to be kind.*

I believe Jesus was real—his work, his words, his presence. His ideas were radical: love your neighbor, show kindness, and resist judgment. And how deeply ironic that his message of love was received as a threat. Two thousand years later, it is still often the case. His insistence on compassion is not unique; other prophets across faiths tried to give us the same message. Again, humanity has been handed the same invitation—to calm the bear through love—and repeatedly, we've turned away.

We've learned to treat kindness as weakness. Of course, we would, as long as we believe we need an enemy. To the old brain, an enemy demands strength; weakness invites danger. We armor instead of open, defend instead of connecting. The idea that we could be safe without power still feels biologically unsafe.

But Jesus modeled the opposite. He ate with lepers, tax collectors, the poor, the downcast, and the outcast. He sat beside prostitutes and those labeled "unclean." He did not comment on body size, cleanliness, sexual orientation, or moral perfection. He met people where they were—with presence, not performance. He saw dignity where society saw contamination.

How easily that part of the story has been lost. The Jesus who touched the untouchable, who broke bread with the excluded, would barely recognize the systems that now claim his name. He came to quiet the Fear Bear in the temple, yet fear remains one of religion's loudest sounds.

For some, his message was liberation. For others, it was destabilizing. Because when your safety has always come from control, love feels dangerous.

And so once again, the old brain pushed back. Those who most needed certainty—those whose nervous systems had been built on rules and hierarchy—saw compassion as chaos. They mistook calm for weakness, curiosity for disobedience, and mercy for moral collapse.

This is the human dilemma I see echoed in my clients' stories every day. Many of them long to believe in a loving God, but the image they inherited is one of vigilance and wrath. "I can't relax," one said softly. "Even when I pray, I'm afraid I'll get it wrong." Another whispered, "It's hard to feel loved when the rules are louder than the relationship."

That's the old brain still running the show—mistaking control for care, punishment for protection.

But if we look closely, the story of compassion is also the story of neurobiological evolution. Something new was emerging: the idea that connection, not compliance, is what truly keeps us safe. That love—not law—is what quiets the bears. Every act of forgiveness, every story of inclusion, was the new brain learning to override millennia of fear conditioning.

Jesus modeled what a regulated nervous system looks like in the face of threat. He stayed present when others fled. He touched those society deemed untouchable. He refused to return violence with violence. His calm was not passivity—it was mastery. It was the parasympathetic made flesh.

And yet, as happens so often with trauma and truth, his presence was intolerable to the system still driven by fear. The temple couldn't integrate compassion any more than the old brain could integrate uncertainty.

And so, once again, fear did what fear always does when it feels its control slipping: it attacked what it could not understand.

I sometimes wonder what would happen if one of those prophets—Jesus, the Buddha, Muhammad—walked among us again. Would we recognize them, or would we scroll past them, certain that wisdom couldn't possibly look that ordinary?

My sense is we'd do what frightened tribes have always done: question, mock, label, and divide. I've even heard people call Jesus "too woke" lately—one of the major prophets of compassion, dismissed for sounding too gentle. It's a strange irony, but also proof of how powerful the bear still is. The old brain, when dysregulated, doesn't trust tenderness. It mistakes compassion for weakness, nuance for danger. The prophets asked us to love one another; the bear keeps asking us to choose sides.

The tragedy, of course, is that this message was never meant to be complicated. Every tradition I've studied—Judaism, Christianity, Islam, Buddhism, and beyond—began with the same biological wisdom: compassion regulates fear. The original teachers didn't ask us to sort or condemn; they asked us to love, to feed, to forgive.

I sometimes wonder what would happen if faith communities returned to those roots—not to the rules that built the fences, but to the rhythms that calmed the body. To remember that mercy is regulation, that hospitality is safety, and that judgment is the quickest way to wake the bears.

But fear rarely surrenders its power easily. And every time love tries to steady the temple, fear finds a new form to inhabit.

Fear Bear and the Zealots

Every time compassion enters the temple, fear eventually rises to meet it. When love threatens control, the old brain roars.

Zealotry is what occurs when fear and faith fuse so tightly that the nervous system can no longer distinguish between devotion and defense. Historically, the Zealots were a sect of first-century Jews who believed violent resistance was the only way to preserve purity and protect their people from Roman oppression. They weren't villains; they were terrified. Their world was unstable, occupied, and uncertain. And in that instability, their biology sought certainty—the only way it knew how—through control, boundaries, and aggression.

In psychological terms, **zealotry is the old brain's trauma response dressed in sacred language.** It's hypervigilance disguised as holiness, fight-flight translated into faith. It's what happens when the body's need for safety hijacks the spirit's search for meaning. Zealotry isn't born from strength; it's born from panic — a dysregulated attempt to build safety by erasing uncertainty.

The Zealots believed safety could only come through purity and power. They clung to law and tradition as if the world depended on it—because to their nervous systems, it did. When Jesus spoke of forgiveness, they heard weakness. When he ate with sinners, they saw betrayal. When he taught non-violence, they felt the chaos of helplessness. To them, compassion wasn't divine— it was dangerous.

It's easy to condemn them from afar, but they were doing what frightened nervous systems always do: **trying to regulate through control.**

When fear is high, the mind searches for proof that its vigilance is justified. The Zealots found that proof in scripture. They quoted verses of judgment and vengeance, reinforcing their activation with the illusion of divine endorsement.

The same pattern repeats in every era. In my clinical work, I see people caught in similar loops— using faith, ideology, or politics to organize their anxiety. Clients often say, "I know God is love, but I still feel like

I'm one mistake away from being cast out." That's the Zealot reflex: the body's demand for certainty overwhelming the soul's longing for peace.

And fear, as it always does, cherry-picks its evidence. The Zealots emphasized the passages of scripture that aligned with their arousal—"an eye for an eye," "vengeance is mine"—while ignoring the verses that called for mercy, rest, or forgiveness. The text didn't change; **the reader's state did.** The frightened brain will always find a theology that justifies its fear.

If we could hear their voices now, the Zealots might say things that sound hauntingly familiar:

"If we stop drawing lines, everything will fall apart." "Without judgment, there's no order."

"Mercy is weakness. Discipline keeps us safe." "Biology is irrelevant—God decides who belongs."

These are not ancient arguments. They echo in modern pulpits, parliaments, and comment sections—whenever fear disguises itself as righteousness. The modern Zealot may wear a suit instead of a robe, but the biology is the same: a hyperactivated nervous system trying to survive uncertainty by controlling the narrative.

Zealotry doesn't arise from a lack of faith; it arises from a fusion of faith and fear. The body cannot tolerate ambiguity, so it demands clear boundaries—good and evil, saved and damned, us and them. The tragic irony is that the very faith meant to unite becomes the weapon that divides.

And yet, beneath that rigidity is pain. Zealots, ancient or modern, are not evil people—they are frightened people whose bodies never learned to rest. They defend certainty because uncertainty feels like death. In trauma work, we call this *over-coupling*—when fear and safety become so entangled that you can no longer tell them apart.

From a biological perspective, zealotry is not a flaw of belief but a misfiring of the survival instinct. It is the nervous system, overreaching for safety, seizing control of the sacred.

In our own time, this same pattern has grown louder, merging faith-based zealotry with political tribalism. Each system—religious and political—activates the same circuitry of fear and belonging, amplifying one another until they create a single, massive collective bear. Both claims offer safety, identity, and moral certainty. Both whisper to the old brain: *Your survival depends on choosing a side.* And once the old brain believes that dialogue feels dangerous, curiosity feels like betrayal, and empathy becomes a threat to the tribe.

This is why modern zealotry feels so volatile—it's not just about belief anymore; it's about biology. When political identity fuses with spiritual identity, disagreement registers in the nervous system as danger rather than discourse. The brain treats opposing ideas like predators. It's no longer *us versus them* in theory; it's *safe versus unsafe* in the body.

And zealotry knows no single faith. **Fear does not discriminate.** Every religion has its own version of the Zealot—whether it's Catholic extremism, Opus Dei's austerity, militant nationalism woven into Hinduism or Islam, or rigid fundamentalism within evangelical Christianity. Each tradition has its factions who turn the search for safety into a crusade for control. The faces and scriptures differ, but the biology is identical: frightened bodies mistaking rigidity for refuge.

That is the ultimate evolution of zealotry: when fear hijacks both faith and governance until they speak in the same language—danger, danger, danger. The sermon and the campaign rally merge, and the old brain believes it is fighting for survival.

The deeper truth is that even scripture and politics can be read from two different bodies: one ruled by fear, and one rooted in love.

The first builds walls; the second builds bridges. The first seeks protection; the second seeks connection. The words may be the same, but the nervous system determines their meaning.

When the frightened body reads the text, it builds another temple to control.
When the regulated body reads it, it begins to build a home for compassion — *a message Jesus himself would likely have signed off on.*

Fear Bear and the Cross

The crucifixion wasn't the end of fear—it was just its next evolution.

When love became too radical, fear learned to wear the mask of respectability. It traded sandals for uniforms, temples for nations, and began preaching safety in the language of loyalty.

The old brain didn't disappear with the resurrection story; it just found new symbols to guard. Where once it sought salvation, now it sought sovereignty.

The bear doesn't care whether it kneels before a cross or salutes a flag—it only wants to know who belongs and who doesn't.

What began as tribal survival now hides behind the word "patriotism," still promising safety through sameness, still confusing unity with uniformity.

The Old Brain Writes Its Myths Through the New Brain

The old brain doesn't know what a nation is. It doesn't understand scripture, law, or ideology. It knows only hunger, fear, and the relief of belonging.

When it feels threatened, the new brain rushes in like a narrator desperate to make sense of the panic. It builds stories to explain the unease — stories about good and evil, purity and danger, us and them.

Those stories become politics and religion, banners and creeds, tribes and "truths."

It's not that belief itself is bad. The impulse to organize meaning is one of the most beautiful things about being human. But the trouble starts when the story forgets what it was written for — when it stops soothing fear and starts feeding it.

Then the old brain takes back the wheel, using the new brain's words as weapons. And we call it conviction.

Maybe that's why our arguments about God and government feel so primal.

Because underneath the theology and ideology, two nervous systems are just trying to feel safe.

In tribal times, that need for safety took shape as leadership. Someone had to organize the hunt, guard the perimeter, and decide who spoke for the group when danger approached. Politics, in that sense, is ancient biology—the old brain's way of managing fear through hierarchy. What began as survival coordination became structure, then allegiance, then ideology. The flag, like the temple, is simply the modern symbol for the same ancient need: to belong to something strong enough to keep the bears away. And when the temple walls no longer feel wide enough to hold our fears, we build larger ones—nations, parties, ideologies. Politics becomes the new parish, the modern temple where the same old nervous system seeks protection through allegiance. The flags change, but the physiology doesn't.

Fear Bear and the Flag

Every nation tells itself a story about virtue and danger. Every frightened nervous system wants a team. Religion was simply the first vessel for that process; politics, nationalism, consumer culture, and online identity tribes are the others. Each offers the same nervous-system bargain: belong, and you'll be safe; question, and you'll be alone.

In tribal times, leadership was a matter of survival. Someone had to decide who hunted, who guarded, who spoke for the group when danger came. Politics began there — not in ideology, but in biology. The old brain craved order and predictability, and so hierarchy became the tribe's nervous system, a way to organize fear.

Over time, that survival structure evolved into governments, nations, and parties. We still look for someone to protect us, to make sense of chaos, to keep the bears away.

Politics is the old brain scaled up — a collective way of deciding who keeps the tribe safe. But fear is a faster recruiter than reason. The moment leaders realize the nervous system responds more to threat than to calm, the Bear learns to campaign. Safety becomes strategy. Fear becomes currency.

I've said throughout this book that the old brain doesn't care about being right; it cares about being safe. It doesn't quote scripture or campaign slogans; it scans for threat and signals for belonging. The new brain then translates that instinct into stories — about loyalty, faith, and freedom. And once we mistake safety for certainty, the map becomes sacred. To question it feels like betrayal. To lose it feels like death.

That's why the same biological wiring that once drove faith now fuels politics. Both systems were built to soothe uncertainty, but risk becoming the very sources of fear they were meant to quiet. The flag, like the cross, began as a symbol of belonging; now both are used as tests of purity

Patriotism itself once meant love of one's home — a sense of care and shared fate. But the old brain's hunger for safety twists that love into vigilance. We start to scan not for shared humanity, but for who's "in" and who's "out." It's the same tribal circuitry, only amplified by mass communication. The bear no longer needs a forest; it has a broadcast network.

Even the weather is politicized now. Growing up in Maine, snowstorms were part of life — sometimes a foot or more overnight. Today, every forecast comes with ominous music and urgent banners, as if the sky itself has become the enemy. Fear sells. It mobilizes. And the nervous system keeps tuning in because vigilance feels safer than calm.

The same pattern plays out in consumerism. The market doesn't just sell products; it sells belonging. We're told we need the latest phone, the right shoes, the right body, the right brand — not because the items matter, but because they mark who's in the tribe. The fear of missing out isn't just social; it's biological. The old brain reads exclusion as danger, so the marketplace obliges, offering us one more purchase, one more scroll, one more hit of reassurance: *You still belong.*

And yet, the cost of all that certainty is exhaustion. Our nervous systems live in a constant low- grade alarm state. Patriotism, politics, and consumer culture all whisper the same promise — that safety can be earned through alignment — while quietly stoking the fear that safety can be lost through dissent.

I often remind clients: the old brain has no party affiliation. It doesn't care about your flag, your faith, or your feed. It cares about pulse and breath, tribe and threat. When it feels danger, it will choose certainty over curiosity every time.

The irony is that the more frightened we become, the more we look for differences — and the less we notice how similar we are. We keep mistaking tension for truth, vigilance for virtue. While human cultures, identities, and traditions remain richly diverse, the nervous system beneath them is shared — and the challenge is learning to experience difference as richness rather than as a threat to the old brain. Because, despite all the noise, the same biology beats inside all of us.

I'm not on the side of left or right, conservative or progressive. I'm on the side of humankind — the part of us that's trying to remember what safety feels like without needing an enemy.

Recap: The Old Brain Still Drives the Bus

If there's one thing I want the reader to take from this section, it's this: **the old brain is still driving the bus.** (Some days, I worry the wheels might be coming off—that's the whole reason I started writing this book.)

Religion, politics, consumer culture—all of it began as our collective attempt to make the world feel safe and predictable. Those systems weren't born from malice; they were born from biology. Certainty, belonging, and order help calm the body. Predictability lowers the pulse. These are good things for the nervous system.

But the old brain doesn't speak in words or ideologies; it speaks in sensations—tightness, racing heart, alertness, tension. The new brain, with all its language and meaning-making, tries to explain what the body is feeling. It builds stories to make sense of the unease: stories about God and government, good and evil, us and them.

That's where most people get lost. They assume the frontal cortex—the "smart" part of the brain—is running the show. But it's not. The new brain is mostly a narrator, trying to translate what the body already feels. It gives voice to the old brain's alarms.

This isn't just true for religion or politics; it's true for trauma, too. When someone has lived through a threat, their body learns to stay ready. The old brain keeps scanning for danger, and the new brain scrambles to make sense of why.

That's why distorted beliefs—whether personal or political—are so often body-based. They start as a feeling, and only later become a philosophy.

So, when we look at ideology, outrage, or certainty, we're really looking at biology—an ancient nervous system trying to stay safe in a modern world. The meanings we attach are the new brain's attempt to make sense of what the old brain has already decided. While human cultures, identities, and traditions remain richly diverse, the nervous system beneath them is shared — and the challenge is learning to experience difference as richness rather than as a threat to the old brain.

Until we understand that, we'll keep mistaking intellect for insight, and conviction for calm. The truth is simpler: the body feels first, and the story follows. We've built whole civilizations out of that same biology. And somewhere along the way, the systems meant to steady us began to inherit our anxiety.

When the Systems Became the Symptoms

It's worth pausing to see what went wrong with the great systems we built to keep ourselves safe.

For years, I thought the problem was them—the churches, the governments, the markets—each too hungry for power or profit. But through the lens of the biology of trauma, the picture shifts.

Ideology often functions like a self-soothing mechanism for unresolved threat responses. In therapy, I've seen it countless times: people who've endured trauma start to identify with the pain they survived. "I became what happened to me," they say. It's not a weakness; the body seeks control amid chaos. It's a way to give form to what feels uncontainable.

Healing begins when they can separate who they are from what happened to them.

Humanity's institutions never made that separation. Faith was meant to quiet fear; politics to protect the tribe; commerce to sustain the group. Each began as an act of regulation—but in trying to master fear, they absorbed it. They began to identify with the trauma they were built to soothe. Religion became fear's voice. Politics became fear's armor. Commerce became fear's distraction. What started as protection hardened into control.

These systems are not villains. They are frightened bodies, built from frightened bodies. They mistake vigilance for safety and power for peace—the same reflex I see in trauma survivors every day. Their failure isn't moral; it's biological. They were designed to help the tribe feel safe enough to rest, but they forgot how to rest themselves.

When safety becomes synonymous with control, the body of the species never truly relaxes. We end up worshipping the symptoms of fear instead of healing its cause. The work ahead— individually and collectively—is to remember what safety was for in the first place: not to control, but to rest.

Bridge to Chapter 6: Rest and Play

If fear was once the architect of our systems, then rest and play were their first blueprints—the body's natural ways to reset. But fear makes both difficult. When the nervous system is locked in vigilance, stillness feels unsafe, and joy feels careless. Fear does not know how to be idle; it keeps the muscles tight and the mind scanning.

That's why even rest and play have become new bears. In a culture that confuses motion with meaning, we've learned to defend instead of delight. We fill every pause, schedule every breath, and call exhaustion productivity. Yet rest and play were never luxuries. They were the oldest biological assurances that danger had passed, that the tribe could exhale together around the fire.

To reclaim them is not to escape responsibility; it's to remember what safety feels like. The next chapter begins there—with the bears we've made from rest and play, and how learning to soothe them might be the first step in healing the collective body of our species. Because in the end, real safety has nothing to do with winning — it's about resting without an enemy.

Key Takeaways

- **The old brain is still driving the bus.** Our systems — religion, politics, commerce — were all born from biology's simple goal: to keep us safe. What began as protection became control when fear stayed in the driver's seat.
- **Ideologies are nervous-system stories.** Beliefs about "us and them," good and evil, right and wrong, are often attempts by the new brain to make sense of what the body already feels. Fear in the body becomes doctrine in the mind.
- **Systems mirror trauma.** Just as trauma survivors confuse vigilance with safety, institutions built to calm fear often absorb it. Faith becomes fear's voice, politics its armor, commerce its distraction.
- **Safety was meant to be a feeling, not a rule.** True regulation doesn't come from certainty, borders, or creeds — it comes from a body that feels safe enough to rest.
- **Certainty soothes, but it can also trap.** The nervous system loves predictability, but when certainty becomes rigid, it fuels division and control rather than peace.
- **The highest expressions of safety**—and the most powerful biological regulators—are <u>love, compassion, care, and non-judgment</u>. These are not weaknesses; they are signs of a nervous system strong enough to stay open.
- **The work ahead is soft, not hard.** Healing the collective body begins not with new ideologies, but with loosening our grip on old ones — breathing where we once defended.

Impression

This chapter invites the reader to recognize that what we call "belief systems" are often nervous- system responses dressed in meaning. By tracing fear back to its biological roots, the reader learns that true safety is not found in control or certainty but in the capacity to rest, connect, and extend compassion. In the end, safety is not a position to defend — it's a feeling to remember.

Before you turn the page, take one last slow breath. The next section isn't about thinking harder — it's about feeling what safety might actually mean.

Contemplation — The Certainty of Safety

We've spent this chapter watching how the old brain's fear gave rise to the new brain's temples and flags — the stories and systems built to quiet that fear. It's easy to lose faith in faith itself after seeing how much damage fear can do when it hides inside meaning.

But maybe the problem was never belief — it was what we believed would keep us safe.

Certainty feels comforting for a reason: it steadies the body. It tells the nervous system, *'You're secure, you belong.'* That's not a weakness. That's biology doing its best to keep us calm. I'm not asking you to give up your certainties — only to hold them a little more softly.

To notice, just for a few breaths, whether they're still giving you peace... or quietly feeding your fear.

What if the only real certainties are not based on our differences, but on what we share in kind — things like love, compassion, care for one another, and non-judgment? I know — for many, those words sound fragile, even naïve. We've been taught that safety comes from standing firm, from drawing lines and defending them.

But here's the quiet paradox: it takes far more strength to stay open than to stay armed. Love requires endurance. Compassion requires courage. Non-judgment is not the absence of conviction; it's the discipline of staying curious when fear begs you to close.

These are not the traits of the weak — they are the nervous system's highest expressions of safety.

Would that make you feel less safe — or more?
Would it make you more defensive — or more open?
Would it threaten your beliefs — or bring them home?

It's okay if the question stirs something. That's just the body checking whether it's safe to loosen its grip. Notice if you can stay with that feeling, even for a moment — curiosity without collapse. Allow your body to respond before your mind does. Notice if it softens, exhales, or releases tension. That's what real certainty feels like.

We've spent most of history trying to overcome fear with the very tools that keep it alive — sorting, judging, killing, shaming. But none of those things regulate the body; they only recycle its panic. Every act of exclusion might quiet fear for a moment, but it deepens it over time.

The nervous system can't feel safe by destroying what it fears — only by remembering connection. That's why love, compassion, care, and non-judgment aren't soft ideals; they're the only forces that truly interrupt the fear cycle. They don't erase evil by denying it — they *out-regulate* it. They bring the body, and maybe the world, back into rhythm.

Imagine a culture built on that kind of safety — where belonging doesn't depend on fear, where sameness isn't the price of peace. The impulse to divide, to find difference, is just another way the nervous system searches for certainty.

But love, compassion, care, and non-judgment don't need sides — they work everywhere, for everyone. We've been taught that certainty lives in systems, in doctrines, in borders and creeds. But biology tells a quieter truth: safety was never meant to be a rule — it was meant to be a feeling, a felt sense.

And feelings, unlike laws, can be shared without limit.

We'll return to this idea in the final chapter, when we explore what it means to build a collective nervous system rooted in those truths.

For now, hold the question.
Not as a challenge — but as a resting place.

Before you turn the page, take one last slow breath.
Notice the space between inhale and exhale — the brief, quiet pause where nothing needs to be proven or defended.
That's what safety feels like when it isn't built on fear. That's where the next chapter begins — in the radical possibility of resting without an enemy.

Chapter 6: Resting and Playing Without an Enemy

"Rest is not idleness, and to lie sometimes on the grass under trees on a summer's day... is by no means a waste of time."
— *John Lubbock*

"It is in our leisure that we reveal the quality of our souls."
— *Plato*

"Arbeit macht frei."

Work will set you free.

Those German words were welded in iron above the entrance to Auschwitz — one of the most infamous Nazi concentration camps of World War II. Beneath that arch, millions of people were starved, enslaved, and murdered. The slogan was a lie—a cruel manipulation meant to disguise horror as order. It told prisoners that obedience and labor could buy safety, when in truth, it was only a cage.

It's uncomfortable to begin a chapter about rest and play this way, but the two are inseparable. Before we can truly rest, we often have to remember how to play. I include this story because the message carved above the gates of Auschwitz didn't begin there—it was simply the darkest expression of an idea much older: that worth must be earned through work.

The belief that worth must be earned through toil has echoed through centuries of culture and faith. You can still hear its softened version today: work *harder. Stay busy. Don't stop. You'll be somebody if you earn it.*

That's why I sometimes tell clients that the sign still hangs over our lives—just invisible now, written into our schedules, our identities, our worth. The modern cage isn't made of iron bars; it's made of calendars, emails, and expectations. Step outside of it—slow down, take a nap, or play—and many people fear they'll lose not just income, but identity. *Who am I without work?* They ask. And beneath that question is the old brain whispering: *If you stop, you won't be safe.*

I've heard it hundreds of times in my practice:

"I just have to be productive." "I can't sit still. If I don't keep moving, I'll fall apart."

These aren't moral failings; they're survival codes. The old brain has learned that belonging depends on producing. In a culture that worships motion, stillness feels like danger.

I'm not against work. I've done my share of fifty-, sixty-, and even eighty-hour weeks. Work can be meaningful, grounding, and good for us. But somewhere along the way, we forgot that its purpose was to serve life—not replace it.

I grew up in a Franco-American household that prized hard work above all else. My parents taught perseverance and pride, but also fear of stillness and play. My father used to say, "Play is what you do when the work is done."

"But Dad," I'd protest, "the work is never done." He'd smile and say, "Exactly." (Insert Emoji here, free choice- bewildered, confused, baffled)

Many of my clients grew up under the same themes. They equate rest and play with laziness, stillness with failure. They sell back vacation days, brag about exhaustion, and feel guilty when they pause. When I ask them to practice sitting still for ten minutes, they look at me like I've lost my mind. But their bodies tell the truth: their nervous systems don't believe they'll be safe if they stop.

Biology disagrees. Muscles don't grow when we lift weights—they grow when we rest. Each repetition creates micro-tears, and it's only during recovery that strength forms. Without pause, the muscle frays. The same is true for the mind. The same is true for the soul.

When we never stop working, we lose the very thing work was meant to protect: our humanity. The body collapses: the mind turns on itself. We begin to confuse exhaustion with purpose and busyness with belonging.

The phrase *"Work will set you free"* was a lie then, and it's a lie now.

Work can sustain us, yes—but when it becomes identity, it becomes captivity. The old brain, in its hunger for certainty, mistakes constant effort for safety. But safety was never meant to be earned through exhaustion.

The truth is that freedom begins when the body no longer has to prove it deserves to exist.

So, before we talk about rest, we have to talk about safety again—not the kind that comes from locked doors, bank balances, or temples, but the kind that comes from regulation, connection, and predictability in our relationships.

The Exhausted Tribe

In the food chapter, we fed the bear. We saw how nourishment, control, and shame tangled into the same survival script—how the body's need for food was turned into a moral argument. But food was never the enemy. It was just one of the old brain's many ways of asking, *Am I safe yet?*

If food is how the bear tries to fill the emptiness, rest is how it dares to surrender.

And that, in today's world, might be the most radical act left.

We've built an entire civilization that runs on adrenaline and self-doubt. Our nervous systems are marinated in caffeine, deadlines, and digital alarms that promise productivity but deliver panic. We call this progress, but what we've really built is a collective hypervigilance—a species that cannot exhale.

The problem is that adrenaline, cortisol, and other stress hormones were never meant to be permanent residents in the bloodstream.

They were designed for short bursts—to help us sprint, fight, flee, or focus—and then subside once safety returned. But most of us never return. The bear never leaves the room; it just changes costumes. We live in a constant state of activation, our bodies quietly flooded with the chemistry of emergency.

Over time, that chemistry becomes corrosive. Chronic stress has been linked to cardiovascular disease, immune suppression, inflammation, metabolic disorders, digestive problems, and even changes in brain structure (McEwen & Karatsoreos, 2015). The same hormones that once saved us from predators now make us sick. We were built for survival, not for *sustained* alarm.

In session after session, I meet people who are successful by every social measure yet feel like failures if they rest. They wake up tired, work through lunch, collapse into bed, and wonder why joy feels like an afterthought. They've learned to see exhaustion as evidence of value. They're not lazy; they're loyal—to a system that tells them belonging is earned through depletion.

The body disagrees. The nervous system doesn't measure worth in output; it measures safety in signals. When the old brain senses danger, it keeps us in motion. When it feels safe, it lets us rest. But we've confused motion with meaning. We've built economies, institutions, and entire identities on the adrenaline of "almost enough."

The result is what I call **the exhausted tribe**—a global body of people too tired to feel, too busy to play, too wired to rest. Like trauma survivors, we've learned to equate vigilance with virtue. The bear doesn't chase us anymore, but we keep running anyway.

Sleep becomes optional. Play becomes childish. Stillness feels unsafe. Even in abundance, the nervous system acts as if scarcity is one step behind.

And this exhaustion isn't just personal—it's inherited. The same way trauma patterns pass through families, cultural patterns of overwork and fear pass through generations. My grandparents came from farms and logging camps, where survival depended on labor. My parents grew up believing that hard work was moral work.

My generation inherited both the pride and the panic of that belief. And now I see my clients living it daily—eyes on the clock, hearts in their throats, convinced that stopping means slipping.

But the truth is simple: rest is not the reward for survival. It's part of it. The old brain was never built for endless motion.

In the wild, activity was followed by recovery: hunt, eat, nap, play, repeat. That rhythm kept the species alive. We've replaced it with constant vigilance and occasional collapse. No wonder the bear is pacing.

Decades of research confirm what the body already knows. Chronic sleep deprivation disrupts nearly every regulatory system—impairing memory, emotional balance, immune function, and even moral reasoning. Matthew Walker's *Why We Sleep* (2017) notes that humans are the only species that deliberately deprives themselves of rest, and that consistent sleep loss increases the risk of depression, anxiety, obesity, cardiovascular disease, and accidents (Killgore, 2010; Walker, 2017; Van Dongen et al., 2003). Even a single night of poor sleep heightens amygdala reactivity by up to 60 percent, meaning our fear center literally grows louder when the body can't recover (Yoo et al., 2007).

When we refuse to rest, we don't just burn out—we lose access to the higher parts of the brain entirely. Creativity, empathy, and curiosity— all of them require a regulated body. Without rest, the new brain can't do its job. It can't dream, imagine, or connect.

The cost isn't just emotional—it's economic. A RAND Corporation study estimated that insufficient sleep costs the U.S. economy more than $400 billion annually in lost productivity, healthcare costs, and accidents. Yet the solution isn't complicated or high-tech. It's ancient. Rest and Play—those simple biological regulators—are free, renewable, and available to everyone.

If the tribe could relearn those rhythms, we might not only become emotionally healthier but also physically and socially healthier. The cure for collective burnout might not lie in a new pill, policy, or productivity app, but in permission—the courage to rest without guilt and play without purpose.

That's why reclaiming rest isn't indulgence; it's repair. It's how we remember what safety feels like without needing an enemy to guard against.

Play: The Forgotten Regulator

If rest is how the body remembers safety, play is how it remembers joy.

And yet, play is the most under-prescribed form of nervous-system medicine we have.

Play is practice for freedom. It's how mammals rehearse trust, creativity, and social bonding. Even adult wolves chase, dolphins surf waves for fun, and elephants play-fight with their trunks. Ravens roll in the snow to feel it. Chimpanzees tickle their young. Even rats giggle at ultrasonic frequencies when they play (Panksepp, 1998). Play is not a luxury of higher life forms — it's the **signature of safety** in the animal kingdom. When the old brain finally believes danger has passed, the body plays.

Humans, however, are the only species that feel the need to **schedule** joy. We built schools, corporations, and calendars so tightly wound that we had to rename play: *training, networking, productivity breaks*.

The bear doesn't stop needing play just because we renamed it. It just grows hungrier for it.

The Education of the Anxious Tribe

I see it now in children's nervous systems. Parents of kindergartners talk about their child "getting behind." Nine-year-olds describe "study anxiety."

By middle school, I see the first panic attacks. I've had children vomit before mandatory state testing — their bodies literally rejecting the stress their culture won't let them discharge.

That's biology, not weakness. Vomiting is the nervous system's way of *clearing the decks* — the body diverting energy from digestion to defense.

When the test becomes a bear, the body prepares for battle.

This is the model we're giving our children: Your worth is your score. Your tribe accepts you if you produce. Your safety depends on performance.

And adults wonder why the next generation can't rest. They were trained out of it.

I watch educators — loving, devoted people — caught in the same trap. Their stress mirrors the students'. "We have to get the material in," they say, as if knowledge can override biology. Less recess. More test prep. Fewer arts. Less breathing room. The body becomes a vehicle for the head, the old brain forgotten in the rush to feed the new.

But the old brain doesn't care what you know. It only wants to know you're safe, accepted, fed, and allowed to breathe.

That's the tragedy: our systems of learning have become systems of threat. The drive to "achieve" has outpaced the biology of becoming. The result? We are raising anxious, over-activated nervous systems that later show up in therapy as exhausted adults — people who did everything "right" and still don't feel safe.

The Science — and Power — of Play

The research on play is unequivocal. Neuroscientist Jaak Panksepp (1998) identified a distinct *play* circuit in the mammalian brain — one that lights up the same reward pathways as food and affection. Play releases endorphins, dopamine, and oxytocin — the chemicals of connection and safety. Dr. Stuart Brown (2009) found that people who lack play in childhood are more likely to suffer from depression, rigidity, poor stress tolerance, and even aggression in adulthood.

And Steve Gross, LCSW — founder of the *Life is Good Playmaker Project* — has shown how play helps traumatized children rebuild trust and self-regulation. Through spontaneous play, he writes, "children remember what safety feels like" (Gross, 2021). But I want to be clear — the kind of play Steve teaches isn't random or chaotic. It's intentional. It's designed to be safe, collaborative, and connecting — the type of play that restores a sense of *"we belong."*

This isn't just fun for fun's sake. It's play with purpose. Each activity is structured to reintroduce safety to the nervous system through movement, rhythm, and shared laughter. Because movement, as we know, is one of the body's oldest antidotes to anxiety, depression, and trauma. Steve's approach helps children reconnect to that truth: that motion regulates emotion, and that connection — not correction — is what steadies the system.

The play he teaches carries intention. Every activity, every burst of laughter, is a rehearsal for trust — a way of helping both children and caregivers remember that healing begins not in words, but in *felt safety shared between bodies.*

On a personal note, I've had the privilege of seeing Steve's work in action. I've watched early-childhood providers being trained in his model, and what struck me most was the parallel process unfolding in real time. As they learned to bring play to children, they began to rediscover it in themselves. Smiles widened. Laughter returned. You could almost see their nervous systems resetting — the very medicine they were preparing to offer was already working on them. I can personally attest to that feeling in my own body; every time I've been part of a training Steve led, I've felt my own system exhale. (Go Playmakers!!)

In conversations with Steve, I've come to deeply admire his conviction that play is not simply a child's pastime but a biological intervention — an antidote to the ACE Study itself. If adverse childhood experiences can wire the body for defense, then play can rewire it for safety. His work reminds us that healing doesn't begin with insight or instruction; it begins with experience. And if we want to change children's nervous systems, we must also model that change in the adults who care for them.

Across the country — and around the world — Steve's approach is helping early childhood caregivers and educators use play as a powerful preventive modality: a way to reach the old brain before fear hardens into lifelong protective patterns.

Power Play — Resilience in Schools

"Power play" is a term most people know from hockey.

During a power play, the advantaged team has more players on the ice — a moment of leverage, pressure, and opportunity to score. But that's not the kind of power play I'm talking about.

The kind of power I'm talking about is the power of connection—the strength that emerges from play that is intentional, safe, and collaborative.

Steve Gross's work with play, though centered on early childhood, offers an approach that could easily scaffold practices in primary and secondary schools as well. Not necessarily through the same activities he uses, but through the same philosophy: if you want to build resilience in children, increase the amount of cooperative play they experience.

It's not the one-off celebrations that create lasting safety or belonging. Those moments may be fun, but true connection grows through consistent, shared experiences—where play becomes a daily language of trust, not an occasional event.

When novelty or "special days" are offered as solutions to deep stress, they may soothe anxiety for a moment, but they don't build the structure that real resilience requires. True resilience isn't born from a single day of joy; it's built through the daily repetition of safety—relationships, boundaries, routines, and trusted adults who keep showing up.

Be deliberate about the kinds of games you create. Choose play that fosters teamwork, mentorship, and shared joy rather than competition or exclusion. Build activities that nurture belonging instead of hierarchy. And don't mistake this kind of play for dullness just because no one's being beamed with a dodgeball—the laughter and connection that emerge from collaborative play are far more powerful than the adrenaline spike of scoring a goal.

The high comes not from victory, but from interconnectedness. And to be clear, I'm not against competitive play—I grew up with it, I've played it, and I still love watching competitive sports (turns out I'm much better at watching than actually playing them). There's a time and place for that energy. But the kind of play that strengthens the old brain—the kind that regulates, settles, and reconnects us—is the play that builds collaboration, safety, and connection.

We forget how powerful that pull toward play can be — even in war. In December 1914, during World War I, British and German soldiers laid down their weapons on Christmas Day. They climbed out of their trenches, crossed the frozen stretch of no man's land, and began to play soccer. They shared food, sang songs, and for a few hours remembered they were human. Then, when dawn came, they returned to their orders — to the "more important" business of killing each other.

That brief ceasefire — that game — may have lasted only a day, but it revealed something profound about us: play is one of the few forces strong enough to silence fear, even if only for a moment. And it's tragic how easily we, as adults, forget that. For a single winter's night, men who were told they were enemies sang the same songs, laughed at the same jokes, and shared the same food. The war resumed the next morning, but the illusion cracked—it was never the men who needed to be enemies, only the systems that told them to be. After all, we always seem to think we need an enemy, don't we?

If soldiers could find peace through play for a day, schools could find it for a lifetime.

(The 1914 Christmas Truce — when British and German troops paused fighting to share food, songs, and a soccer match — is documented in Stanley Weintraub's Silent Night: The Story of the World War I Christmas Truce (2001).)

Even in humanity's darkest chapter, play persisted. In the barracks of concentration camps — including Auschwitz — children played pretend with scraps of wood, paper, and imagination (Dwork, 1991). They built invisible worlds, reenacted life before the fences, and whispered laughter between shadows. Psychologists studying their resilience believe these moments of play were not denial, but defiance — the nervous system's final act of remembering what it means to be human in a place designed to erase it.

I've seen this same truth—in a much safer setting—like in Steve's trainings. Even as an adult, the experience is transformative — the kind of joy that resets your nervous system and reminds you what safety feels like. This kind of intentional play matters now more than ever. Many of today's children come from across the world, some from war-torn regions or unstable homes. Play becomes their universal language; laughter becomes their bridge. It's how human beings, regardless of origin or trauma, remember they belong.

Imagine schools where teachers play alongside students — running, laughing, pretending, rediscovering that shared humanness. Children light up when adults join in; it tells them the world is safe enough for everyone to be silly together. That's what I mean by a true power play — one that restores connection, not control.

It can't be said enough—if you want to build resilience in our children, let them play more. Learning will come easier. There will be less bullying, less violence, and more cooperation. The more interconnected we are, the quieter the old brain becomes. Those modern bears lose their grip, and schools become what they were meant to be — safe places to grow, not survive.

I know what many educators or parents might be thinking: "Come on, Paul — grades matter. Hard work matters." And of course they do. But we can't keep ignoring the biology beneath the books. Children's nervous systems crave the same things ours do: safety, connection, movement, and joy. When we overlook those needs, we teach kids to ignore their bodies, too — to equate their worth with achievement rather than aliveness.

Play isn't a distraction from learning. It's the foundation for it. It shapes the brain, calms the body, and builds the kind of resilience no standardized test could ever measure.

Research shows that play improves immune function, lowers cortisol, strengthens memory, and increases social bonding (Burghardt, 2005; Panksepp, 1998). Play literally restores the biology that constant vigilance wears down.

The Cost of Losing Play

When we strip play from education, we're not just cutting recess — we're cutting regulation. We're creating nervous systems that can't downshift, children who associate learning with danger, and adults who believe that stillness equals failure.

And the pattern continues. Those children grow into adults who schedule every minute, fill silence with screens, and call exhaustion normal. They become parents who tell their own children, *"Play when the work is done."* But as I learned long ago, the work is never done.

The irony is that the simplest tools for healing our collective stress — rest and play — cost nothing. They don't require technology, privilege, or politics. They require only permission. Play and rest are not escapes from responsibility; they are rehearsals for safety.

If we could relearn them at scale—as families, classrooms, and workplaces—we might not just be happier but healthier. Imagine a culture in which regulation is built into the day, in which play is recognized as medicine, and in which adults' model for children that the body's wisdom matters as much as the minds.

Health care costs may drop.
Maybe anxiety rates would fall.
Maybe the tribe could finally exhale.

The truth is that the old brain never stopped needing play. It's how the body remembers the difference between living and merely surviving.

Play reminds the body that life can be safe and spontaneous. Rest takes that lesson one step further — it asks us to feel safe doing nothing.

For a species built on vigilance, that might be the hardest task of all. We've learned to rest only when the danger is gone, yet the old brain keeps watch, waiting for permission that never comes.

The next question, then, is not just how to rest —but whether we can learn to rest without needing a threat to justify it.

Resting Without an Enemy

We've already seen what happens when rest disappears from the human story — the body breaks down, the mind frays, and the tribe forgets its rhythm. But understanding the science of rest isn't the same as feeling safe enough to rest.

The old brain was never built for peace. It evolved for movement, vigilance, and survival. When danger passed, it rested — but only until the next rustle in the grass. Stillness, to the primitive nervous system, was a risk. To rest meant to trust. And trust, for many of us, feels unsafe.

When clients tell me they "can't stop," they're describing more than a habit — they're describing a body that doesn't yet believe it's allowed to rest. The same adrenaline that once fueled escape now drives ambition, productivity, even perfectionism. We've turned vigilance into virtue. The bear no longer chases us; it motivates us. We've built an entire culture on that same chemistry — rewarding exhaustion as proof of worth.

The Adrenaline Society

In earlier chapters, we explored how chronic activation—the body's constant surge of stress hormones—reshapes both biology and behavior. When cortisol and adrenaline never reset, they begin to erode the very systems they were meant to protect.

Sleep is usually the first casualty. It's the most essential form of biological recovery, yet the one we treat as optional. Many of my clients talk about sleep the way they talk about hobbies—something they'll get to if there's time. They stay up late "to get more done," not realizing that every lost hour of sleep quietly taxes their immune system, their memory, and their emotional balance.

When the body is chronically deprived of deep sleep, it stops repairing tissue, consolidating memory, and processing emotion effectively. The amygdala grows louder, the prefrontal cortex quieter — meaning we become more reactive, less reflective, and biologically less resilient (McEwen, 2007; Walker, 2017; Yoo et al., 2007). We call it irritability, burnout, or poor focus, but at its core, it's a nervous system starved for rest.

Sleep suffers. Immunity falters. Inflammation rises. The heart and mind grow weary. The body that was built for bursts of danger now lives in a state of perpetual readiness — a body at war with its own chemistry.

This is the nervous system of a culture that confuses safety with speed, that fears stillness because stillness feels like vulnerability. We even hear it in our language: *restless*, *idle hands*, *power nap*, *recharging*. Even our words for rest are mechanical — productivity-adjacent.

The old brain, flooded with stress hormones, doesn't distinguish between a predator and an email inbox. The body's alarm system was built for lions, not deadlines — yet the response is the same: heart rate up, muscles tight, digestion paused, breath shallow. Over time, living in this state of vigilance becomes an illness in itself.

We start calling it anxiety, burnout, chronic pain, autoimmune flare, or depression. But beneath those names is the same biology — a nervous system that can't downshift. And so, we medicate the symptoms rather than treating the cause. We forget that safety isn't something we think our way into; it's something we feel our way back to.

Rest as Regulation

To rest is to allow the parasympathetic nervous system — the body's "rest and digest" branch — to take the wheel again. It's not laziness; it's recalibration. (Porges, 2011).

Sleep is the body's most powerful regulator — the nightly therapy session built into our biology. It's when the brain consolidates memory, clears metabolic waste, and resets emotional tone (Walker, 2017). During deep sleep, the amygdala quiets, the prefrontal cortex strengthens its grip, and the nervous system rebalances after the chaos of the day. Without enough of it, everything — from empathy to immune function — begins to fray.

But rest isn't only about sleep. It's about stillness — the ability to pause without the presence of danger. It's about the body relearning that the absence of threat is not itself a threat.

I often tell clients: You can't rest if your body doesn't believe you're safe. For many, this lands as revelation. They've been chasing calm as if it were a mindset rather than a bodily state. But the nervous system has its own timeline. Safety must be felt before it can be chosen.

When people begin to practice true rest — unguarded rest — their bodies often rebel at first. Anxiety rises. The mind searches for something to fix or finish. That's just the bear pacing the edge of the forest, wondering why we've stopped running.

What Real Rest Looks Like

Rest isn't passive. It's active recalibration. If rest is regulation, then real rest is the nourishment of the parasympathetic nervous system — the part of the body that whispers, "It's safe now." This is sometimes called the rest-and-digest system, and its activation allows for repair, digestion, and immune recovery after prolonged stress (Porges, 2011; McEwen, 2007). When the sympathetic nervous system — the fight-or-flight branch — remains dominant for too long, cortisol and adrenaline remain elevated, and the body loses the ability to reset.

Chronic activation is now linked to cardiovascular disease, autoimmune inflammation, depression, and even impaired memory (Sapolsky, 2004; McEwen & Gianaros, 2011). Sleep, in particular, is the body's built-in antidote — the nightly recalibration that turns survival back into stability (Walker, 2017).

Real rest restores this balance. It's how we move from defense to repair, from vigilance to vitality.

Three Markers of Real Rest

1. **Improved vagal tone.**
   The vagus nerve acts like the body's internal brake pedal. When it's engaged, heart rate slows, digestion resumes, and emotional regulation improves. Studies show that high vagal tone correlates with resilience, empathy, and stress recovery (Porges, 2011; Thayer & Lane, 2009).

2. **Synchronized breath and heartbeat.**
   As the parasympathetic system re-engages, breathing and heart rhythms begin to align — a state called *respiratory sinus arrhythmia*. Slow, intentional breathing increases vagal activity and lowers stress hormones quickly (Lehrer et al., 2020; Zaccaro et al., 2018).

3. **Systemic repair.**
   When the body truly rests, digestion, immunity, and cellular repair resume. Deep sleep is one of the most restorative states known—it clears metabolic waste from the brain via the glymphatic system and resets emotional tone (Walker, 2017; Xie et al., 2013). Chronic lack of rest, on the other hand, is associated with elevated inflammation markers such as IL-6 and CRP, reduced immune function, and accelerated aging (Irwin, 2015).

Cultivating Rest at Scale

To rest without first needing a threat to justify it, we must intentionally rebuild the conditions that let the body feel safe enough to stop. Somewhere along the way, rest was hijacked by threat-based permission—something we grant ourselves only when we've reached the edge. Science consistently shows that small, intentional pauses throughout the day can interrupt stress physiology — improving attention, lowering cortisol activity, and helping reset heart rate variability (Brosschot et al., 2018).

These practices help restore rhythm:

- **Micro-pauses:** 30- to 60-second breaks to breathe, stretch, or feel one's feet on the ground — training the nervous system to toggle between activation and ease.

- **Rhythmic movement:** Gentle walking, yoga, or dance can activate vagal pathways through patterned motion (Streeter et al., 2012).

- **Co-regulation:** Sharing space with calm others — what social neuroscientists call "limbic resonance" — helps nervous systems synchronize (Cozolino, 2014).

- **Guided stillness:** Practices like mindfulness or progressive relaxation shift the brain from beta-wave vigilance to alpha-wave calm, enhancing parasympathetic dominance (Tang et al., 2015).

- **Safe context rest:** Environments where stillness is socially permitted — classrooms with quiet corners, workplaces with rest breaks — send powerful cues of collective safety (Siegel, 2012).

Why This Matters Beyond the Individual

When enough bodies learn to rest, a culture begins to heal. Stress contagion — the spread of dysregulation through social networks — reverses when calm becomes the dominant signal (Cozolino, 2014; Wirth & Schultheiss, 2006).

Imagine classrooms that pause for breath, workplaces that reward recovery, homes where stillness isn't mistaken for laziness. That's how the collective nervous system begins to recover. Rest isn't retreat; it's repair.

The old brain will always scan for danger, but the new brain can now whisper back: *We're safe enough to stop running.*

Bridge to Chapter 7: The Comparison-Status Bear

Rest was never meant to be the end of the story — it was meant to be the reset. When the body finally exhales, something remarkable happens it begins to look for connection again. Safety makes space for curiosity, and curiosity leads us back into relationship.

But in a world built on scarcity and hierarchy, even connection can become a form of competition. The same biology that seeks belonging also craves recognition. Once the tribe feels safe, the old brain doesn't stop asking *"Am I secure?"* — it starts asking *"Am I valued?"*

That's where the next Bear appears.

The Comparison-Status Bear doesn't roar with fear; it whispers comparison.

It feeds on subtle hierarchies — grades, titles, followers, trophies — anything that tells the nervous system, *"You matter more if..."* And while it may seem more civilized than the fears of hunger or war, its effects are just as corrosive: stress hormones rise, empathy falls, and belonging fractures into ranking.

Neuroscience shows that the same reward circuits that once fired for food and safety now light up for approval and prestige. Dopamine — the brain's "seek more" chemical — doesn't distinguish between discovering berries or getting likes.

It rewards anticipation, not satisfaction (Berridge & Kringelbach, 2015). That means the moment we achieve status; the brain's craving resets. We scroll, strive, or perform again — chasing the same neurochemical spark that once kept our ancestors alive.

In the language of the nervous system, status is just safety wearing fancier clothes. It's the old brain's way of saying, *"If I can't be the strongest, maybe I can be the most admired — and the tribe will still keep me."* But when belonging becomes conditional, the cost is regulation itself. The tribe can't exhale together if everyone's trying to stand taller.

If the last chapter asked whether we could rest without an enemy, this next one asks whether we can connect without competing.

Chapter 6: Key Takeaways

- Rest and play are not luxuries — they are biological necessities.

- Stillness is not weakness; it's recalibration.

- Play restores connection — within ourselves and with others.

- Permission is the medicine. Giving yourself and others space to rest and play softens the bears and strengthens resilience.

Impression

This exercise invites you to gently challenge the inherited messages that equate worth with productivity. By engaging in stillness and non-competitive play, you give your body a chance to relearn safety — a prerequisite for regulation, healing, and connection. Through both rest and play, the nervous system discovers that safety isn't earned through control; it's remembered through permission.

Exercise — LET THE BEARS PLAY

Step 1: Notice the Messages

Take a few minutes to reflect on the messages you learned growing up — from school, family, church, or culture — about *work*, *rest*, and *play*.
What were you told about "doing nothing"?
Was it lazy, shameful, or dangerous?

Write down a few of those bears — the inner voices that whisper, *"You haven't done enough,"* or *"You don't deserve to stop."*

Step 2: Trace Their Origins

Ask yourself: *Where did these messages come from?*
Who taught them to you — and who taught them to *them*?
You'll likely find a long lineage of inherited fear — generations who believed that safety could only be earned through effort. Recognizing the inheritance loosens its grip.

Step 3: Practice Rest — On Purpose

Once a week, set aside 10–15 minutes to do absolutely nothing. No emails. No "quick tasks." No multitasking disguised as rest. Sit or lie still and give your body explicit permission to stop.

If your mind drifts to your to-do list, come back to your senses: Feel the chair beneath you, the air against your skin, the rhythm of your breath. Each exhale is a tiny truce with your own vigilance. You're not doing nothing — you're doing something profoundly biological: teaching your old brain how to rest.

Work up from once a week to a few times a week, maybe daily. And for god's sake, don't turn this into another productivity contest.

If you catch yourself thinking, *"I'm wasting time,"* smile and remind yourself: "I'm doing something for my health — for my nervous system

— for my bears." You might be surprised how much quieter they become when you stop chasing them.

Step 4: Invite Play Back In

Find small, simple ways to play.

Not competitive play but play that connects — **joy without winners.** Be silly. Move. Paint. Dance badly (I am good at that). Laugh loudly.

Remember the soldiers in World War I, who paused on Christmas Day to share food and play soccer. For a few brief hours, even enemies remembered they were human.

That's the power of play — **it interrupts fear long enough for connection to take hold.**

Step 5: Reflect and Integrate

Imagine what that same spirit could do in your home, your classroom, or your workplace. You don't need a holiday truce — just a few minutes of courage to let your bears play.

Reflection Prompts

- What beliefs about rest or play still feel "off-limits" to you?
- How does your body react when you try to stop moving?
- What kind of play — quiet, silly, creative, relational — makes your nervous system exhale?
- Who in your life might need permission to play, too?

Closing Reflection

The world will wait — your nervous system won't.

Chapter 7 – The Lost Tribe: Scarcity, Status, and the Search for Safety

"We were never meant to do this alone,"
Pinette Field Notes—2025

Somewhere along the way, we forgot that we were built to belong to each other. Our species survived not because we were the fastest or the strongest, but because we were the most connected. We faced danger together, shared food, mourned together, and celebrated together. Survival wasn't a solo project; it was a communal nervous system regulating itself through shared purpose and care.

Then something changed. The first time a human stored grain instead of sharing it, a new story began—one about *mine and yours*. The moment food could be stored; it could also be withheld. Safety became something you could own. Scarcity—once a condition of nature— became a belief about one another. The tribe began to fracture.

Status and competition emerged from that fracture. They weren't born from greed; they were born from fear—the nervous system's way of organizing insecurity. When we could no longer trust the tribe, we began to prove ourselves rather than connect. Over time, those patterns hardened into systems. Capitalism wasn't a mistake; it was an adaptation—a way to coordinate survival in groups too large to know by name. It worked brilliantly until fear began running the show. When the old brain leads, collaboration shrinks, and safety becomes a scoreboard.

Money became the modern form of stored grain—our currency of safety. The brain doesn't know that numbers on a screen aren't baskets of food; it reacts the same way: protect, compare, accumulate. But where ancient sharing soothed the body, modern accumulation often amplifies anxiety. The harder we try to secure safety on our own, the less safe we feel.

If the tribe once gathered around a fire, today we gather around a feed. Social media has become the new campfire of comparison—bright, endless, and strangely lonely. We scroll not to see each other, but to measure ourselves. In therapy, I hear it weekly: "I was on Facebook…" and what follows is rarely joy. The images of happier families, richer lives, better bodies—all interpreted by the nervous system as proof that belonging is slipping away. When we can't compete, we defend by dismissing: "They're not really that happy." That isn't cruelty; it's protection.

Because anyone can post anything, we've learned to treat posting itself as proof. Fear pushes us to declare certainty—opinions, beliefs, identities—because certainty feels like safety. The act of posting becomes an attempt to make it true. Someone else, equally afraid, posts back from their own alarm. Fear recruits; it motivates; it spreads—a collective threat response disguised as discourse. The nervous system doesn't rest in that loop; it arms. And once armed, curiosity dies, replaced by the comfort of being right.

The Comparison-Status Bear

It's not just fear that drives the cycle—it's comparison. I sometimes call it The Comparison-Status Bear—the part of us that prowls for proof of worth. Status and competition feed it. So do our screens.

Many of my clients ask whether they may take out their phones so they can "show me" something—as if truth now resides inside the glass. They scroll through photos, posts, and comments like evidence: "Look at this family." "Can you believe this?" Then the comparisons spill out: "They're better than me… smarter than me… richer than me." It's a long list. And beneath every one of those lines lives the same old message: I might not be enough.

When they hold out the screen, I often ask quietly, "Do you see the sorting happening?" Because it's not just what they're looking at—it's what's happening inside them as they look.

The judging. The ranking. The unconscious dividing of the world into better and worse, safe and unsafe, valuable and not. Many have internalized this sorting so completely that they no longer notice it. As if it weren't enough that society sorts and judges us, now we've learned to do it to ourselves.

And it shows up in the body. I can see it happen in real time: as a client unlocks their phone, their breathing shortens, their chest tightens, their jaw sets. The nervous system braces, anticipating a threat that never comes but always feels nearby. The bear wakes up, pacing behind the eyes.

This isn't vanity or weakness—it's biology misfired. When worth and safety become tied to comparison, the old brain assumes danger is near. It reads every post as a potential exclusion from the tribe. Every smiling face becomes evidence of someone else's safety and, therefore, your possible rejection.

Many people now have more "connections" through a screen than in person. And that's a problem, because the nervous system doesn't regulate through pixels. As Stephen Porges reminds us, safety cues come from tone, facial expression, and eye contact—from living faces, not filtered ones. The phone offers information without co-regulation, stimulation without safety, contact without connection. We're trying to feed an emotional body on digital calories—it fills us, but it doesn't nourish.

Even small things can spark the bear—a vacation photo, a promotion, a new relationship. The old brain reads each as a social hierarchy: who belongs, who's secure, who might be left behind.

The comparison-status bear whispers: if they have more, you'll have less. It's the same scarcity story in new clothes. And because that tension feels productive—like motivation—we scroll again, hoping the next post will reassure us. But the bear never leaves full; it only leaves hungrier.

And in that hunger, something essential erodes. Worth becomes performance. Attention becomes currency. We start living not to connect, but to compete—for proof that we exist, that we matter, that we are safe.

The Return of the Small Tribe

Yet even in this noise, the old design hasn't disappeared. You can still see it—at the family dinner table, in a pickup basketball game, a recovery group, a choir, a therapy circle, or two friends on a porch after a long day. These are our *micro-tribes*—small repair stations inside modern chaos. They don't look heroic, but they are the nervous system's survival code replaying itself in miniature. Every time people share laughter, stories, or silence, something ancient recalibrates: *We are safe together, for now.* The tribe was never lost; it's just scattered into smaller rooms.

The Body as Tribe

Remembering begins in the body. Regulation isn't a concept—it's choreography.

Our physiology still speaks the language of the tribe: rhythm, breath, synchrony, touch, eye contact, movement. A shared laugh. A song. "Regulation is not found in status or comparing, but instead in *the status of plentiful connections.*" Even matching another's breathing for a few seconds signals the old brain that we belong.

The body is the first and last village we inhabit. When we move, hum, dance, or sit quietly beside another regulated body, we are rebuilding the tribal map cell by cell. You don't have to chant around a fire to activate it. You just have to notice the small cues of safety your system recognizes: a steady tone, a face that softens, a moment when you and another person exhale at the same time. That's the nervous system remembering home.

Curiosity as Strength

None of this means becoming sentimental or naïve. Connection isn't a luxury or a moral posture; it's a biological discipline. Empathy and curiosity are not soft—they're regulated.

A fearful brain defends; a regulated brain inquires. That's why curiosity is such a powerful form of strength—it keeps the conversation, and the species, from closing its fists. In every era, the people who could remain curious the longest were the ones who kept communities from breaking apart entirely.

Curiosity opens the door; regulation keeps it open long enough to build something new.

Rebuilding Ourselves

So, what now? We don't need to overthrow systems or preach utopia. We need to re-regulate within the world we already inhabit. The tools are the same ones we began with in Chapter 1—the ones that fill the coping bucket.

But this time, we return to them knowing what's at stake: each calm nervous system is a small act of infrastructure. The breath, the pause, the rest, the simple tending of the body—these are not just personal habits; they are social repairs.

Before we can rebuild the tribe, we must rebuild capacity. A calm nervous system isn't a weakness; it's a form of quiet leadership. The more of us who can stay grounded long enough to choose connection over certainty, curiosity over comparison, and presence over performance, the more the collective begins to steady.

That's the work ahead—refilling what leaks out, remembering what holds us together, one regulated breath at a time.

Closing Reflection

Maybe the real measure of evolution isn't how much we can accumulate, but how gently we can live among each other. The modern tribe won't look like the old one, and that's all right. What matters is whether we can still recognize the ancient signals of safety—tone, laughter, eye contact, breath—and answer them. The work ahead isn't to rebuild what was lost, but to remember what was never supposed to be forgotten: that regulation is love in biological form. Every calm nervous system is a small light left burning in the dark.

Bridge to Chapter 8 — The Coping Bucket

Before we can calm the collective, we must strengthen the individual container.

The next chapter turns inward—toward the simple, practical ways we refill our own reserves of calm, rest, and resilience. These are not self-improvement techniques; they're acts of nervous-system maintenance, the same ones that once kept our ancestors steady in the face of hunger and storms. We'll look at how to recognize when our bucket is leaking, what drains it, what restores it, and how one regulated body can begin to steady the field around it.

Key Takeaways

- **Scarcity rewrote safety.** Once food could be stored, fear learned to hoard, and belonging began to fracture into competition.

- **Status and comparison are fear's modern uniforms.** The old brain still chases tribal worth but now mistakes visibility and accumulation for safety.

- **Screens amplify the scarcity story.** Social media and digital connections often simulate community while bypassing the safety cues the body needs.

- **The comparison status bear feeds on judgment—especially self-judgment.** Many of us have internalized society's sorting into our own inner dialogue.

- **Real regulation happens face-to-face, body-to-body.** Tone, rhythm, and synchrony are the languages of safety.

- **Curiosity is courage.** In a world ruled by certainty, staying curious is the new act of strength.

- **Healing begins locally.** Every grounded breath, every calm exchange, is a structural repair in the collective nervous system.

Transition to Exercise

If you've ever felt that low-grade hum of unease while scrolling, you already know what I mean by the Comparison-Status Bears. You can almost feel them waking up—the tiny flickers of tension, judgment, envy, or fear of being left behind. Rather than analyzing it from a distance, let's slow it down and actually notice what's happening in real time.

The next exercise isn't about giving up technology or pretending you're above it. It's about learning to feel the old brain in motion—how quickly it reaches for safety through comparison, and how easily it can be soothed by connection.

Exercise: Calming the Comparison-Status Bears

You might not expect a chapter exercise to start this way—but grab your phone.
Yes, really. Open the social media app you usually gravitate toward. (*Bet you didn't see that one coming.*)

Step 1: Scroll and Notice

Start scrolling as you normally would, but this time, pay attention to your *body*.

Notice what happens as you move through the posts. Maybe it's a smiling family that seems "the happiest of happy," or a headline warning about some group we're told to fear, or a friend announcing another promotion or showing off their "stuff."

As you scroll, listen to your inner narration:

"They must be happier."
"They have more."
"I'm not as smart."
"Those people are dangerous."

Each of those small zings and twinges is data. That tightening in your chest, the little ache behind your eyes—these are signs your **old brain** is scanning for threat, scarcity, and belonging: *Do I still fit in? Do I still matter? Am I still safe?*

You've just met the Comparison-Status Bear—the part of you that mistakes other people's highlight reels for survival maps.

Step 2: Rewire the Feed

Keep your phone, but this time, open a search window and type "random acts of kindness."

Watch a few short videos or read a few stories. Notice what happens in your body again.

Does your breath drop lower? Do your shoulders soften a little? That warmth or steadiness is your nervous system regulating. The body distinguishes between competition and connection.

Now imagine practicing those small acts yourself: smiling at a stranger, holding a door, paying it forward, offering a kind word. Can you picture what your old brain might say?

"Hey, thanks—that feels safer."

What you're feeling isn't sentimentality. It's the biology of safety coming back online.

Step 3: Choose Your Feed Wisely

If you noticed a difference—if that sense of calm felt real—consider a small adjustment.

You don't have to abandon social media entirely; that's not realistic. But you can limit the feeds that consistently activate your bears. Unfollow a few comparison triggers. Mute a few panic merchants.

Then fill that reclaimed space with content that evokes curiosity, humor, compassion, or learning—anything that reminds your nervous system of connection rather than competition.

Over time, these small acts of digital hygiene become nervous-system hygiene. You'll start to recognize how often the bears show up and, more importantly, how quickly they settle when you feed them safety instead of status.

Pause & Reflect: What Did You Notice?

Take a moment—before you put the phone away—to reflect on what your body told you.

- What sensations stood out when you scrolled the first time? Where did they live in your body?

- What changed when you shifted from competition to compassion?

- Which feeds or images wake your comparison bears the fastest?

- What kinds of interactions, stories, or people leave you feeling calmer, warmer, or more connected?

Now zoom out for a second. Imagine your body as part of a larger ecosystem of nervous systems. Every time you calm your own, you quietly shift the field around you. This is where self-regulation becomes social repair.

You don't have to silence every bear. You have to notice them—and feed them safety instead of scarcity. That's the same foundation we'll build on next: refilling your coping bucket, so there's enough calm in your system to meet the world without losing yourself.

PART III

Taking Action

Chapter 8 – What Was Never Lost: Refilling the Coping Bucket

"We arrive in this world with birthright gifts—then we spend the first half of our lives abandoning them or letting others disabuse us of them. Then if we are awake, we spend the second half trying to recover and reclaim them."
— Parker J. Palmer, *Let Your Life Speak*

Listening to What the Body Has Been Saying All Along

Much of what we call coping isn't about learning something new; it's about listening to what the body has been trying to tell us all along. The body is the first responder to stress and the first to signal when capacity is running low—yet most of us don't hear it until we've already crossed into depletion.

Regulation begins with recognition: tightness, fatigue, restlessness, withdrawal—these are not weaknesses but messages. This chapter explores how to rebuild capacity by attending to those signals, refilling what's been drained, and restoring the body's role as both messenger and ally.

In clinical terms, this is how we move from survival management to sustainable regulation—learning to trust that what was never lost can, in fact, be felt again.

Revisiting the Old Brain

By now, you've likely learned a great deal about your own biology—specifically, the language and priorities of the old brain. My hope is that this knowledge has helped you recognize what the old brain really cares about: staying alive, staying safe, and staying connected.

That primal drive for survival is incredibly powerful. It has kept our species alive through millennia, yet in modern life we've drifted from that awareness. We've mistaken sophistication for separation, forgetting that the old brain's mission—to keep us alive—is not outdated. It's sacred.

The new brain—our prefrontal cortex—is extraordinary, but it has limits. We cannot think ourselves out of thirst, logic ourselves out of hunger, or reason our way out of exhaustion. Only the body can meet those needs. Understanding this boundary between intellect and biology is key to self-regulation.

And beyond understanding, my hope is that you've felt some of these truths in your body—the tightening in your chest as you read about fear, the breath that deepened when you read about safety, the moment you recognized your own "modern bears" and realized that taming them was never about elimination—it was about understanding, calming, and coexisting.

Knowing Is Not Enough

Many clients tell me, "I know better—why aren't things changing?" My response is always the same: because knowing isn't enough. Knowledge without action is just more data in the frontal cortex. Transformation requires that what we know becomes what we practice.

We're not trying to force the old brain to behave; we're learning to respect its rhythms. Self-care isn't a luxury—it's biology. The goal isn't to dominate our primitive impulses but to partner with them, integrating the wisdom of both brains—the instinctual and the intentional.

In the next chapter, I'll expand on this idea of partnership—how the same principles that help us calm our own nervous system can extend inward toward deeper listening, where understanding becomes collaboration rather than control.

Refilling the Coping Bucket: Returning to Basic Biology

The most powerful forms of self-care are not novel—they're ancient. They are the biological rituals that once kept our ancestors alive:

- **Hydration.** The body's call for balance is simple yet often ignored. Water replenishes energy, concentration, and mood—small, tangible proof that biology doesn't need to be complicated to be wise.

- **Nutrition.** We are animals designed for scarcity, not grocery aisles. Skipping meals or using food to self-soothe are both ways of trying to regulate through the wrong channel. Respecting hunger is respecting life.

- **Rest.** Sleep is not laziness; it's repair. Each hour of rest reaffirms safety to the nervous system.

- **Movement.** The body was made to move, to play. Movement burns anxiety's excess energy, releases endorphins, and reclaims joy from fear.

- **Connection.** A smile, tone of voice, eye contact, touch—these are forms of co-regulation. We forget that belonging is a biological event.

- **Elimination.** Respect the body's need to eliminate waste; don't ignore it.

These are not small acts; they are sacred ones. They refill the coping bucket by restoring what chronic stress drains from us daily.

Hebb's Law and the Body's Lesson in Learning

You may notice some repetition in these pages—that's intentional. Hebb's Law in neuroscience states, "neurons that fire together wire together" (Hebb, 1949). The brain learns through repetition—but the body feels its way there first.

When I first learned to drive, I gripped the steering wheel so tightly my knuckles turned white. My driver's-ed instructor looked over and said, "Paul… you can let go of the steering wheel a little bit."

That tension wasn't just anxiety—it was my nervous system's response to uncertainty. My body was protecting me from the unfamiliar. Over time, with practice, I loosened my grip. What once felt foreign became automatic.

That's Hebb's Law in motion: through repetition and safe exposure, neurons draw closer together, and the body learns that new can be safe. This is why practicing regulation feels awkward at first. Even healthy change can register as a threat until the nervous system experiences it enough times to believe it.

Reading these ideas once won't transform anything. Living them repeatedly will. Each time you honor thirst, rest, hunger, or connection, you strengthen a neural bridge toward regulation. You teach your system that safety can be rehearsed—and remembered.

From Insight to Action

Filling the coping bucket begins with attention to biological cues—thirst, hunger, fatigue, the need for touch, for stillness, for laughter. But it also means becoming intentional about practices that support those needs:

- Conscious breathing and grounding
- Journaling for emotional release and meaning making
- Movement—dance, stretching, walking, yoga
- Resting without apology
- Choosing play and connection over productivity when possible

These are not indulgences. They are the maintenance rituals of regulation. Use your new brain to plan and your old brain to feel. Self-care that honors both is not self-improvement—it's self-integration.

Stumbling Across the Four Pillars: Love, Compassion, Caring, and Non-Judgment-The Compass

Up to this point, we've explored what keeps the old brain alarmed—those modern bears of scarcity, shame, comparison, and fear—and what begins to settle it again: connection, curiosity, and safety. And now it's time to name the practices that hold all of that together.

And honestly? I didn't discover them so much as *crash* into them. Something started to click while I was writing Chapter 5—especially the part on religion—and layering that with everything I already knew from biology, neuroscience, psychology, and two decades in the therapy room.

But the real moment didn't feel elegant at all. "Stumbled" is too generous. I tripped, twisted, and went forehead-first into a metaphorical light post. And that light post was an old 1998 article by Stephen Porges titled, **Love: An Emergent Property of the Mammalian Autonomic Nervous System (Porges, 1998)**

The very title itself had the word *love* in it, which was enough to grab me. But the content stopped me cold. It didn't just support what I was beginning to see—It confirmed it.

Suddenly, it all snapped into place.

Love, compassion, caring, and non-judgment weren't "virtues," or "nice ideas," or "spiritual slogans." They were **biological states. Autonomic realities.** Not abstract wishes—but the actual physiological conditions under which humans regulate, connect, heal, and become themselves fully.

And here's the wild part: this was published *before* the internet as we know it. Before social media. Before our modern bears exploded into a 24-hour firehose of judgment and comparison, the culture simply wasn't ready for what that article was pointing to. Not unlike the prophets—repeating the same message for millennia, and we keep missing it.

Ever since hitting that "light post," I haven't been the same (in a good way, mind you).

When I say love, compassion, caring, and non-judgment create safety, I mean they're not lofty ideals — they're what a safe nervous system looks like. They are biological regulators (and yes, I keep repeating that on purpose).

These states calm the threat system, widen our window of tolerance, soften shame, restore clarity, and rebuild trust—in ourselves, in others, and in life itself. They are not decorative. They are required. They are how the nervous system stabilizes.

The Biology Behind It (as simple as possible)

If this sounds surprisingly simple, that's because the biology is simple. Porges' work shows that humans move through three basic physiological states:

• **Ventral vagal** — safety, connection, curiosity, compassion, presence, clear thinking.
• **Sympathetic** — fight-or-flight: fear, judgment, defensiveness, irritability.
• **Dorsal vagal** — shutdown: collapse, numbness, withdrawal, hopelessness.

And here is the part almost no one learns:

We shift between these states based on how we treat ourselves.

When we rest, feed ourselves, hydrate, breathe deeply, move, play, connect, and speak to ourselves with warmth rather than attack, the body reads these as *signals of safety* and moves toward a ventral vagal state.

When we criticize (judge) ourselves, push without rest, compare, hustle, shame, ignore our needs, or obey the modern bears, the body reads these as *signals of threat* and shifts into sympathetic or dorsal survival.

In other words:

Love, compassion, caring, and non-judgment are nervous-system states expressed as behaviors that pull the body back toward safety.

And if this polyvagal-theory stuff feels abstract, let me give you a real-life example one I have lived many times as a parent (did I mention I have five kids?). And don't worry if you're not a parent; I'm fairly certain you've felt this too.

If you've ever heard an infant cry, you've felt your sympathetic nervous system activate.

Infants are born with a fully functioning sympathetic system but only a rudimentary parasympathetic system. A baby comes into the world with distress fully online and safety still under construction. So, they borrow a caregiver's ventral vagal system until their own is strong enough to take over.

A baby cannot self-regulate. Their entire nervous system depends on external regulation.

And you know this in your body. Think about how hard it is to ignore a crying baby. That sharp sound cuts straight through thought and lands in your physiology—your chest tightens, your attention spikes, your whole system moves toward action. This is exactly what Porges means by **neuroception**: the body detects distress before the mind interprets it.

That's biology, not choice. And almost instantly, notice what happens next.

We soften our voice.
We pick the baby up.
We sway.
We offer warmth, eye contact, and rhythm.

These aren't random instincts; they are ventral-vagal cues of safety— the exact behaviors Porges describes in the **social engagement system.** One nervous system offering calm, so another can borrow it.

In small tribes, if a parent wasn't nearby, another adult stepped in—not only out of compassion but because a baby's distress dysregulated the entire group. Soothing the infant soothed the tribe. This is co-regulation in its most ancient form, and we still feel it today.

The same biology drives the Four Pillars. When we meet fear with warmth, tone, presence, and connection—whether with a baby or with ourselves—we activate the pathways that guide the body back into safety. We shift from sympathetic activation toward the ventral vagal state, where healing can finally take root.

Once we're in ventral vagal, our body becomes a tuning fork for others. Safety resonates. Calm spreads. Regulation is contagious. This is co-regulation—not a metaphor, but biology.

This is the engine behind the Four Pillars.
Not morality.
Not mindset.
Not willpower.
Just the old brain doing what it was designed to do when it finally feels safe.

This is the piece people rarely connect until it's spelled out: What we do for infants is exactly what we must learn to do for ourselves. We don't outgrow the need for safety cues — we take over the job. And once you understand that something becomes very clear:

The Feedback Loop

Here is the simplest way I can describe it:

How you treat yourself determines your autonomic state,
And your autonomic state determines how you treat yourself.

It is self-reinforcing in both directions:

Care → Ventral → More Care
Judgment → Survival → More Judgment

The Four Pillars are both the **path into** ventral vagal safety.
and the **expression of** ventral vagal safety.

They are the nervous system's native language.
They are what humans naturally become when we are not trapped in fear.

Think of the Four Pillars as a **compass.**
Keep that image close—we're going to need it when we get to the mountains in Chapter 10.

I hope that this book becomes a kind of nervous system literacy course: a way back to emotional safety, community co-regulation, compassion that doesn't collapse, less shame, more understanding—a way to be human with less suffering.

What Survival Mode Looks Like

When the old brain gets stuck in sympathetic or dorsal activation, it does what it was built to do: sort, judge, defend. Judgment isn't a moral failure—it's the old brain scanning for danger. Hypervigilance, anger, rigidity, shutting down… these are survival states, not character flaws.

The antidote?
Similarity. Connection. Warmth. Familiarity.
Signals of safety.

These shift the autonomic state back toward a ventral vagal state.

What Ventral Vagal Looks Like (the Four Pillars in action)

Love.
Compassion.
Belonging.
Community.
Attachment.
Forgiveness.
Patience.
Openness.
Sorting dissolves.
Judgment weakens.
Rigidity softens.

Curiosity returns.
Connection becomes possible.

One regulated nervous system at a time.

And how do we transmit that ventral state? As we have discussed in previous pages, through what Stephen Porges calls the Social Engagement System—the coordinated use of facial expression, tone of voice, eye gaze, head movement, and the vagal brake, which together signal safety to another human being (Porges, 1998). In other words, the cues we already use every day —our eyes, our tone, our breath, our pacing, our presence, our softness.

These are not mysterious tools. They're the exact tools that make therapy effective. When our physiology shifts into what Porges calls "immobilization without fear," we activate safety in others.

People then access the Four Pillars.
—not because they tried,
—not because they're "good people,"
—but because their biology recognized safety.

The Four Pillars are simply what mammals become when we are no longer afraid.

They are the nervous system's original design.

Humans cannot heal in fear.
We heal in safety.
We cannot transform into judgment.
We transform into compassion.
We cannot grow in chaos.
We grow through co-regulation.
We cannot thrive in shame.
We thrive in connection.

This is biology—not philosophy.

Here's What Surprised Me Most

Every field of human knowing has been saying this all along.
Not metaphorically.
Not symbolically.
Literally.

Biology and spirituality were never opposites—they were always describing the same thing. The core teachings of the world's wisdom traditions are actually descriptions of a regulated nervous system.

What we once called virtues are physiological states.
What we once called sins are states of fear or dysregulation.
What we assumed were "choices" were often nervous system constraints.

Human goodness is not earned.
It is unlocked through safety, connection, co-regulation—the Four Pillars.

When the old brain feels safe, people become who they truly are.
When the old brain is afraid, people do things that don't reflect their character at all.

It has always been fear vs. safety.
Old Brain vs. New World.

And now, with this compass in hand, we can finally begin to navigate. And as we do, we discover something remarkable: every field of human knowing has been pointing to this same map.

The Four Pillars Across Every Field of Human Knowing

Biology

When the body feels safe, the ventral vagal system comes online.
Breathing steadies.
Tone softens.
Gaze widens.
The prefrontal cortex returns.

In other words:
Love is what the nervous system looks like when it stops bracing for threat.

Neuroscience

Compassion quiets the amygdala.
Non-judgment activates the prefrontal cortex.
Caring increases vagal tone.
Warmth synchronizes heart rhythms.

Neuroscience keeps discovering what prophets described in metaphor:
A regulated nervous system creates the conditions for wisdom.

Psychology

Attachment theory, trauma therapy, IFS, somatics, and polyvagal theory all agree:
Humans heal in environments of attunement, safety, and presence.

Not pressure.
Not punishment.
Not fear.

Psychology's translation is simple:
We regulate through love.
We dysregulate through fear.

Evolutionary Biology

Mammals survive through co-regulation—huddling, grooming, orienting, soothing.
Care is not a moral virtue. It is the oldest survival strategy we have.

Philosophy

Stoics, Buddhists, and humanists all echo the same idea:
Clarity requires calm.
Wisdom requires regulation.

Theology

Before religion was used as a moral authority, it was trauma medicine.
"Be not afraid."
"Love one another."
"Do unto others…"
"Judge not, lest ye be judged…"
— not as a threat, but as a reminder that judgment activates fear, not connection.

The prophets weren't teaching behavior management.
They were teaching fear management — how to keep the old brain from eating us alive.

I cannot repeat this enough: the Four Pillars aren't virtues.
They are nervous-system instructions.

That's why they endure.
That's why their teachings stabilize people across centuries.
That's why they feel familiar when you hear them—because they're encoded in our biology.

The prophets weren't delivering moral lectures.
They were teaching down-regulation as a path to staying human. They were trying to provide nervous system literacy in the language of the time.

Certain Certainty

Love, compassion, care, and non-judgment weren't chosen because
they're "nice."
They were chosen because they stabilize the human nervous system —
individually and collectively.

They are the only states in which we can think clearly, love
generously, play honestly, and live without fear.

They are **not** sentiment.
They are **not** weakness.
They are **not** softness.

They are biology.
They are regulators.
They are the only certainty we have.

Turning the Four Pillars Inward

Here's where the work begins: turning those same pillars toward
yourself.

How do you practice love, compassion, caring, and non-judgment
toward your own body?

For many of my clients, this is the most challenging task.
They come in echoing the voices of trauma and culture:

I'm too heavy.
I'm not smart enough.
I don't make enough.
I'm not lovable.

They've internalized the modern bears—status, productivity,
comparison—and now use those same metrics to judge their worth.

But those judgments aren't biological truths; they're cultural noise.
The old brain never asked us to be perfect.
It only asked us to stay alive and connected.

Practicing self-compassion means trading judgment for curiosity.

Instead of, "I should've stayed late; I'm lazy," try, "I've done enough. It's time for rest." Instead of, "I shouldn't need comfort," try, "My body is asking for soothing—that's human."

I can't tell you how many times a week I coach clients to practice these four states toward themselves. It's often the hardest habit to break; those bears roar to drown out our regulatory skills.

So, I invite them to permit themselves—to rest, to laugh, to play. To make sleep a priority, not an afterthought. To notice how often they compare themselves to others—on a screen or in the world—and to feel what that comparison does inside the body.

You can't always change what shows up on your feed. But you *can* change how you speak to yourself, how you treat your body, and how you respond to your own biology.

You have all the control you need. What's usually missing is permission—something I keep offering until it begins to take root.

Why the Four Pillars Matter

Love, compassion, caring, and non-judgment aren't sentimental—they're **stabilizing**.
They regulate physiology the same way deep breathing or safe touch does.

They remind the body that it belongs, even when the world feels uncertain.
How we treat ourselves becomes rehearsal for how we treat the world.

Each gentle thought toward your own biology fills your coping bucket a little more—
and maybe begin to refill the collective one too.

Personal Bears

I want to pause for a moment and share some self-disclosure. Writing this book was never about having it all figured out. Many of my clients imagine that I've reached some summit of wisdom, sitting on high and dispensing advice to the masses, far from it. I am human. I have an old brain.

Like everyone else, I live in a world bombarded by social messaging about how I should live, how I should appear, what I should be as a man, a therapist, a human. I'm not immune to the influences of the very constructs I've been writing about. I have my own bears.

Yes, I may be more familiar with them than some because of what I do—but that doesn't make me exempt. The work is the same: not fighting the bears but respecting and calming them. Writing this book helped me identify a few I hadn't noticed before.

And don't think I haven't done my share of judging and sorting—because I have. But here's the difference: I try to catch myself. I try to focus on understanding. That word—**understanding**—is in the subtitle of this book for a reason.

Shame, too, is no stranger to me. For much of my life, I've struggled with feeling bad about my basic needs—resting, hungering, wanting comfort. That's one of my bears. I know what it's like to shame myself for simply being human. But I've learned that practicing loving, caring, compassionate, and non-judgmental self-acceptance is one of the most powerful antidotes to shame. It's what I coach my clients to do: understand the source of the shame, name it, and reflect on the need you were trying to meet. That's where healing begins.

I think it's time we stop beating up on the old brain. To borrow from Rodney Dangerfield: "I get no respect, no respect!" Maybe it's time we start giving it some.

Writing the chapter on religion and politics was especially clarifying. I realized how caught up I had become in the chaos of the news cycle—the fear, the perceived threats—and how easily that led me to more sorting and judging. Through the writing, I found clarity. I began to see that much of what we're witnessing—whether in politics, religion, or social tension—is really a search for certainty.

And I learned to live with a new truth: the only things that are truly certain are love, compassion, caring, and non-judgment. That realization became my foundation.

That doesn't mean I no longer get triggered—I still feel it in my body: the tight chest, the churn in my stomach. However, I now have solid ground to return to. I understand that people are afraid that the systems once designed to soothe and protect us have, in many ways, become the very sources of threat. And I get it now, truly. And I hope that, through these pages, others can arrive at this place as well. This chapter is about listening to our biology, our needs, our impulses, and, as the next chapter will explore, to what the old brain is trying to tell us through all the noise.

Rewriting Our Relationship with the Old Brain

For too long, we've treated the old brain like an unruly child to be tamed. But the truth is, it has always been loyal. It seeks safety, connection, and continuity.

Our task is to listen differently—to say: "I hear you. I'll drink some water soon." "It's okay to want touch—it's biology, not weakness." In doing so, we begin to befriend what once felt primitive. We build a new partnership between survival and awareness.

Lessons from the End of Life

Australian palliative-care nurse Bronnie Ware spent years listening to her patients' reflections and compiled them in *The Top Five Regrets of the Dying* (2012). Their regrets were remarkably consistent:

- "I wish I'd had the courage to live a life true to myself, not the life others expected of me."

- "I wish I hadn't worked so hard."

- "I wish I'd had the courage to express my feelings."

- "I wish I had stayed in touch with my friends."

- "I wish that I had let myself be happier."

No one said, "I wish I'd sent more emails," or "worked more overtime." At the edge of life, the truth becomes simple: what mattered most were connection, laughter, and rest.

Ware's book is a quiet plea from those at life's threshold to those still racing through it—to listen sooner.

The Call to Action

The invitation of this chapter is clear:

- Listen to your biology.
- Respect your old brain.
- Practice the Four Pillars with yourself.
- Tend to your personal bears with compassion.
- Fill the coping bucket daily.

Because when we calm our own system, we begin to hear what it's been trying to tell us all along. The next chapter turns inward—into the rhythms, impulses, and signals of the old brain itself—and into what happens when we finally learn to listen rather than react.

Resonance

My hope—my goal, my wish—is that these pages become something readers truly resonate with.

Resonating means producing a deep, lasting response—emotional, intellectual, or physical. When something resonates, it vibrates in harmony with something else. The word comes from the Latin *resonance*, meaning "to sound again." When we say an idea or experience resonates with us, we mean it echoes something already inside us—it feels familiar, true, or meaningful on a deeper level.

The success of these pages won't be measured in sales or social media chatter, but in the depth of resonance they evoke. If this book becomes mere information, then I've missed the mark. My work has never been about information alone—it's about transformation that settles into the body.

I've watched resonance happen in real time. I see it in my clients' bodies when these concepts take root—the moment their posture shifts, their chest opens, their tone lightens. There's a spark of relief, even awe. It's not just that they understand something; it's that their biology agrees.

That is my measure of success for this book: to witness change not only in thought, but in body, in nervous system, in lived experience. My continued hope is that these words ripple outward—first in individuals, and maybe, if we're fortunate, across our collective nervous system as well.

Key Takeaways

- **Self-care is biology, not luxury.** The old brain's needs—hydration, nourishment, rest, movement, connection—are not optional; they're the foundation of regulation.

- **Knowing isn't enough.** Insight must become practice. Real change begins when awareness is lived, not just understood.

- **Repetition rewires.** According to Hebb's Law, the brain learns safety by repeatedly experiencing it.

- **"Love, compassion, caring, and non-judgment are regulatory acts."** They calm the threat system and widen our window of tolerance.

- **Shame is not a flaw—it's a signal.** Naming and understanding it transforms self-criticism into self-respect.

- **Partnership is the goal.** We are learning to work WITH our old brain, not against it—respecting its rhythms while guiding it with intention.

- **Resonance matters more than information.** Transformation happens when ideas are felt in the body and echoed in real life.

Exercise — Filling the Cup

Take a few quiet minutes today—no agenda, no timer.
Notice how your body feels after reading this chapter. Ask yourself:

1. **What drains me most right now?**
   (Overwork, disconnection, judgment, fear, lack of rest?)

2. **What fills me fastest?**
(Moments, however small, that bring ease, warmth, or laughter?)

3. **How can I honor my biology this week?**
Choose one simple action—drink water, stretch between tasks, get an early night, text a friend to connect—and commit to it as an act of partnership with your old brain.

4. **Pause and notice.**
As you follow through, sense your body's feedback—breath easing, shoulders softening, heart rate slowing.
This is your old brain saying THANK YOU.

5. **Practicing the Four Pillars with Yourself.**

Set aside a few quiet minutes. This is not about fixing anything — it's about practicing safety.

Think of a moment from today when you felt stressed, self-critical, tired, or overwhelmed. Nothing dramatic — just real.

Now, move slowly through the Four Pillars as if you were comforting a child, a client, or a close friend.

Love
Place a hand on your chest or take a slow breath.
Say to yourself: "I'm here. I'm allowed to be human."
Let your tone soften, even if it feels unfamiliar.

Compassion
Ask gently: "What was hard about that moment?"
See if understanding replaces criticism.

Caring
Ask: "What does my body need right now?"
Water? Movement? Rest? A pause?
Choose one small act of care and follow through.

Non-judgment
Notice any critical thoughts that arise and let them pass without arguing with them.
Try: "This is a nervous system moment, not a character flaw."

Pause again and notice what changes in your body — even slightly.
A softer breath. A quieter mind. Less tension in the shoulders.

That is your coping bucket being refilled.

This practice may feel awkward at first. That's normal. The nervous system learns safety the same way it learned fear — through repetition.

The Four Pillars are not something you achieve.
They are something you practice toward yourself, one moment at a time.

This simple practice marks the start of a partnership.
In the next chapter, we'll stay with that dialogue—learning how to listen more closely to the old brain itself, to the instincts and signals beneath thought, and what they're really trying to protect.

A Brief Note on Polyvagal Theory:

Polyvagal Theory is not without its critics and continues to evolve, as all scientific models do. The very word theory reminds us that it is not a settled or final map of human physiology.

But whatever refinements or debates emerge around vagal pathways, its central insight remains consistent and well supported: safety opens us to connection, and fear constricts us. That principle is echoed across biology, neuroscience, attachment research, and decades of clinical practice.

Even Stephen Porges has emphasized that Polyvagal Theory is an evolving framework, not a finished doctrine. And while aspects of the model continue to be examined and debated, the patterns themselves are unmistakable. I witness them every day in my therapy office.

Whatever language we use, the lived reality is the same: safety opens people, fear constricts them. Connection regulates. Judgment destabilizes. Compassion restores. I see these principles in action, session after session — individually and collectively — and that embodied truth is impossible to ignore.

Chapter 9 – Listening to the Old Brain for Understanding

The Practice of Compassionate Awareness

"When one nervous system finds safety, it can lend it to another."
— *Author unknown*

From Knowledge to Listening

In the last chapter, we focused on refilling—restoring what the nervous system loses when we ignore the body's calls for balance. Now, we turn toward listening.

Listening is where knowledge becomes wisdom. It is the quiet act of hearing the old brain without trying to correct it, debate it, or outthink it.
When we listen, we make space for the full conversation of our biology—its fears, hungers, impulses, and longings.

The goal here isn't mastery; it's understanding. Understanding means that when the old brain speaks in tightness, heat, craving, or fatigue, the new brain responds not with judgment but with curiosity. Listening, in this sense, is both a practice of regulation and a practice of reverence.

The Discipline of Listening

True listening requires the very things modern life discourages, which are stillness, time, and silence.

Our culture teaches us to interrupt—to fill space, to fix, to optimize. But the nervous system doesn't speak the language of speed; it speaks through rhythm and sensation.

Listening to the old brain asks us to slow the tempo until we can sense what's underneath the noise: the heartbeat that races when safety feels distant, the shallow breath of vigilance, the ache for connection we sometimes mistake for weakness.

This kind of listening is not passive—it's active attunement, a partnership between the new brain's awareness and the old brain's messages.

When we do it well, we begin to sense when our system is over-threatened versus under-nourished—and we can respond accordingly.

Why Listening Matters

In therapy sessions, I often notice a client's nervous system answering long before their words do. Their tone softens when they feel seen. Their shoulders lower when I mirror their breath. That's the body listening. That's biology recognizing safety.

This is especially true when I'm using EMDR. More than the words my clients share during processing, it's the story their body tells that guides the work. Sometimes I'll gently point it out:

"You're telling me one story with your words, but your body is telling me another. Can you notice that?"

That moment of noticing often becomes the turning point. Awareness deepens, defenses soften, and new meaning begins to form. It's in those moments—when the words and the body finally begin to speak the same language—that healing accelerates.

The theme is simple but profound: **listen to the body.** It's always been telling the truth—it just needed someone to listen. Listening is how the brain learns it's not alone. It rewrites the internal story from *"Something's wrong with me"* to *"Something in me is speaking."*

That small linguistic shift changes the entire chemistry of the moment—less cortisol, more oxytocin, less defense, more openness.

Listening and Shame

Shame thrives in silence.
It tells us to hide our needs, to apologize for our impulses, to keep our hungers secret.

Listening interrupts that secrecy. When we meet shame with awareness instead of avoidance, we discover that its message isn't *"You're broken"*—it's *"You're scared of being cast out."*

In the therapy room, we name the shame. We bring it out into the open—not with judgment, but with understanding. I often say to clients, *"You are not broken. You are human."*

I can't tell you how often I hear, *"Sorry I'm crying," "Sorry I'm angry," "Sorry I feel this way."* And I gently remind them, *"What do you have to be sorry for? This is the perfect space for all of it—for tears, for anger, for whatever needs a voice."*

Together, we practice what it means to feel without apology. The goal isn't to suppress emotion but to unlearn the reflex of shame—to replace *sorry* with self-acceptance, and to bring that same **non-judgment home to the self.**

Understanding this transforms shame from a verdict into a signal. It becomes something we can care for rather than something we must conquer.

As I wrote earlier, **understanding is the antidote to shame.** Listening is the method by which that antidote is delivered.

Listening as Daily Practice

To listen to the old brain is to build small rituals of awareness into daily life:
• **Morning check-in:** Before reaching for your phone, notice your first breath. Is it shallow or full?
• **Body pause:** When tension arises, ask, *what are you trying to tell me?*
• **Hunger scan:** Before eating, pause—am I physically hungry, emotionally empty, or seeking stimulation?
• **Relational moment:** When someone speaks, listen with your body as well as your ears.

Each small act of listening expands your window of tolerance. It's repetition in the service of connection.

Listening to Others Begins Here

The way we listen to ourselves becomes the model for how we listen to the world.

When we practice non-judgment internally, we can carry that same posture outward—to partners, colleagues, communities, and even those we disagree with.

Listening to our own old brain teaches us the humility needed for collective regulation. Before we can co-regulate, we must learn to self-regulate.

Before we can hold the fear of another, we must make peace with the fear in ourselves.

This is where empathy begins—not as an ideal, but as a biological event.

Key Takeaways — Chapter 9

• Listening is how knowledge becomes wisdom — when we stop correcting the old brain and begin understanding it, regulation can begin.

• The body often speaks before words do — sensation, impulse, and emotion are the nervous system's language of safety and threat. Ultimately, this book is about <u>listening to the body.</u>

• Understanding is the antidote to shame — shame is not proof that something is wrong with you; it is a signal that something inside you needs care.

• Compassionate awareness changes the internal story — moving from judgment to curiosity shifts the nervous system from defense toward connection.

• Small moments of listening build regulation over time — brief daily pauses to notice breath, tension, hunger, or emotion expand the window of tolerance.

• Learning to listen to yourself makes empathy possible — self-regulation becomes the foundation for co-regulation and connection with others.

Exercise —Listening to the Old Brain for Understanding

Set aside **15–30 minutes**—longer if you can—to sit quietly with what you've learned from these pages.

This is not a quick task or worksheet; it's a conversation with your nervous system.

1. Return to the Body — With Love, Compassion, Caring, and Non-Judgment

Begin by finding stillness. Breathe. As you recall what you've read in earlier chapters—and in this one—bring those four guiding principles inward: **love, compassion, caring, and non-judgment.**

Notice where your body responds—perhaps a tightening in your chest, a flutter in your stomach, or subtle "zingers" of sensation.
These are not intrusions; they are your body's language, quietly inviting you to listen.

2. Name the Bears

Reflect on the *modern bears* that have roamed through your thoughts—the inner voices whispering, *I'm too heavy… not smart enough… not lovable… not enough.*

Write them down. These are not truths; they are learned constructs and echoes of fear. Naming them brings them into the light, where they can no longer rule from the shadows.

3. Acknowledge Shame

Pause to notice where shame shows up in your body or your thoughts. Then ask gently:

- What need was I trying to meet when I felt this?
- What fear was I protecting myself from?
- How can I meet that need with kindness instead of criticism?

Remember, **understanding is the antidote to shame.** Shame is not weakness—it's simply a signal that a need has gone unheard.

4. Reframe the Message

For each critical or fearful thought, craft a compassionate response: You may have said some of these things to yourself or something similar.

- "I'm too lazy." → "My body is asking for rest."
- "I shouldn't need anyone." → "Connection is how humans survive."
- "I'm not enough." → "I'm learning to honor my limits and my needs."

- "I'm too heavy." → "My body has carried me through more than most will ever know—it deserves gratitude, not punishment."

- "I'm ugly." → "My body tells the story of everything I've lived through—it deserves care, not critique."

- "I'm unlovable." → "Love isn't earned by perfection; it grows in authenticity and presence."

- "I always mess things up." → "I'm learning, not failing. Mistakes are data, not definitions."

- "I don't deserve happiness." → "Happiness isn't a reward—it's a right that my nervous system can relearn."

- "I'm weak for feeling this way." → "Feeling is strength—it means my system is still open and alive."

- "No one understands me." → "Maybe I can start by understanding myself, gently."

Each reframe turns an old survival pattern into a new act of respect for your biology. These aren't just "nice sentiments" — they're acts of regulation, even if they don't feel true right away.

5. Identify Biological Priorities

List a few tangible ways to honor your old brain this week:
• Drink water regularly.
• Protect your sleep and create evening routines that help you unwind.
• Move your body daily — even gentle stretching counts.
• Allow play, silliness, or quiet rest without guilt.
• Limit the chase for productivity as proof of worth.
• Pause when eating — notice the experience without judgment.
• Invite safe touch back into your life — a hug, a hand squeeze, a brief embrace. The body recognizes safety through contact long before the mind does.

And when it feels right, allow sexuality to be part of that connection too — not as performance or escape, but as an act of wonder, presence, and understanding.

These are not luxuries; they are biological acts of self-preservation.

6. Make a Commitment

Write a short plan—no perfection required—of how you'll
work *with* your old brain instead of against it.
Let your **new brain** serve as a gentle guide, helping to plan and
remind, not criticize or control.

7. Practice with Others

Share what you're learning. Teaching these ideas to someone else—
explaining "the bears," the nervous system, or the old brain—helps
you integrate them more deeply. Each time you model self-kindness,
you invite co-regulation.

8. Feel the Resonance

As you practice, notice how your body responds when you act in
alignment with your biology.
Maybe your breath deepens, your shoulders soften, your tone lightens.
Those are not coincidences—they are **signs of resonance.**
They tell you the old and new brain are finally working together.

Closing Reflection

Real change isn't cognitive—it's *felt*.
Let your new brain hold the map, but let your old brain decide when
you've truly arrived.
When understanding becomes something you can feel in your body,
that's when regulation begins to take root.

The Quiet Conversation

If Chapter 8 was about filling the coping bucket, Chapter 9 is about
learning to hear the *sound* of that water inside you—when it's running
low, when it's overflowing, when it's steady.

Listening is how the nervous system feels respected.
And when respect becomes the tone of our inner life, understanding
becomes possible—within us, and soon, between us.

Bridge to Chapter 10 — The Collective Nervous System

When one nervous system finds safety, it can lend it to another. In the next chapter, we'll explore what happens when this listening expands beyond the individual—how the same biology that connects one heartbeat to another can also repair what has fractured in the world around us.

Chapter 10- The End of Fear, The Beginning of Us-The Honest Beginning

"Community is a place where the connections felt in our hearts make themselves known in the bonds between people, and where the tuggings and pullings of those bonds keep opening our hearts."

— *Parker J. Palmer*

I didn't begin this book from peace. I began it from anger and fear.

It was my way of shouting into the noise, trying to make sense of the hate, the violence, the judging and sorting that seemed to fill everything. My clients were echoing that same tension, that same fear, which only made the urgency inside me grow louder. I felt it in my body — the chaos, the overwhelm, the need for certainty. Maybe you've felt it too.

At first, I thought I would explain why I was right and why others were wrong. But somewhere along the way, I started hearing my own tone. I was sorting. I was judging. I was chasing certainty — just like everyone else.

But something shifted deep in me back in Chapter 8, when I stumbled onto the Four Pillars. And in that moment, it stopped being about winning the argument or being right. It became about the only kind of certainty that actually creates peace:

Love. Compassion. Care. Non-judgment. The highest expressions of safety.

As Kristin Neff (2003) reminds us, self-compassion isn't indulgence — it's the act of meeting our own suffering with the same kindness we'd offer someone we love. The Four Pillars extend outward and inward, turning what appears to be softness into physiological strength.

What struck me — and has stayed with me — was how universal this truth is. These aren't just therapeutic principles; nearly every moral, spiritual, and philosophical tradition has been circling the same core idea for millennia.

Love, compassion, care, and non-judgment are not new. They're ancient biological truths dressed in the language of theology.

This is what the major prophets spoke of, including what Jesus embodied — not doctrine, but regulation. He didn't sort or condemn; he co-regulated through presence. When he encountered fear, he didn't escalate it; he softened it.

Remember, every tradition has its own version of this: *the calm nervous system as sacred ground.* What we call virtue may simply be the biology of safety made visible.

These are not weaknesses; they are signs of a nervous system strong enough to stay open. Because in the end, safety is not just a physical state — it's the body's quiet way of remembering what love has been trying to teach us all along: that peace isn't found through power, but through presence.

And I realized: this was the peace I had been searching for from the beginning — peace grounded not in ideology but in biology. When our most basic needs are met — food, water, warmth, touch, connection, play, rest — the old brain finally stands down. The body knows: we are safe enough.

If we each learn what calms our own system — and we offer that safety forward — then maybe the ripple becomes a wave. Maybe a calmer individual's nervous system can help calm a collective one.

And as I wrote those words, I realized I was feeling them. My body softened.

With clients, I noticed I was listening differently — breathing, pausing, nodding instead of rushing to fix. When clients spoke of chaos, I could finally say, "I get it," and truly mean it.

We're all searching for safety through certainty. All the bears were born from that instinct: *If I can define clearly who is "us" and who is "them," then I'll know where I belong.* And belonging feels good.

But sorting and judging only make us feel safer for a moment — and then they feed the very fear we're trying to escape.

That's the cycle.

I'm not angry anymore.

I'm still a little afraid — not of the world, but of what happens if we don't learn to calm our collective nervous system.

Mostly, I feel sad — sad that in our search for safety, we've mistaken our differences for danger. But maybe that sadness is also a clue — a reminder of how much we still belong to one another.

We're the same tribe, after all. We always have been.

The Great Misdirection

We live in a time when division is packaged as identity.
When certainty is mistaken for safety.
When the loudest voice in the room becomes the measure of truth.
This is the great misdirection: showing us how to feel safe by telling us who to be afraid of.

Our social media feeds, our news cycles, our neighborhoods—they all become battlegrounds.
Us vs. them.
Good vs. bad.
Right vs. wrong.
If you're not with us, you're against us.
If you're unsure, you're in danger.

And so, we tighten our chests.
We pick sides.
We sharpen our tongues.
We impersonate certainty to keep the old brain quiet.

But here's what's really happening underneath:

Ideas have become modern bears.

Once, words about how we vote, how we look, who we love, how we
worship, and where we come from were just that — words.
Descriptions of human variety. Differences to understand, not dangers
to survive.

Now the old brain reacts to a pronoun, a word, a belief, a protest sign,
a hairstyle, a holiday tradition — as if it were a predator in the grass.

The old brain doesn't understand metaphors.
It can't tell the difference between disagreement and danger. Between
a person with a different opinion and a threat to survival.

We have been so bombarded, so overwhelmed, that concepts have
become threats.

Even the word "we" — the notion that we are a single species sharing
a single fate — has become suspicious.
We don't talk about *us* anymore.
Only the fractured versions: *our* group, *our* tribe, *our* side.

There is no unified "we."
Only divided we, which defies the very meaning of the word.

That's the danger of the misdirection:

We think we're defending truth.
We're defending *ourselves*.
But what we're really defending is the illusion of safety.

If you're here, reading this, you've begun to notice that maybe the
loudest battle isn't out there. It's inside— in your body, your nervous
system, your old brain — in that felt sense that something isn't safe.

And maybe, just maybe, the peace you've been chasing doesn't live in winning. It lives in being allowed to sit down.
So before we go any further, take a breath.
Feel your shoulders drop just a bit.

Notice that you're still here. Still safe enough to keep going.

What I Hope You've Learned So Far

If you've come this far, I hope a few things have begun to settle in.

That the fears and impulses you carry aren't "bad" — they're primal wiring doing their best to keep you safe and alive in a world of circuitry that moves too fast. The Old Brain isn't trying to ruin your life; it's trying to save it.

That many of the things we label *good* or *bad* are really just social rules designed to create certainty — beliefs repeated so often that the Old Brain starts treating them as truth. Beliefs become reflexes. Culture becomes biology.

Our sorting and judging give the nervous system a false sense of order. When life feels uncertain or threatening, the Old Brain reaches for categories: right or wrong, us or them, safe or unsafe, a search for clarity. It's an ancient survival reflex trying to find its footing in a complex world. For a moment, it works—certainty feels like safety, calm; the story feels complete. But the relief is short-lived, because every time we divide the world this way, we shrink it. Each judgment isolates us a little more, which makes the world feel even less safe — and the Old Brain doubles down, sorting harder, judging faster, chasing the illusion of safety it just lost. Maybe we can begin to see that we don't need an enemy — especially not each other — but co-regulators in the same search for peace.

Sorting for certainty becomes its own kind of addiction loop. Each new difference spotted brings a rush of reassurance: *I'm right. I'm safe.* But like any high, it fades quickly, and soon we're chasing the next one. At first the differences are obvious — color, body size, sex, ethnicity — but because it's never enough, we keep looking. Eventually, we start hunting for micro-differences, subtle cues that mark who's "in" or "out," until we see differences everywhere. The craving for certainty blinds us to what is shared, what is human, what is alike.

Faith, politics, even personal values can offer real grounding when they orient us toward meaning and care. But when conviction hardens into certainty — when belief becomes a wall instead of a bridge — the Old Brain mistakes that rigidity for protection. What began as safety becomes separation. The nervous system doesn't realize it's defending against its own fear. The only way out of that loop isn't more judgment; it's curiosity and compassion — the two forces that regulate rather than restrict.

And this is where I think back to the chapter on safety and the work of Stan Davis. The truth is, we don't teach our children how to get along with people they *don't* get along with — whether those differences are cultural, personal, or simply temperament. Sadly, that same pattern persists in adults. The binary belief of friend or foe fuels the search for differences. But survival — both personal and collective — depends on learning a third category: classmate, neighbor, coworker, citizen. We don't have to like each other to live well together. We just have to stay in connection long enough for safety to take root.

Some say sorting is God's way, but the stories that endure — whether from faith or history — tell a different truth. The ones who healed, who fed, who reached across the line didn't *sort* first; they *saw* first. That's the difference between fear's version of safety and love's. Biology echoes the same lesson. Our species survived not through exclusion but through cooperation — even when that cooperation was rough, uneven, and far from perfect. The nervous system doesn't calm when it wins; it calms when it connects. Fear sorts to feel safe; love regulates to stay human.

By now, you've met the bears — the ones hiding beneath hunger, shame, sex, comparison, certainty, exhaustion, and fear. You've learned to spot them, name them, and even soften toward them. What began as a Bear Hunt turned out not to be a hunt at all, but a remembering. Along the way, you may have discovered that the bears were never just ours; they belong to the whole tribe. They move through families, workplaces, and nations — old fears dressed in new stories. The work isn't to destroy them, but to see them clearly, together, and, most importantly, to understand them. When we recognize that our growls sound the same, something ancient in us exhales. That shared awareness is how a collective nervous system begins to heal — not through conquest, but through compassion.

Underneath all of this, we are wired to connect. Touch, belonging, relationship — they're not luxuries; they're Old-Brain-approved regulation tools. Polyvagal Theory reminds us that connection is the original safety signal.

And maybe most of all, I hope you've felt — even for a moment — that when you calm your own system, you create a little more space for others to calm too. That is how change begins: not by force, but by biological resonance — or in simpler terms, a felt sense of safety.

You've now reached a central truth of this book — and the foundation of what it means to become an ambassador: someone who understands that resonance is bidirectional.

It's how fear spreads.

And it's also how calm spreads.

Old Brain → resonance → trigger
New Brain → resonance → regulation

It's synchronized biology, not ideology.
Same wiring — just intentionally pointed toward a different outcome.

Healing happens at the speed of connection.
Regulation is the root of compassion, and compassion is the root of change.

But understanding something in theory is one thing.
Letting it change you — that's something else entirely.

Writing this didn't just teach me about the human nervous system.
It taught me about my own.

What Writing This Taught Me

When I began writing, I thought I was studying others — their fears, their impulses, their bears. But the deeper I went, the more I realized I was studying myself.

My Old Brain was right beside me the whole time — trying to protect me from being wrong, from being misunderstood, from being alone on the "outside" of any group. It wanted a side to choose. It wanted a clear enemy. It wanted the comfort of certainty.

It wanted what every human nervous system wants:

Safety.

The more I learned, the more I saw — and the more I felt — in my clients, in my community, in my country, and even in my own family — that most of our conflict isn't really about issues.

It's about people trying not to feel afraid.

The people I disagreed with weren't villains.
They were humans whose Old Brain was ringing the same alarm mine was.

And the moment that clicked, something softened.

My anger melted into curiosity.
My judgment melted into compassion.
My certainty melted into something far more spacious — understanding.

I realized I didn't just want to feel "not afraid." I wanted **us** to feel not afraid.

Because fear isolates. But calm connects.

And once I understood how **my** nervous system responded to threat... I could suddenly see how **ours** responded too.

That's when the scope of this book shifted.
What if it's not only individuals who are dysregulated?

What if our collective nervous system is stuck in survival mode? And once I saw that... there was no unseeing it.

Because before we became a world of strangers, we were a tribe.

The Two Tribes — Then and Now

A. The Old Tribe

Long before screens, politics, and social-media tribes, there was just *the* tribe.
We survived because we had each other.
We shared food. We shared danger. We shared touch.
The sound of the fire was the sound of safety.

Caring, kindness wasn't a virtue — it was resource distribution.
Lovingness wasn't romance — it was attachment that kept infants alive.
Non-judgment wasn't moral — it was trust.
Curiosity wasn't optional — it was how we found water, berries, and better shelter.

We didn't need a sermon to teach compassion. Biology taught us that connection = survival.
We shared laughter.
We shared struggles.
We even shared shit.

Tribal life wasn't a utopia. We shared food, fire, and story — but we also fought, exiled, and sometimes killed. (And I doubt they had many club-control policies back then.) Both compassion and cruelty were acts of survival, born from the same nervous system that could open in empathy one moment and close in fear the next.

The fire came later — both literal and symbolic — as the gathering place where safety, story, and nervous systems intertwined. Our ancestors didn't just share warmth; they shared regulation. Our nervous systems evolved together.

B. The Modern Tribe

Then society changed faster than the Old Brain could update its software.

Now we sort. We judge. We hoard.
We panic-scroll. We outrun ourselves.

We live in a collective nervous system stuck in permanent fight-or-flight — hyperconnected digitally, disconnected biologically.

We have abundance, yet feel scarcity in our bones.
We have neighbors, yet feel alone in our homes.
We have global communication, yet no shared language of safety.

Infrastructure researchers warn it would take just two weeks of disruption — no trucks, no fuel, no supply chains —for society to unravel into survival mode again.

Two weeks from status updates... to *status as threat*.

How did we survive when we needed each other for every breath — yet now, surrounded by plenty, we turn away?

Because when we stopped depending on each other, our bodies never got the memo.

A Traumatized Collective Nervous System

(Hypothesis #2)

This is the second hypothesis I offer in this book — one that emerged naturally as I followed the biology from individuals to communities, and then to the wider world.
What if humanity itself functions like one vast nervous system — capable of trauma, dysregulation, and healing?

We already know that two nervous systems can change each other. Therapists call this co-regulation — we breathe, soften, mirror, and safety spreads. Every therapy modality depends on that truth. The techniques help, but the relationship does the regulating.

If two people can co-regulate… why not more?
Why not a family? A neighborhood? A nation? A planet?

That question led me to a realization I haven't seen articulated in quite this way:
We don't just live in a society.
We live inside a collective nervous system.

Not metaphorically — biologically.

Social neuroscience shows how we absorb each other's emotions — nervous systems syncing whether we intend to or not (Herrando, 2021). Mirror neuron systems help our brains match and mirror the actions, expressions, and even stress of people around us (Decety & Jackson, 2004). Emotional states in crowds can cascade rapidly — panic propagates from person to person as brains attune to perceived danger (Kramer et al., 2014). Our brains even synchronize their rhythms during interaction — literally firing in rhythm together (Hu et al., 2017).

Porges shows that autonomic regulation and social engagement shape how we attach and co-regulate with one another. If that same biology repeats across many people, it suggests these regulatory processes can ripple outward — from caregivers to families, from families to communities, and eventually into culture itself (Porges, 2011).

This isn't a brand-new idea in the abstract — scholars have long discussed collective mindsets — but here's the key distinction: I'm not talking about a spiritual concept. I'm talking about biology at scale.

A collective nervous system is:

- A network of human bodies trying to detect safety or danger together
- Reacting to shared threats
- Resonating with the same fear
- Becoming traumatized together

And if a single nervous system can get stuck in survival mode... so can a collective one.

This isn't finished science. It's a hypothesis — an invitation to notice patterns we are already living:

- Hypervigilance
- Outrage cycles
- Numbing through media and distraction
- Social avoidance and isolation
- A world that feels "on-edge"
- A species bracing for the next blow

Tell me that doesn't sound familiar.
When enough bodies don't feel safe individually...
Society stops feeling safe collectively.
Trauma doesn't stay inside one person's skin.
It spills outward. It resonates. It scales.

And the Old Brain — our ancient threat-detector — isn't built to handle global information, existential fear, or 24/7 crisis alarms.
So it defaults to what it knows:
Survive. Protect the tribe. Identify the enemy.
Which brings us here — the unavoidable conclusion:
Our collective nervous system is stuck in a trauma response.
And once I saw that... I could only think of one next question:
What if we looked at society the same way we look at PTSD?

When a Society Meets the PTSD Criteria

Collective PTSD — Chronic & Complex

If this were a single client sitting in my office, I'd say we're showing classic signs of PTSD — chronic, complex, and unrelenting.

Because PTSD isn't really about what happened.
It's about what the nervous system has had to survive.

And right now, our collective nervous system looks like a client who has:

- been exposed to threat repeatedly
- never had time to recover
- lost a stable sense of safety
- started seeing danger everywhere

Let's walk through the actual DSM-5 diagnostic criteria for PTSD — and you tell me if any of this sounds familiar.

Criterion A — Exposure to Threat or Trauma

To diagnose PTSD, there must be exposure to actual or threatened death, serious injury, or sexual violence—either directly, by witnessing it happen to others, by learning that it occurred to a close family member, or through repeated exposure to distressing details (as often happens in professional roles such as first responders, journalists, or therapists). These events must fall outside the range of ordinary human experience, evoke intense fear, helplessness, or horror, and cause significant disruption in a person's ability to live and function.

Ask yourself:

- How many mass shootings have you seen in the news over the past few years?
- How often do you encounter videos of violence before breakfast?
- How many times has your body braced watching strangers get hurt?
- How much fear have you absorbed — not from personal experiences — but from the collective ones?
- Our nervous systems were never meant to handle:
- schools doing active shooter drills
- threats of war in every headline
- real-time footage of harm spreading around the world
- families worrying if their kids will come home today

As you read that list, notice what your body is doing.

We're not hearing about danger anymore.
We're witnessing it — again and again — in full sensory detail.

The Old Brain does not distinguish:

"This is happening on my street" vs.
"This is happening on a screen."

It only asks one question:

Am I safe?
Increasingly, the answer is **no**.

Criterion B — Intrusive Symptoms

PTSD causes the mind to relive danger even when it isn't present. For the collective?

- Outrage cycles
- Breaking news alerts
- Replayed footage
- "Never forget" narratives
- Communities re-triggered every time another trauma echoes the last
- Intrusions are no longer private nightmares. They are shared — across entire populations.

Criterion C — Avoidance

When the world feels unsafe, the nervous system avoids what hurts. Individually, PTSD looks like:

- shutting down
- isolating
- refusing reminders of trauma

Collectively, it looks like:

- political polarization
- echo chambers
- blocking and unfriending
- "I want to disconnect from everyone and everything" energy

Avoidance feels protective. But it shrinks our world.

Criterion D — Negative Thoughts & Mood

Trauma rewrites beliefs:

"I can't trust anyone." "The world is dangerous." "People are terrible."

Look around:

- compassion fatigue
- cynicism as culture
- collapsing belief in institutions
- high mistrust across groups

- loneliness as an epidemic

The Old Brain thinks pessimism = protection. But pessimism becomes prison.

Criterion E — Alterations in Arousal & Reactivity.

This is where the trauma body **acts out**:

- Hypervigilance
- Hair-trigger reactions
- Rage outbursts
- Poor sleep
- Constant scanning

Sound familiar? As a society:

- We rage-scroll
- We panic-buy
- We blast each other online
- We assume bad intent fast
- We snap at tiny threats
- We are tired *all the time*

We are a species living like our lives are on the line — every day.

If this were one client...

As my client, across from me in session, I would look you in the eyes — gently, steadily — and say:

> "Your body has been in survival mode for too long. You are not flawed, or weak — you are overwhelmed."

If you apply that same compassion to all of us, the conclusion becomes clear: The collective body is locked in fight, flight, or freeze.
And here's the part that gives us hope:

If a society can mirror trauma, it can also mirror healing.

Not through arguments.
Not through ideology.
But through safety, co-regulation, and time.

Which brings us to what matters most:
Which brings us to something essential — maybe *the* most essential thing:

Good Ole Brain Compassion: You're Overwhelmed, Not Broken

If you were my client sitting across from me in session, I would remind you that "You're not broken. You are overwhelmed."
Because the Old Brain — that ancient guard dog inside you — was built for very specific kinds of danger:

- predators in the brush
- sudden attacks
- short bursts of terror
- run → hide → shake it off → return to the fire

It was designed for short-term survival, not long-term fear. But modern danger?
Modern bears? They don't leap from bushes.

They glow and scream from screens. They follow us home.
They repeat — every hour, every day, every year.
And your Old Brain is doing exactly what evolution taught it to do:

"If something might kill you...focus on it. Stare at it. Don't look away."

So, it keeps watch. All night. All day. Without rest.
Survival mode gets the job done —but it is a miserable place to live.
Survival mode means:

- Sleep is shallow
- Joy is muted
- Curiosity is gone
- Play feels dangerous
- The connection feels risky
- Danger is everywhere

Survival mode is: "Just get through the day."
Clients come to my office and whisper, "I feel like a crazy person."

And every time, I say: "You are not crazy. Crazy is what happened to you."
You are responding perfectly to a world that has been anything but.

Your Old Brain thinks it's helping —that hypervigilance equals protection —because it's one job is to keep you alive.

It doesn't care:

- If you look at irrational
- If you seem dramatic
- If others judge you
- If your coping makes sense

All it cares about is: "Did we survive today?"
And here's where the shame tries to move in:
We look at our coping — the food, the substances, the scrolling, the isolation — and we label ourselves:

- weak
- dramatic
- broken
- "too much"

But those aren't failures. Those are strategies.
Strategies created by a mind that loves you enough to keep you alive through anything.

The Old Brain doesn't need punishment. It needs permission.
It needs a place to finally say: "Something scared me.
And I didn't know how to stop being scared."

I tell my clients: "Your old brain has a story to tell — and it's stored in sensations, not sentences. It's doing exactly what it was meant to do: survive."

It's a story told through tight chests, jumpy reactions, sleepless nights, tears you can't quite explain.

And every single time a client hears this… shoulders drop.
Their breathing loosens.
Their eyes soften.
Because for the first time, they understand: they weren't failing.
This isn't a weakness.
This is your body remembering what your mind tried to survive.
And now — as a species — we are all surviving together.
Our old brains are on high alert… not because we are flawed… but because the world has been frightening.
This isn't where the story ends — it's where the healing begins.

The Compass

Do you still have that compass from Chapter 8?
No worries if you need to flip back and remind yourself—go ahead, I'll wait.

…Got it? Good.

You're going to need it here.

That compass is more than a metaphor. It's what will make this next landscape navigable. In simple terms, it looks like this:

The Compass — Ventral Vagal (The Four Pillars)
The Mountains — Threat, culture, modern bears, collective dysregulation
The Navigation — Co-regulation, compassion, the ripple effect

This is our biological map.

The earlier chapters helped you see the terrain ahead—the steep mountains of fear, the cultural cliffs, the loose gravel of shame, the fog of uncertainty, and the sudden drop-offs shaped by our modern bears. These are the conditions we move through every day. The mountains aren't just obstacles out there somewhere; they form the landscape of our inner world as well.

And the compass—the Four Pillars, the ventral vagal state—is what might give us an actual chance of finding our way.

Because when we shift our internal state into a ventral vagal state, something remarkable happens. We gain access to an experience we often label as emotion, but which, I believe, is deeply biological: **hope.**

Yes, hope.

Hope itself may be a mammalian autonomic event—a natural consequence of what the Four Pillars restore inside us. And here's what matters most:

Hope moves.
It shifts.
It travels.
It spreads.

Just like fear.
Just like safety.

Once our nervous system feels even a small dose of hope, it ripples outward—through our tone, our eyes, our presence, our pacing, the softness in our gestures. And that ripple can reach others, changing their internal landscape as well.

This is why the compass matters.
This is what the rest of this chapter will explore.

The Ambassador – A Biological Invitation (Felt Sense)

We've reached a point where understanding isn't the finish line — it's the doorway. What comes next isn't moral instruction or spiritual philosophy. It isn't politics. It's biology. The nervous system is non-negotiable. You can disagree with ideas, but the body will always tell the truth. And that truth is this:

- Regulation spreads.
- Dysregulation spreads.
- Connection spreads.
- So does fear.

So, before we talk about changing the world, we have to begin with a quieter revolution — inside your own skin.

Take a moment and thumb back through this journey. Remember when something in a chapter made your chest tighten, or your jaw clench, or your breath stop short? That was your Old Brain raising a paw: *"Hey — that's one of my bears."*

And remember when something softened you — a spark of recognition, a moment of "Oh... that makes sense"? That was your nervous system receiving a safety signal.
You weren't just learning.
You were *feeling*.

That's been the whole point.
Knowledge changes thoughts.
Felt sense changes lives.

I've watched it for years in my therapy room. When a client understands something intellectually, it's interesting. But when they understand it in their body, when fear eases even a little and safety takes one small breath... that's healing.

 It is the sacred moment I get to witness — the nervous system remembering something ancient:

"I was never meant to survive alone."
And here's the leap we are making now:
If dysregulation can spread person-to-person... then regulation can too.
That is what an ambassador is —not someone who carries a doctrine, but someone who carries a feeling.

You begin with yourself:

Love?
Caring, kindness toward your own fear.
Compassion toward your own survival strategies. Care for your own signals.
Non-judgment toward your own imperfections.

You teach your nervous system:

"I am safe enough inside myself."
From that state, you can step toward another nervous system.
When you soften your eyes instead of narrowing them... When you listen without rushing to correct...When you let curiosity replace certainty...
When you allow differences without assigning danger... Their Old Brain hears:
"I am safe enough with you."
Not because you agreed.
Not because you convinced them.
Not because you won the point.

But because your biology offered them a better state to borrow.
That's how healing moves: One breath regulating the next.
One steady presence calming a room. One nervous system lowering its guard —and another following suit.

Not ideology.
Biology.

We've tried moralizing ("Be nicer").
We've tried logic ("Here's why you're wrong").
We've tried shame ("Only bad people think that").
None of that regulates the Old Brain.
All of it inflames it.

You don't calm modern bears with better arguments.
You calm them by being someone they feel safe around. That's the sequence:
Regulate yourself. Then regulate between.

Then watch the room change.

Not: "Be better. Behave better."
But: "Be regulated enough to choose better."
This is empowerment, not perfection.
Agency, not criticism. Resonance, not coercion.

You don't have to change your beliefs.
You don't have to surrender your tribe.
You don't have to abandon identity.

Just don't sacrifice your nervous system —or someone else's —for the illusion of certainty.

We don't heal the world by winning debates.
We heal it by letting our biology lead.
Because beneath every argument and opinion and label, we all share:

- the same Old Brain
- the same chemistry
- the same fear of not belonging
- the same desire to survive

Different beliefs.
Same species.
Different thoughts.
Same needs.
Difference was never the danger. Fear was.

And fear can change — as soon as one nervous system signals: "It's safe enough to be human here." That's the Ambassador's work.
Not to convert.

But to co-regulate.
Not to erase disagreement.
But to create enough safety to hold it together.
Not to craft perfect beliefs.
But to breathe in a way that invites life into the room.

Imagine what could happen if each of us found just three people — friends, coworkers, family — and shared not the theory, but the felt experience you've had while reading this book. The moment your chest softened. The moment your Old Brain stopped bracing. The moment you remembered: "Most people are just trying not to feel afraid." Three people sharing with three more...then three more... And suddenly calm travels faster than fear. Not a movement of ideas. A movement of nervous systems. A quiet, unstoppable contagion of safety. And if you're thinking, "I'm not sure I felt it..." That's okay.

Just try the Four Pillars anyway.

Because **Love isn't weakness** — it is courage born of safety.
Compassion isn't agreeableness — it's steadiness in the face of fear.

Care isn't coddling — it's anchoring the body before it collapses.
And non-judgment isn't passivity — it's choosing curiosity over defense.

If you give someone the gift of feeling regulated in your presence...
You have already changed their world.

This is the new activism: Not protest first — presence first.
Not fixing people — facing people.

Not certainty —safety.
Your nervous system is not small.
It is contagious. You are not one person in a broken world.
You are one node in a healing network that is older than history.
and smarter than fear.

So here, near the end, is the real invitation:
Become the calm your tribe can borrow.
Become the reminder that we survive together.
Become the Ambassador your biology designed you to be. This isn't utopian.
This isn't sentimental.

This is the oldest science we've ever lived. And it just might save us.

The Chorus of Us-*Hopeful • Connected • Quietly Courageous*

If you listen closely — beneath the noise, beneath the shouting and certainty — you can still hear the sound of something ancient.
The sound of humans gathered near a fire.
The crackle of warmth.

The hush of night. The soft rhythm of breathing that says:
"We are safe enough to rest."
We have forgotten that sound for a while.
Our Old Brains have been working overtime, guarding the tribe as if danger lives everywhere. But safety was always meant to be a shared experience.
Not earned.
Not argued for.

Not withheld until agreement.
Just felt.

Together.

We are a nervous system stretched across the whole world — still learning how to regulate at scale. Still learning how to trust. Still learning that connection is not the enemy of difference. Still learning that fear is not the same as truth.
And yet — look how far we've come.

You are here, reading these words.
Feeling your breath again.
Remembering something your biology knew before language: We survive by calming each other.
If your nervous system softened even a little on this journey —if something in you loosened, even briefly —then you are already part of what comes next.

Because regulation doesn't stay inside one body.

It ripples.
It spreads.
It invites.

One steady presence can change a room.
One moment of compassion can shift a day.
One nervous system at peace can become a refuge.

And peace — real peace — is simply a collection of regulated moments, shared. Real peace is a regulated collective nervous system. And when that happens, we may finally experience what could be called "collective wellbeing" (Kemp et al., 2022).

So, here is the final invitation:
Sit a little closer to the fire.
Let your shoulders drop.
Let your breath widen.
Let yourself be human with other humans.
And when someone near you feels afraid...
when their words come out sharp or certain or small...
offer your nervous system before you offer your opinion.

You don't have to convert them.
You don't have to fix them.

You just have to help their Old Brain feel a bit less alone.
Because that is how a species heals —not all at once, but one body
remembering safety
in the presence of another.

We are not done becoming.
We are not done learning how to be together.
We are not done discovering how much we belong.
Fear may have been our first language.
But safety is our oldest one.

Breathe.

Stay open.
Let them borrow your calm.

And when the world feels too loud again —
Look for the ones near the fire.
Look for the Ambassadors.
Look for us.

We are the chorus. We always were. And now...
we remember.

Mountains in My Mind — The Passage

When I began this book, I thought it was about conquering something—climbing the mountains in my mind, proving I could rise above the chaos.
But the more I wrote, the more I kept thinking of the Chris Stapleton song *Mountains of My Mind* and the way he sings about never quite reaching those internal peaks.

Somewhere in the writing, something shifted.
I slowly realized it was never about reaching the peaks at all.
I didn't need to climb the mountains.
There was a path through them.

And that discovery — that calming — changed everything. It turns out I wasn't looking for a summit; I was looking for a way forward. A way to finally feel at home in my own nervous system. A way I've quietly been searching for my whole life.

Maybe that's why I became a social worker in the first place — to help others, yes, but also to find myself. To find my way. Writing this book gave me that path.

I've crossed the rugged pass. Not without fear. Not without effort. Not without the moments where the trail disappeared, and I had to feel my way forward through the dark.

But now I understand what I didn't fully grasp when I started: The mountains weren't there to be conquered. They were there to be walked together.

So, if you feel ready — even a little — I hope you'll take a few steps on this path yourself. You won't be alone. I've left lanterns along the way, so you don't get lost.

And when you arrive — whenever that is — I'll be waiting by the fire with a warm smile and a space held by the four pillars we've built — love, compassion, care, and non-judgment — steady enough for you to rest your feet.

Appendix A:

The Four Pillars & The Physiology of Peace

Why Love, Compassion, Care, and Non-Judgment Are Biological Necessities — Not Moral Niceties

Throughout this book, I've returned to a simple truth:
Human beings cannot thrive in a nervous system dominated by fear.
Sorting, judging, withdrawing, defending — these are not character flaws but biological threat-responses.

What calms that system is equally biological.

The Four Pillars—**Love, Compassion, Care, and Non-Judgment**—are not sentimental ideas.
They are forms of *regulation*.
Across biology, psychology, neuroscience, and spirituality, these same principles repeatedly appear as the states in which humans become wise, relational, and fully alive.

What follows is an overview of how each pillar operates in the body, and why they matter not only for personal well-being but for the collective nervous system we all participate in.

1. LOVE — The Biology of Safety

Love is not merely an emotion; it is the body's most advanced safety signal.

When love is present, the **ventral vagal system** activates:

- breath slows
- facial muscles soften
- vocal tone warms
- The prefrontal cortex (our reasoning and relational center) comes back online.
- The amygdala quiets

Love pulls us out of defense and into openness.
It tells the old brain: *"You are safe enough to connect."*

Why this matters:
A regulated system does not need to judge, sort, or defend.
Love removes threat at its biological root.

2. COMPASSION — The Antidote to Fear

Compassion shifts the nervous system from protection to presence.

Neuroscience shows that compassion:

- reduces amygdala activation
- increases vagal tone
- expands the window of tolerance
- enhances empathy and perspective-taking
- releases oxytocin, deepening social connection

Compassion doesn't excuse suffering — it meets it.
It transforms fear into understanding.

Why this matters:
Compassion interrupts the cycle of reactivity.
It opens space for reflection, nuance, and shared humanity.

3. CARE — Our Oldest Survival Strategy

Long before modern society, mammals survived through **co-regulation**:
huddling, grooming, soothing, orienting, and watching over one another.

Care is not a moral virtue.
It is an **evolutionary necessity**.

When we care for others or receive care:

- cortisol drops
- immunity strengthens
- heart rhythms synchronize

- trust increases
- The nervous system stands down.

Care satisfies the oldest biological requirement we have:
"Do I belong somewhere?"

Why this matters:
Belonging turns off threat responses faster than logic ever can.

4. NON-JUDGMENT — The Physiology of Openness

Judgment is a threat-reduction strategy.
When the world feels unsafe, the old brain categorizes everything into:
safe/not safe, us/them, right/wrong.

Non-judgment:

- increases prefrontal cortex activity

- reduces limbic reactivity

- stabilizes emotional regulation

- increases tolerance for ambiguity

- supports curiosity over fear

Importantly, non-judgment doesn't mean passivity or permissiveness.
It means the nervous system is regulated enough to stay *open*.

Why this matters:
We cannot learn, listen, or love from inside a threat response.
Non-judgment makes a relationship possible.

Why These Four Pillars Appear in Every Wisdom Tradition

Psychology calls them regulation.
Neuroscience calls them safety signals.
Evolutionary biology calls them survival strategies.
Theology calls them love, mercy, grace, and compassion.
Philosophy calls them virtues.

Different languages.
Same biological truth.

Every field of human understanding has been pointing to the same nervous-system realities all along.

Before religion was moral instruction, it was trauma medicine:

- "Be not afraid."
- "Love one another."
- "Judge not…"
- "Peace be with you."

These weren't doctrines.
They were **regulatory strategies** disguised as spiritual teachings.

The Collective Nervous System

While these pillars transform individual biology, they also shape the collective.

When one person brings Love, Compassion, Care, and Non-Judgment into an interaction:

- heart rates synchronize
- tone shifts
- mirror neurons adjust
- threat decreases
- connection increases

Calm is contagious — just as fear is.

The Four Pillars are how an individual's nervous system becomes part of a calmer *collective* one.

The Takeaway

The Four Pillars are not virtues.
They are **biological necessities**.

They are what the nervous system looks like when it is at its strongest—
awake, open, steady, and connected.

They are the states in which humans think clearly, love generously, play honestly, and live without fear.

They are, quite literally, the physiology of peace.

And if enough of us practice them, even inconsistently, the ripple becomes a wave.

Because every regulated person becomes one less frightened person in the world—
And that is how the collective nervous system begins to heal.

REFERENCES

Note: *The following works informed and inspired the ideas presented throughout this book. While every effort has been made to ensure accuracy and faithful representation, this text is an interpretive synthesis intended for reflection and education—not a clinical manual. Some scientific concepts are summarized or paraphrased from publicly available abstracts and review articles when full access to primary sources was limited. If any detail is imperfect or a citation incomplete, I ask that it be read in the spirit in which this book was written, with respect, good faith, and an honest attempt to bridge science, story, and the old brain's lived truth. Above all, these references are included not to establish certainty, but to show lineage—to acknowledge the researchers, clinicians, and thinkers whose work continues to deepen our shared understanding of the human nervous system and its capacity for healing.*

Ainsworth, M. D. S., Blehar, M. C., Waters, E., & Wall, S. (1978). Patterns of attachment: A psychological study of the strange situation. Hillsdale, NJ: Erlbaum.

Allen, S. M., & Hawkins, A. J. (1999). Maternal gatekeeping: Mothers' beliefs and behaviors that inhibit greater father involvement in family work. Journal of Marriage and the Family, 61(1), 199–212.

Armstrong, L. E., Ganio, M. S., Casa, D. J., Lee, E. C., McDermott, B. P., Klau, J. F., Jimenez, L., Le Bellego, L., Chevillotte, E., & Lieberman, H. R. (2012). Mild dehydration affects mood in healthy young women. The Journal of Nutrition, 142(2), 382–388.

Bagemihl, B. (1999). Biological exuberance: Animal homosexuality and natural diversity. St. Martin's Press.

Bailey, J. M., Dunne, M. P., & Martin, N. G. (2000). Genetic and environmental influences on sexual orientation and its correlates in an Australian twin sample. Journal of Personality and Social Psychology, 78(3), 524–536.

Bancroft, J. (2005). The endocrinology of sexual arousal. Journal of Endocrinology, 186(3), 411–427.

Bartlik, M. T., Goldstein, A. T., & Meston, C. M. (Eds.). (2018). Integrative sexual health. Oxford University Press.

Bauman, Z. (2007). Consuming life. Polity Press.

Baumeister, R. F., Catanese, K. R., & Vohs, K. D. (2001). Is there a gender difference in the strength of sex drive? Theoretical views, conceptual distinctions, and a review of relevant evidence. Personality and Social Psychology Review, 5(3), 242–273.

Berridge, K. C., & Kringelbach, M. L. (2015). Pleasure systems in the brain. Neuron, 86(3), 646–664.

Berridge, K. C., & Robinson, T. E. (2016). Liking, wanting, and the incentive-sensitization theory of addiction. American Psychologist, 71(8), 670–679. https://doi.org/10.1037/amp0000059

Berry, A., Brady, S. S., Burgio, K. L., Cunningham, S. D., Gahagan, S., James, A. S., Kane Low, L., & Newman, D. K. (2025). Associations between U.S. women's toileting behaviors and lower urinary tract symptoms: A cross-sectional analysis of Rise for Health study data. Journal of Women's Health. Advance online publication. https://doi.org/10.1089/jwh.2024.0743

Bordo, S. (2003). Unbearable Weight: Feminism, Western Culture, and the Body. University of California Press.

Bowlby, J. (1969). Attachment and loss: Vol. 1. Attachment. New York: Basic Books.

Boyd, Robert, and Peter J. Richerson. The Origin and Evolution of Cultures. Oxford University Press, 2005.

Brosschot, J. F., Verkuil, B., & Thayer, J. F. (2018). Generalized Unsafety Theory of Stress: Unsafe environments and conditions inhibit parasympathetic activity. Psychophysiology, 55(9), e13223. https://doi.org/10.1111/psyp.13223

Brown, B. (2012). Daring Greatly: How the courage to be vulnerable transforms the way we live, love, parent, and lead. Gotham Books.

Brown, S., & Vaughan, C. (2009). Play: How it shapes the brain, opens the imagination, and invigorates the soul. Penguin.

Burghardt, G. M. (2005). The Genesis of Animal Play: Testing the Limits. Cambridge, MA: MIT Press.

Carmichael, M. S., Warburton, V. L., Dixen, J., & Davidson, J. M. (1994). Relationships among cardiovascular, muscular, and oxytocin responses during human sexual activity. Archives of Sexual Behavior, 23(1), 59–79.

Carson, E. A. (2023). Prisoners in 2022 – Statistical tables (NCJ 306273). Bureau of Justice Statistics, U.S. Department of Justice.

Centers for Disease Control and Prevention. (2024, May 16). Intimate partner violence, sexual violence, and stalking: Quick facts — Data from the 2016/2017 NISVS; updated fact sheet. https://www.cdc.gov/intimate-partner-violence/about/index.html

Cohen, S., & Wills, T. A. (1985). Stress, social support, and the buffering hypothesis. Psychological Bulletin, 98(2), 310–357.

Cohen, S., Miller, G. E., & Rabin, B. S. (2001). Psychological stress and antibody response to immunization: a critical review of the human literature. Biopsychosocial Science and Medicine, 63(1), 7-18.

Copeland, W. E., Wolke, D., Angold, A., & Costello, E. J. (2013). Adult psychiatric outcomes of bullying and being bullied by peers in childhood and adolescence. JAMA Psychiatry, 70(4), 419 426. https://doi.org/10.1001/jamapsychiatry.2013.504

Corona, G., Rastrelli, G., Monami, M., Meserole, E., Jannini, E. A., Balercia, G., Sforza, A., Forti, G., Mannucci, E., & Maggi, M. (2013). Frequency of sexual activity and cardiovascular risk in subjects with erectile dysfunction: Cross-sectional and longitudinal analyses. Andrology, 1(6), 864–871. https://doi.org/10.1111/j.2047-2927.2013.00139.

Cozolino, L. (2014). The neuroscience of human relationships: Attachment and the developing social brain (2nd ed.). W. W. Norton.

Crompton, L. (2003). Homosexuality and civilization. Harvard University Press.

Cunningham, G. R., Stephens-Shields, A. J., Rosen, R. C., Wang, C., Bhasin, S., Matsumoto, A. M., Parsons, J. K., Gill, T. M., Molitch, M. E., & Farrar, J. T. (2016). Testosterone treatment and sexual function in older men with low testosterone levels. The Journal of Clinical Endocrinology & Metabolism, 101(8), 3096–3104. https://doi.org/10.1210/jc.2016-1645

Davis, S. (2007). Schools where everyone belongs: Practical strategies for reducing bullying (2nd ed.). Research Press.

Decety, J., & Jackson, P. L. (2004). The functional architecture of human empathy. Behavioral and Cognitive Neuroscience Reviews, 3(2), 71– 100. https://doi.org/10.1177/1534582304267187

Dickerson, S. S., Mycek, P. J., & Zaldivar, F. (2008). Negative social evaluation, but not mere social presence, elicits cortisol responses to a laboratory stressor task. Health Psychology, 27(1), 116–121. https://doi.org/10.1037/0278-6133.27.1.116

Dim, E. E., & Lysova, A. (2022). Male victims' experiences with and perceptions of the criminal justice response to intimate partner abuse. Journal of Interpersonal Violence, 37(17–18), NP13067–NP13091

Ditzen, B., Neumann, I. D., Bodenmann, G., von Dawans, B., Turner, R. A., Ehlert, U., & Heinrichs, M. (2007). Effects of different kinds of couple interaction on cortisol and heart rate responses to stress in women. Psychoneuroendocrinology, 32(5), 565–574.

Dixson, A. F. (2012). Primate sexuality: Comparative studies of the prosimians, monkeys, apes, and humans. Oxford University Press.

Domina, T. et al. (2024). "Universal Free School Meals Might Improve Discipline Rates." Education Week.

Dunbar, Robin. Grooming, Gossip, and the Evolution of Language. Harvard University Press, 1996.

Dwork, D. (1991). Children With a Star: Jewish Youth in Nazi Europe. Yale University Press.

Eckstein, M., Mamaev, I., Ditzen, B., & Sailer, U. (2020). Calming effects of touch in human, animal, and robotic interaction — scientific state-of-the-art and technical advances. Frontiers in Psychiatry, 11, Article 555058. https://doi.org/10.3389/fpsyt.2020.555058

Eisenberger, N. I. (2012). The neural bases of social pain: Evidence for shared representations with physical pain. Psychosomatic Medicine, 74(2), 126–135.

Fashemi, B., Delaney, M. L., Onderdonk, A. B., & Fichorova, R. N. (2013). Effects of feminine hygiene products on the vaginal mucosal biome. Microbial Ecology in Health and Disease, 24(1).

Fazio, L. K., Brashier, N. M., Payne, B. K., & Marsh, E. J. (2015). Knowledge does not protect against illusory truth. Journal of Experimental Psychology: General, 144(5), 993–1002. https://doi.org/10.1037/xge0000098

Felitti, V. J., Anda, R. F., Nordenberg, D., Williamson, D. F., Spitz, A. M., Edwards, V., Koss, M. P., & Marks, J. S. (1998). Relationship of childhood abuse and household dysfunction to many of the leading causes of death in adults: The Adverse Childhood Experiences (ACE) study. American Journal of Preventive Medicine, 14(4), 245–258. https://doi.org/10.1016/S0749-3797(98)00017-8

Field, T. (2010). Touch for socioemotional and physical well-being: A review. Developmental Review, 30(4), 367–383. https://doi.org/10.1016/j.dr.2011.01.001

Field, T. (2014). Touch. Cambridge, MA: MIT Press.

Fischler, C. (1988). Food, self, and identity. Social Science Information, 27(2), 275–292.

Floyd, K. (2006). Communicating affection: Interpersonal behavior and social context. Cambridge University Press.

Frappier, J., Toupin, I., Levy, J. J., Aubertin-Leheudre, M., & Karelis, A. D. (2013). Energy expenditure during sexual activity in young healthy couples. PLOS ONE, 8(10), e79342. https://doi.org/10.1371/journal.pone.0079342

Ganio, M. S., Armstrong, L. E., Casa, D. J., McDermott, B. P., Lee, E. C., Yamamoto, L. M., Marzano, S., Lopez, R. M., Jimenez, L., Le Bellego, L., Chevillotte, E., & Lieberman, H. R. (2011). Mild dehydration impairs cognitive performance and mood of men. British Journal of Nutrition, 106(10), 1535–1543.

Gordon, N. (2018). School nutrition and student discipline: Effects of universal school meals (NBER Working Paper No. 24986). National Bureau of Economic Research. https://www.nber.org/papers/w24986

Grewen, K. M., Anderson, B. J., Girdler, S. S., & Light, K. C. (2003). Warm partner contact is related to lower cardiovascular reactivity. Behavioral Medicine, 29(3), 123–130. https://doi.org/10.1080/08964280309596065

Gross, J. J. (1998). The emerging field of emotion regulation: An integrative review. Review of General Psychology, 2(3), 271–299.

Gross, S. (2021). The power of play: A pediatrician's perspective on playful learning. In D. R. Weisberg, K. Hirsh-Pasek, R. M. Golinkoff, B. Scipione, & D. L. Golinkoff (Eds.), The Playful Classroom: The Power of Play for All Ages. Philadelphia, PA: Temple University Press.

Gulledge, A. K., Gulledge, M. H., & Stahmann, R. F. (2003). Romantic physical affection and relationship satisfaction. American Journal of Family Therapy, 31(4), 233–242.

Gurven, M., & Hill, K. (2009). Why do men hunt? A reevaluation of "Man the Hunter" and the sexual division of labor. Current Anthropology, 50(1), 51–74. https://doi.org/10.1086/595620

Hafner, M., Stepanek, M., Taylor, J., Troxel, W. M., & van Stolk, C. (2017). Why sleep matters: The economic costs of insufficient sleep. RAND Corporation. https://doi.org/10.7249/RR1791

Hambach, A., Evers, S., Summ, O., Husstedt, I. W., & Frese, A. (2013). The impact of sexual activity on idiopathic headaches: An observational study. Cephalalgia, 33(6), 384–389.

Hamilton, M. (2010). Sex disparities in arrest outcomes for domestic violence. Journal of Interpersonal Violence, 25(8), 1340–1357. https://doi.org/10.1177/0886260509340541

Hanks, C. (Director). (2025). John Candy: I Like Me [Film]. Amazon Studios/Maximum Effort (Prime Video).

Hawkley, L. C., & Cacioppo, J. T. (2010). Loneliness matters: A theoretical and empirical review of consequences and mechanisms. Annals of Behavioral Medicine, 40(2), 218–227.

Hebb, D. O. (1949). The organization of behavior: A neuropsychological theory. Wiley.

Henrich, J. (2015). The Secret of Our Success: How Culture Is Driving Human Evolution, Domesticating Our Species, and Making Us Smarter. Princeton University Press.

Herrando, C., & Constantinides, E. (2021). Emotional contagion: A brief overview and future directions. Frontiers in Psychology, 12, 712606.

Hines, M. (2011). Gender development and the human brain. Annual Review of Neuroscience, 34, 69–88.

Hirschel, D. (2008). Domestic Violence Cases: What research shows about arrest and dual arrest rates. U.S. Department of Justice, Office of Justice Programs, National Institute of Justice.

Hirschel, D., & McCormack, P. D. (2021). Same-sex couples and the police: A 10-year study of arrest and dual arrest rates in responding to incidents of intimate partner violence. Violence Against Women, 27(9), 1119–1149.

Hochschild, A. R. (1983). The managed heart: Commercialization of human feeling. University of California Press.

Holt-Lunstad, J., Smith, T. B., & Layton, J. B. (2010). Social relationships and mortality risk: A meta-analytic review.PLoS Medicine, 7(7), e1000316. https://doi.org/10.1371/journal.pmed.1000316

Hrdy, S. B. (2009). Mothers and Others: The Evolutionary Origins of Mutual Understanding. Harvard University Press.

Hu, Y., Li, X., Pan, Y., Cheng, X., & Yinying, H. (2017). Brain-to-brain synchronization across two persons predicts mutual prosociality. Social Cognitive and Affective Neuroscience, 12(11), 1835–1844.

Huis in 't Veld, E. M. J., & de Gelder, B. (2015). From personal fear to mass panic: The neurological basis of crowd perception. Human Brain Mapping, 36(6), 2338–2351. https://doi.org/10.1002/hbm.22774

Irwin, M. R. (2015). Why sleep is important for health: A psychoneuroimmunology perspective. Annual Review of Psychology, 66, 143–172.

Jeon, H., & Lee, S. H. (2018). From neurons to social beings: a short review of the mirror neuron system research and its socio-psychological and psychiatric implications. Clinical Psychopharmacology and Neuroscience, 16(1), 18.

Johnson, S. M. (2004). The practice of emotionally focused couple therapy: Creating connection. Brunner-Routledge.

Kashi, D. S., Hunter, M., Edwards, J. P., Zemdegs, J., Lourenço, J., Mille, A.-C., Perrier, E. T., Dolci, A., Walsh, N. P., & [additional authors as per full list if known] (2025). Habitual fluid intake and hydration status influence cortisol reactivity to acute psychosocial stress. Journal of Applied Physiology, 139(3), Article 698. https://doi.org/10.1152/japplphysiol.00408.2025

Kemp, A. H., Koenig, J., & Thayer, J. F. (2022). The complex construct of well-being and the role of vagal function. Frontiers in Integrative Neuroscience, 16, Article 925664.

Killgore, W. D. S. (2010). Effects of sleep deprivation on cognition. Progress in Brain Research, 185, 105–129. https://doi.org/10.1016/B978-0-444-53702-7.00007-5

King, M. L. Jr. (1963, August 28). I Have a Dream: speech, Lincoln Memorial, Washington, D.C.

Kramer, A. D. I., Guillory, J. E., & Hancock, J. T. (2014). Experimental evidence of massive-scale emotional contagion through social networks. Proceedings of the National Academy of Sciences, 111(24), 8788–8790.

Lamb, M. E. (1977). Father-infant and mother-infant interaction in the first year of life. Child Development, 48(1), 167–181.

Lamb, M. E. (2012). Fathers, fatherhood, and father–child relationships: Five decades of research. In M. E. Lamb (Ed.), The role of the father in child development (5th ed., pp. 3–25). Wiley.

Långström, N., Rahman, Q., Carlström, E., & Lichtenstein, P. (2010). Genetic and environmental effects on same-sex sexual behavior: A population study of twins in Sweden. Archives of Sexual Behavior, 39(1), 75–80. https://doi.org/10.1007/s10508-008-9386-1

Lastella, M., Miller, D. J., Montero, A., Sprajcer, M., Ferguson, S. A., Browne, M., & Vincent, G. E. (2025). Sleep on it: A pilot study exploring the impact of sexual activity on sleep outcomes in cohabiting couples. Sleep Health. Advance online publication. https://doi.org/10.1016/j.sleh.2024.11.004

LeDoux, J. E. (1996). The Emotional Brain: The mysterious underpinnings of emotional life. Simon & Schuster.

LeDoux, J. E. (2000). Emotion circuits in the brain. Annual Review of Neuroscience, 23, 155–184. https://doi.org/10.1146/annurev.neuro.23.1.155

Lee, R. B. (1979). The!Kung San: Men, Women, and Work in a Foraging Society. Cambridge University Press.

Lehrer, P., Eddie, D., Shaw, K., Lee, F., Zhang, Y., & Moser, M. (2020). Heart rate variability biofeedback improves emotional and physical health and performance: A systematic review and meta-analysis. Applied Psychophysiology and Biofeedback, 45(3), 109–129. https://doi.org/10.1007/s10484-020-09466-

Leitzmann, M. F., et al. (2004). Ejaculation frequency and subsequent risk of prostate cancer. JAMA, 291(13), 1578–1586.

Levin, R. J. (2007). Sexual activity, health and well-being – the beneficial roles of coitus and masturbation. Sexual and Relationship Therapy, 22(1), 135–148.

Levine, P. A. (1997). Waking the Tiger: Healing Trauma. Berkeley, CA: North Atlantic Books.

Lewandowsky, S., Ecker, U. K. H., Seifert, C. M., Schwarz, N., & Cook, J. (2012). Misinformation and Its Correction: Continued Influence and Successful Debiasing: Continued Influence and Successful Debiasing. Psychological Science in the Public Interest, 13(3), 106-131.

Lewis, A. M., Lloyd, J. C., Heaton, J. P., & Jacklin, C. N. (2011). The effect of an acute increase in urge to void on cognitive function. Neurourology and Urodynamics, 30(1), 183–187. https://doi.org/10.1002/nau.20999

Life Magazine. (1954, March 1). The plague of overweight. Life, 36(9), 53–56.

Light, K. C., Grewen, K. M., & Amico, J. A. (2005). More frequent partner hugs and higher oxytocin levels are linked to lower blood pressure and heart rate. Biological Psychology, 69(1), 5–21.

Liu, H., Waite, L. J., Shen, S., & Wang, D. H. (2016). Is sex good for your health? A national study on partnered sexuality and cardiovascular risk among older men and women. Journal of Health and Social Behavior, 57(3), 276–296. https://doi.org/10.1177/0022146516661590

Loos, R. J. F., & Yeo, G. S. H. (2022). The genetics of obesity: From discovery to biology. Nature Reviews Genetics, 23(2), 120–133. https://doi.org/10.1038/s41576-021-00414-z

Major, B., Rattazzi, L., Brod, S., Pilipović, I., Leposavić, G., & D'Acquisto, F. (2015). Massage-like stroking boosts the immune system in mice. Scientific Reports, 5, 10913. https://doi.org/10.1038/srep10913

Malinowski, B. (1929). The Sexual Life of Savages in North-Western Melanesia. Routledge & Kegan Paul.

Maresh, C. M., Whittlesey, M. J., Armstrong, L. E., Yamamoto, L. M., Judelson, D. A., Fish, K. E., Casa, D. J., Kavouras, S. A., Anderson, J. M., & Kraemer, W. J. (2007). Effects of hydration status on hormonal responses to exercise in the heat. Journal of Strength and Conditioning Research, 21(3), 634–642.

Marlowe, F. W. (2010). The Hadza: Hunter-gatherers of Tanzania. University of California Press. – (ethnography on Hadza clothing practices and situational modesty)

Maté, G. (2003). When the Body Says No: Exploring the Stress-Disease Connection. Hoboken, NJ: John Wiley & Sons.

McEwen, B. S., & Lasley, E. N. (2002). The end of stress as we know it (1st ed.). Joseph Henry Press.

McEwen, B. S. (2007). Physiology and neurobiology of stress and adaptation: The central role of the brain. Physiological Reviews, 87(3), 873–904.

McEwen, B. S., & Gianaros, P. J. (2011). Stress- and allostasis-induced brain plasticity. Annual Review of Medicine, 62, 431–445.

McEwen, B. S., & Karatsoreos, I. N. (2015). Sleep deprivation and circadian disruption: Stress, allostasis, and allostatic load. Sleep Medicine Clinics, 10(1), 1–10. https://doi.org/10.1016/j.jsmc.2014.11.007

Mikulincer, M., & Shaver, P. R. (2016). Attachment in adulthood: Structure, dynamics, and change (2nd ed.). Guilford Press.

Miller, J. G., Kahle, S., & Hastings, P. D. (2017). Moderate baseline vagal tone predicts greater prosociality in children. Developmental Psychology, 53(2), 274–289. https://doi.org/10.1037/dev0000238

Morhenn, V. B., Beavin, L. E., & Zak, P. J. (2012). Massage increases oxytocin and reduces adrenocorticotropin hormone in humans. Alternative Therapies in Health and Medicine, 18(6), 11–18.

Mueller, S.M. (2023). Effects of Massages and Other Touch Interventions on Various Diseases. In: Human Touch in Healthcare. Springer, Berlin, Heidelberg. https://doi.org/10.1007/978-3-662-67860-2_8

Neff, K. (2003). Self-compassion: An alternative conceptualization of a healthy attitude toward oneself. Self and Identity, 2(2), 85–101.

Neumark-Sztainer, D., Bauer, K. W., Friend, S., Hannan, P. J., Story, M., & Berge, J. M. (2010). Family weight talks and dieting: How much do they matter for body dissatisfaction and disordered eating behaviors in adolescent girls? Journal of Adolescent Health, 47(3)270276. https://doi.org/10.1016/j.jadohealth.2010.02.001

Oesterling, C. F., Borg, C., Juhola, E., & Lancel, M. (2023). The influence of sexual activity on sleep: A diary study. Journal of Sleep Research, 32(4), Article e13814. https://doi.org/10.1111/jsr.13814

Ogden, P., Minton, K., & Pain, C. (2006). Trauma and the body: A sensorimotor approach to psychotherapy. W. W. Norton.

Packheiser, J., Hartmann, H., Fredriksen, K., Gazzola, V., Keysers, C., & Michon, F. (2024). A systematic review and multivariate meta-analysis of the physical and mental health benefits of touch interventions. Nature Human Behaviour, 8(6), 1088–1107. https://doi.org/10.1038/s41562-024-01841-8

Palmer, P. J. (2024). Let your life speak: Listening for the voice of vocation. Jossey-Bass.

Panksepp, J. (1998). Affective Neuroscience: The Foundations of Human and Animal Emotions. Oxford University Press.

Pfaus, J. G. (2009). Pathways of sexual desire. Journal of Sexual Medicine, 6(6), 1506–1533.

Pierce, H. M., Perry, L., Gallagher, R., & Chiarelli, P. (2019). Delaying voiding, limiting fluids, urinary symptoms, and work productivity: A survey of female nurses and midwives. Journal of Advanced Nursing, 75(11), 2579–2590. https://doi.org/10.1111/jan.14128

Popkin, B. M., D'Anci, K. E., & Rosenberg, I. H. (2010). Water, hydration, and health. Nutrition Reviews, 68(8), 439–458.

Porges, S. W. (1998). Love: An emergent property of the mammalian autonomic nervous system. Psych neuroendocrinology, 23(8), 837-861. https://doi.org/10.1016/S0306-4530(98)00057-2

Porges, S. W. (2009). The polyvagal theory: New insights into adaptive reactions of the autonomic nervous system. Cleveland Clinic Journal of Medicine, 76(Suppl 2), S86–S90. https://doi.org/10.3949/ccjm.76.s2.17

Porges, S. W. (2011). The Polyvagal Theory: Neurophysiological foundations of emotions, attachment, communication, and self-regulation. W. W. Norton.– (social cues and nervous-system shifts)

Prothero, A. (2024, January 31). Universal free school meals might improve discipline rates. Here's how. Education Week. https://www.edweek.org/leadership/universal-free-school-meals-might-improve-discipline-rates-heres-how/2024/01

Puhl, R. M., & Latner, J. D. (2007). Stigma, obesity, and the health of the nation's children. Psychological Bulletin, 133(4), 557–580.

Rapaport, M. H., Schettler, P., & Bresee, C. (2012). A preliminary study of the effects of repeated massage on hypothalamic–pituitary–adrenal and immune function in healthy individuals: A study of mechanisms of action and dosage. The Journal of Alternative and Complementary Medicine, 18(8), 789–797. https://doi.org/10.1089/acm.2011.0071

Regan, P. C. (1996). Rhythms of desire: The association between menstrual cycle phases and female sexual desire. Canadian Journal of Human Sexuality, 5(3), 145–156.

Robinson, K. (2006, July). Do Schools Kill Creativity? [TED Talk]. TED Conferences. www.ted.com/talks/ken_robinson_do_schools_kill_creativity

Rodgers, R., & Chabrol, H. (2009). Parental attitudes, body image disturbance, and disordered eating among adolescents. European Eating Disorders Review, 17(2), 137–145.

Roughgarden, J. (2004). Evolution's rainbow: Diversity, gender, and sexuality in nature and people. University of California Press.

Sahlins, M. D. (1972). Stone Age Economics. Aldine.

Sapolsky, R. M. (2004). Why Zebras Don't Get Ulcers (3rd ed.). Henry Holt.

Sapolsky, R. M. (2017). Behave: The biology of humans at our best and worst. Penguin Press.

Savic, I., & Lindström, P. (2008). PET and MRI show differences in cerebral asymmetry and functional connectivity between homo- and heterosexual subjects. PNAS, 105(27), 9403–9408.

Schore, A. N. (2012). The science of the art of psychotherapy: The Latest work from a pioneer in the study of the development. WW Norton & Company.

Schwartz, A. E., & Rothbart, M. W. (2020). Let them eat lunch: The impact of universal free meals on student performance. Journal of Policy Analysis and Management, 39(2), 376–410. https://doi.org/10.1002/pam.22175

Segerstrom, Suzanne C., & Miller, Gregory E. (2004). Psychological stress and the human immune system: A meta-analytic study of 30 years of inquiry. Psychological Bulletin, 130(4), 601–630.

Shankar, P., Chung, R., & Frank, D. A. (2017). Association of food insecurity with children's behavioral, emotional, and academic outcomes: A systematic review. Journal of Developmental & Behavioral Pediatrics, 38(2), 135–150. https://doi.org/10.1097/DBP.0000000000000383

Sheldon, W. H. (1940). The Varieties of Human Physique: An Introduction to Constitutional Psychology. Harper & Brothers.

Siegel, D. J. (2012). The developing mind: How relationships and the brain interact to shape who we are (2nd ed.). Guilford Press.

Siegle, G. J., Thompson, W., Carter, C. S., Steinhauer, S. R., & Thase, M. E. (2007). Increased amygdala and decreased dorsolateral prefrontal BOLD responses in unipolar depression: Related and independent features. Biological Psychiatry, 61(2), 198–209. https://doi.org/10.1016/j.biopsych.2006.05.048

Sommer V, Thomsen R, Brindle M. Masturbation in Primates. In: Shackelford TK, ed. The Cambridge Handbook of Evolutionary Perspectives on Sexual Psychology. Cambridge Handbooks in Psychology. Cambridge University Press; 2022:133-170.

Spill, M. K., Callison, K., Grynaviski, E., Huang, H., Garcia Vera, V., & Ribar, D. (2024). Universal free school meals and school and student outcomes: A systematic review. JAMA Network Open, 7(6), e2418344. https://doi.org/10.1001/jamanetworkopen.2024.18344

Spitz, R. A. (1945). Hospitalism: An inquiry into the genesis of psychiatric conditions in early childhood. Psychoanalytic Study of the Child, 1, 53–74.

Streeter, C. C., et al. (2012). Effects of yoga on the autonomic nervous system, gamma-aminobutyric acid, and allostasis in epilepsy, depression, and post-traumatic stress disorder. Medical Hypotheses, 78, 571–579.

Tang, Y. Y., et al. (2015). The neuroscience of mindfulness meditation. Nature Reviews Neuroscience, 16, 213–225.

Taylor, S. E., Klein, L. C., Lewis, B. P., Gruenewald, T. L., Gurung, R. A. R., & Updegraff, J. A. (2000). Biobehavioral responses to stress in females: Tend-and-befriend, not fight-or-flight. Psychological Review, 107(3), 411–429. https://doi.org/10.1037/0033-295X.107.3.411

Tejada, A. H., R. I. M. Dunbar, and M. Montero. Physical contact and loneliness: Being touched reduces perceptions of loneliness. Adaptive Human Behavior and Physiology, 6 (3), 292–306. 2020, (Demonstrates touch lowers neglect feelings and loneliness.)

Thayer, J. F., & Lane, R. D. (2009). Claude Bernard and the heart–brain connection: Further elaboration of a model of neurovisceral integration. Neuroscience & Biobehavioral Reviews, 33, 81–88.

Thomas, P. A., & Kim, S. (2021). Lost touch? Implications of physical touch for physical health. Journals of Gerontology: Series B, 76(7), 1344–1352. https://doi.org/10.1093/geronb/gbaa159

Tiggemann, M. (2006). The role of media exposure in adolescent girls' body dissatisfaction and drive for thinness: Prospective results. Journal of Social and Clinical Psychology, 25(5), 523–541. https://doi.org/10.1521/jscp.2006.25.5.523

Turnbull, C. M. (1961). The Forest People. Simon & Schuster.

United States Department of Agriculture, Economic Research Service. (2024, June 13). State universal free school meal policies reduced food insufficiency among children in the 2022-2023 school year. Amber Waves. https://www.ers.usda.gov/amber-waves/2024/june/state-universal-free-school-meal-policies-reduced-food-insufficiency-among-children-in-the-2022-2023-school-year/

Uvnäs-Moberg, K. (1998). Oxytocin may mediate the benefits of positive social interaction and emotions. Psych neuroendocrinology, 23(8), 819–835.

Uvnäs-Moberg, K. (2003). The oxytocin factor: Tapping the hormone of calm, love, and healing. Da Capo Press.

Uvnäs-Moberg, K., Handlin, L., & Petersson, M. (2015). Self-soothing behaviors with particular reference to oxytocin release induced by non-noxious sensory stimulation. Frontiers in Psychology, 5, 1529. https://doi.org/10.3389/fpsyg.2014.01529

van der Kolk, B. (2014). The body keeps the score: Brain, mind, and body in the healing of trauma. Viking.

Van Dongen, H. P. A., Maislin, G., Mullington, J. M., & Dinges, D. F. (2003). The cumulative cost of additional wakefulness: Dose–response effects on neurobehavioral functions and sleep physiology from chronic sleep restriction and total sleep deprivation. Sleep, 26(2), 117–126. https://doi.org/10.1093/sleep/26.2.117

von Mohr, M., Kirsch, L. P., & Fotopoulou, A. (2021). Social touch deprivation during COVID-19: Effects on psychological well-being and craving interpersonal touch. Royal Society Open Science, 8(9), 210287. https://doi.org/10.1098/rsos.210287

Walker, M. (2017). Why We Sleep: Unlocking the Power of Sleep and Dreams. Scribner.

Walker, P. (2013). Complex PTSD: From Surviving to Thriving. Azure Coyote.

Ware, B. (2012). The top five regrets of the dying: A life transformed by the dearly departing. Hay House.

Weintraub, S. (2001). Silent night: The story of the World War I Christmas truce. Free Press.

Whipple, B., & Komisaruk, B. R. (1985). Elevation of pain threshold by vaginal stimulation in women. Pain, 21(4), 357–367.

Wirth, M. M., & Schultheiss, O. C. (2006). Effects of affiliation arousal (hope of closeness) and affiliation stress (fear of rejection) on progesterone and cortisol. Hormones and Behavior, 50, 786–795.

Xie, L., et al. (2013). Sleep drives metabolite clearance from the adult brain. Science, 342, 373–377.

Yoo, S. S., Gujar, N., Hu, P., Jolesz, F. A., & Walker, M. P. (2007). The human emotional brain without sleep—A prefrontal–amygdala disconnect. Current Biology, 17(20), R877–R878.

Zaccaro, A., Piarulli, A., Laurino, M., Garbella, E., Menicucci, D., Neri, B., Gemignani, A. (2018). How breath-control can change your life: A systematic review on psychophysiological correlates of slow breathing. Frontiers in Human Neuroscience, 12, 353. https://doi.org/10.3389/fnhum.2018.00353

ABOUT THE AUTHOR

Paul Pinette is a Licensed Clinical Social Worker with over 22 years of clinical practice and more than 30 years in the mental health field. He was born and raised in Fort Kent, Maine, in Aroostook County, and comes from a strong Franco-American heritage, with French as his first language. These roots continue to shape his grounded, relational approach to work.

Paul entered the mental health field without formal training, beginning his career as a psychiatric technician at a freestanding psychiatric hospital. He also spent several years working on a suicide hotline, providing safety assessments and helping determine appropriate levels of care for individuals in crisis.

He earned his Bachelor of Social Work from the University of Southern Maine in 2002, followed by his Master of Social Work through the Advanced Standing program at the University of New England in 2003. Over the course of his career, Paul has worked in suicide prevention, crisis response services, and private practice. He has also served as a consultant and trainer on improving school climate and bullying prevention, contributing to three large federal grants under the *Safe Schools, Healthy Students* initiative across multiple southern Maine school districts. In addition, he has provided training and consultation on traumatic stress to first responders and continues to offer officer wellness sessions for local law enforcement personnel.

Paul began his private practice in 2003 and continues to serve clients in southern Maine. Over his career, he has worked with several thousand individuals and remains actively engaged in clinical work.

Outside of his professional life, Paul enjoys time with his wife and family, including five children and seven grandchildren. He values long walks, reading, laughter, and—despite the passage of time—still enjoys video games, having started with Pong.

This book began with fear and ends in hope—tracing a path toward regulation, connection, and a more compassionate way of being human.

AUTHOR'S REFLECTIONS

This book was written during a period when the world felt increasingly loud, polarized, and dysregulated—and when many of my clients, and frankly my own nervous system, were struggling to make sense of it all. It began from a place of certainty, from a belief that I understood what was happening and wanted to explain it clearly. What was unexpected was that the process itself would change.

As the pages accumulated, the work shifted from proving a point to listening more deeply—first to clients, then to the body, and eventually to the biology underneath us all. The book you're holding is the result of that transformation.

One part of the process matters enough to name directly. Artificial intelligence was used as a tool while writing this book—much like a sounding board, an editor, or a mirror. At times, it helped clarify language, fix grammar and spelling, tighten sentences, or reflect ideas back so they could be heard more clearly. At other times, it suggested changes that were explicitly rejected. There were moments of friction— places where something might have read "better" on the page but didn't feel embodied or true. In those moments, embodiment was chosen over elegance, and the original words remained.

The artwork associated with this book—including the cartoon caveman with a modern phone and image of a caveman standing on a perched cliff with a bear behind him, overlooking a darker modern city skyline— was created using artificial intelligence, guided intentionally to reflect the themes of the work.

That distinction matters. Because this book did not come from an algorithm. It emerged from lived experience, clinical work, curiosity, and felt understanding. The core ideas—the metaphors, the Four Pillars, the modern bears, the coping bucket, the framing of judgment as fear, and the idea of a collective nervous system—arose through integration, not automation.

One example is worth naming. The 1998 article by Stephen Porges, *Love: An Emergent Property of the Mammalian Autonomic Nervous System*, was not surfaced by any tool. It was encountered during research, and the moment it was read, it landed viscerally. The recognition was immediate—how precisely it was biologically grounded, what had already been forming here. That kind of recognition—like many others in this book—came from lived resonance, not suggestion.

This is shared not to distance the work from the tools used, but to demystify them. Tools can assist thinking, but they cannot replace discernment. They do not feel. They do not live in bodies. They do not know when something is true in the gut.

This book required presence. It required saying no as often as saying yes. It required staying awake to what felt aligned and what did not. Any clarity here is the result of that attention.

The ideas, interpretations, integrations, and conclusions in this book are my own. Any errors are also mine. If something resonates, it is trusted because it reflects a truth that many of us already carry—sometimes quietly—within our nervous systems.

This book is not about having the right answers. It is about remembering what safety feels like, and what becomes possible when we return to it—together.

Paul Pinette MSW

REVIEWS

As I read, I found myself reflecting on how fear has shaped parts of my own life and how easy it is to hold back out of concern about belonging. Your book reopened my awareness of both my own resilience and the resilience we all carry. It's a powerful reminder that we're stronger when we share our stories and step into the circle together.

I found the writing clear and engaging. The reframes, chapter closings, key takeaways, and exercises all worked well.

This book was deeply affirming and gave me practical ways to notice when my biology is "barking" and how to reset. I kept thinking of clients, my family, and friends in life transitions who would benefit from this work. Truly, there is something here for everyone.

Adam Dubay, LCPC

A clear, compassionate guide to how our oldest wiring shapes modern life. Drawing on anthropology, neuroscience, and clinical practice, this book shows that basic needs—safety, sleep, food, hydration, play, and social connection—are not optional comforts but the biological scaffolding of mood, identity, and resilience. It explains why social exclusion still triggers primal threat responses, why play matters for learning and recovery, and how simple, everyday habits refill our coping reserves. Practical, humane, and evidence-informed, this book offers readers small, actionable steps to reclaim balance in a world that often undermines the body's built-in regulators.

Cheryl Demers, LCSW

Paul has woven his real-life insights from clients' stories and struggles into current research to create a brilliant read. His approachable tone makes the science easy-to-understand and feels like a conversation. This book is full of practical exercises and suggestions; I found myself thinking of specific clients and how I could use Paul's guidance in session (not to mention, for myself). A valuable resource for those who work with others and for those who could use some reminders and "Aha's" about being human.

My favorite takeaway:
One steady presence can change a room.
One moment of compassion can shift a day.
One nervous system at peace can become a refuge.

Just might get this printed to hang up - can't wait to see the book printed!

Linda Berg, LCPC

When reading psychology books or periodicals, I tend not to get far in the material before I lose interest. Much of what is available seems overly technical, and researchers discussing their work delve into 'control groups' that could be university students or others paid to take part in their study. What differentiates Paul's work is that there is no 'control group'; only real clients from varying age groups, occupations, and backgrounds seek help with real-world problems. Over two decades of work in the field of stress and trauma provide more data than any short-term study can provide. You have taken 'raw data', distilled down what you have learned over the decades, and delivered an understanding that ordinary people can understand.

The background information on how we are wired from our ancestral roots (old bear), contrasted with what we face today, and the subsequent challenges, makes complete sense, and you did it in plain language with real-life examples. I came away after reading every chapter, learning something. Having an understanding of our primal survival mechanisms and understanding what people face today shines a bright light on why there are so many mental health challenges today.

Thank you for your work. Thank you for helping. Thank you for writing this book. I truly believe this will help many people.

Jack Clements, Chief of Police, Saco, Maine

_ _ _

He who fights with monsters should look to it that he himself does not become a monster. And if you gaze long into an abyss, the abyss also gazes into you.

-F. Nietzsche

* 9 7 9 8 9 9 5 0 8 8 5 0 9 *